August, 79

CONFESSIONS
OF A
CONSERVATIVE

By Garry Wills

Confessions
of a **Conservative**

Garry Wills

DOUBLEDAY & COMPANY, INC./Garden City, New York
1979

Library of Congress Cataloging in Publication Data
Wills, Garry, 1934–
   Confessions of a conservative.
   1. Conservatism. 2. Wills, Garry, 1934–
3. Political scientists—United States—Biography.
I. Title.
JC251.W554   320.5′2′0924 [B]
ISBN: 0-385-08977-5
Library of Congress Catalog Card Number 78–19662

CONTENTS

To
"Natalie C"
in the Alfa Romeo

INTRODUCTION

Being a conservative in America is lonely work, but interesting—to me, if not to others. And it can be confusing—to others, if not to me. Once I was called conservative, but wasn't—or was very imperfectly so. Now that I have reflected on the term, and settled better into it, some want to take it away, to save either it or me from disgrace. I cling to it, nonetheless; and will try to say why.

"Confession" in the literature I grew up with was used not only for admission of guilt but profession of faith, *confessio fidei*. St. Augustine found a wide range of meanings in the word, meanings he treated as a natural cluster. *Apologia* had the same play of senses. One must apologize for what one believes in, to the extent that one's life offers no very good advertisement for it. So, while some might demand a confession to being conservative, I confess my failing so often to be one.

PART ONE

NATIONAL REVIEW DAYS

1 · Going to Meet Buckley

Twenty years back from the time when I write this, I was lying on a bottom bunk in the sweltering "honors dorm"—a converted Victorian home—of Xavier University's campus in Cincinnati. Another student came in, to say I had a call on the house phone from New York. After a secretary's formal checkings at the other end of the line, the dull heat was cut by that higher bounce of voice he saves for the telephone: "This is Bill Buckley. I read what you sent us, and love it, and will run it soon. Could you come to New York and see us?" I mumbled that I didn't think I could. "We would pay, of course." Which changed things. But even so: I had a few days more of summer class, and tickets to the Antioch Shakespeare Festival after that. "Well, after that?" All right.

It didn't seem ridiculous at the time to turn down extra days in New York in order to see some plays. Through almost six years at a Jesuit seminary (from ages seventeen to twenty-two), I had nursed an instinctive love of the theater from a very great distance. Now I was determined to see all the plays I could—first in nearby Antioch, then in Chicago. I concentrated on these targets because New York was, to me, unimaginable. I thought, insofar as I thought of New York at all during that brief phone call, that I would fly in for an interview or something and fly right back. Better Shakespeare in Ohio.

My response seemed odd only in retrospect—when, weeks later, I was reviewing Broadway plays, along with the Shakespeare seasons in Central Park and at Connecticut's Stratford. They were the first professional plays I had ever seen. That may not say much either for my credentials as a reviewer or Mr. Buckley's as an editor; but who am I to criticize him on those grounds? This was just the first of many things I would owe to Bill's foolhardiness. Years later, when Pope Paul issued his encyclical on world peace, Buckley called me to check a quote from Thomas Aquinas —the dictum that Popes may err, in moral decisions, *propter falsos testes* ("because of erring witnesses" to points of fact). The now familiar voice on the phone interjected: "Doesn't testicle come from the same word as witness?" I said yes, then urged him to hold off on a column that would make certain Catholics angrier than ever at Buckley's magazine. He refused: I could hear his typewriter already Latinizing while his shoulder pinned the phone receiver to his head—a familiar sight in his office. Why not hold off a day or two? "Because I don't have *falsos testes.*" Laughter, and a click. Only that kind of bravado explains his offering me the job of cultural editor at *National Review* a few hours after we met.

I arrived in New York during an airport limousine strike (not knowing how typical that would be of later visits there), and had to take a taxi to Buckley's office. The price so horrified me that I offered no tip—and got my first lesson from a New York cabbie. By the time he finished, I would have given him *another* five dollars (so "low" was the fare back then); but he dictated the terms. I escaped happy, no matter what. I was wearing the one suit I owned, a gift of the seminary when I left; it was a winter one, and this was New York in July. Luckily *National Review*'s first office (later abandoned), though cramped and slovenly, was air-conditioned. I waited in a little cubicle for visitors, glassed off from the one large room, with little stalls along the sides, that housed this busy small world of editors. Stuck in my bowl, I took a goldfish view of bustle in and out of stalls, stray interweavings in the middle of the room. My first impression was of youth; but that did not carry over to the man who came to pull me out of my bowl.

I was surprised, for some reason, to find him tall—less preppy-looking than his book-jacket picture had led me to expect; pleasantly disheveled and informal, despite the rich prance and neighing of his voice. Today, many people who meet Buckley for the first time have seen and heard him on TV; but I knew him only, by repute, as a *Wunderkind;* and this tall thirty-two-year-old seemed somehow more normal and adult than the image I had formed of him.

When we went into his office, though, he seemed a bit boyish in the company of fellow editors, each his senior by decades—James Burnham, John Chamberlain, Willmoore Kendall. Buckley sat on his desk, tucked his legs under him, and continued discussion of some policy matter. He showed a deference to others that might belie his superiority on the review's masthead; but he showed the same deference when the conversation circled toward my chair. Buckley asked my opinion. I don't remember what the subject was, but I fear I answered confidently. The others went through the motions, at least, of seriously considering an opinion from this stranger off the street. Those around Bill pick up his manners, acknowledging each other's presence and giving all a hearing. It is one of the things that makes his company so pleasant.

When these editors filed out, Buckley told me he was specially buoyant this day because Whittaker Chambers, after much solicitous wooing, had just agreed to join the staff of *NR* (the office abbreviation becomes inevitable near Buckley). I shared Buckley's elation. Chambers' book *Witness* was the only secular work read aloud during meals in our novitiate refectory. And I had read the book privately after that. In fact, I praised Chambers in the manuscript I had mailed to Bill's magazine. "Are you a conservative, then?" I answered that I did not know. Are distributists conservative? "Philip Burnham tells me they are not." It was an exchange with the seeds of much later misunderstanding.

Buckley asked about my background. I told him I had recently left a Jesuit seminary, and was working on a doctorate in classics with emphasis on Greek theater. "Oh, you must review some plays for us. We just lost our drama critic." Not Willi Schlamm? "Yes." Schlamm was the principal reason I had read *National Review,* and submitted an article to the magazine. He wrote of the theater with great enthusiasm: "Miss Beatrice Lillie enters the stage from a snowy nowhere, and life is good again." He had also carried on a dogged war against Brooks Atkinson of the *Times,* my only other source of Broadway criticism out in the Midwest. Schlamm affected me somewhat as Mencken is said to have struck young readers in the 1920s. I savored his epigrams: "Scientists are people who first build and then buy the Brooklyn Bridge." His words rolled with a jolly noisiness, as when he deplored "the tastelessly genuine Tennessee Williams" of *Orpheus Descending.* Schlamm admired Toscanini's genius and disliked his music—just the right distinction, I thought. In the very last issue of *NR* I had seen, he reviewed the big Picasso retrospective at the Museum of Modern Art (one of the things I was determined to see in New York) and found a basic triviality beneath the godlike versatility. I sang Schlamm's praises to Bill, unaware they had just parted with great bitterness.

He said nothing of that fight, but thought I would be pleased to know one of Schlamm's last tasks at the magazine had been to copy edit my article, which he admired. Then Bill explained the importance of that remark: My piece was on *Time* style, and Schlamm had been an associate of Henry Luce for several *Time-Life* projects. (Later that day, John Chamberlain, the world's gentlest ex-radical and another *Time-Life* escapee, asked if I had worked for any Luce publication. I didn't tell him I had never worked for *any* publication. "You capture the frustrations inside that company so well.")

Schlamm ran a column in the magazine called "Arts and Manners." But for his recent ousting, I would not have been tried at so many congenial tasks, nor offered the "Arts and Manners" column. Bill took me around to meet editors and staff—his sisters Priscilla and Maureen; Suzanne LaFollette, who looked a Helen Hokinson type overlipsticked, but whose conversation remembered incongruous barricades. Burnham, Chamberlain, and Kendall I had met in Buckley's office. Brent Bozell was in Washington. Frank Meyer, the book review editor, was at his eyrie in Woodstock. "You must get some books to review from Frank." Bill lifted the phone. I went into another little booth and waited for Frank to come on the line.

His raspy voice was sleep-phlegmed—it was early in the afternoon (somewhere around two o'clock). He asked me what kinds of books would interest me. Classics and theater. "Can't give you classics. Revilo Oliver takes all those we can handle in the magazine. How about politics?" Sure. He suggested a few titles and said they would be at the office in a day or two.

The rest of the afternoon I spent in Bill's office while he pushed letters and newsclips across his desk, conversing easily while he worked. He made it look natural to be doing two or three things at once. To me, after the enforced somnolence of seminary days, he seemed a one-man version of *Front Page*. Bill was leaving the office early that afternoon, and had already invited me to dinner. We went out to a small foreign car, the first I had ever entered. The constant whirrings down, fussy tuggings, and resumed flight seemed a nuisance rather than a luxury—though in a matter of weeks I would be learning the forward and downward shifts of an Alfa Romeo from a person who is still teaching me things.

I had not realized that going to dinner involved a sixty-mile ride, round trip. (This was long before Buckley purchased Dag Hammarskjöld's old town house in Manhattan.) As the little car dipped down to toll booths and Buckley shot coins at the metal baskets, he asked me questions I was all too happy to answer. My weeks of summer school in Cincinnati had been even more eremitic than the seminary, and here was a busy editor showing interest in my plans and future. Bill asked tactfully if I had left the Church when I left the seminary. I said no, and he looked genuinely relieved. Being Catholic always mattered more to him than being conservative. I told him I had spent my last unhappy years in the seminary reading plays; how I hoped to write a book on Shakespeare after I did a dissertation on Aeschylus. He was curious; and I foolishly talked myself out on the subject of Shakespeare's fools. Bill, though quickly bored, is even quicker to explore anything another person has studied. He can learn from almost anyone. Over the wind I talked loud to his profile. The large eyes and mouth shrank back from the prominent forehead and chin—formed a man in the moon in the resulting crescent. We got onto another interest of mine, opera. He had heard in the theater singers I knew only from records. He regretted there was no opera season in the summer for me to review.

He asked how long I could stay in New York. Just till the middle of August. (I would alter that, later, to early September.) I had left the seminary in April without having applied to any graduate school. A former teacher got me a conditional scholarship at Xavier for the coming year, provided I take accelerated reading courses from the two Greek teachers at work that summer. This had let me in for long hours in a hot library room collating microfilmed manuscripts of St. John Chrysostom. I now had tuition money for the fall, when I would have to earn recommendation to a better graduate school for the doctorate. Bill said if I worked part-time for *NR* he could probably help with my tuition. I thanked him, but said no. I had grown to hate the placidity of Jesuit life; but in these few hours things had accelerated a bit too fast for me, faster even than this little car's takeoff after each toll gate.

At his home outside Stamford, we had a drink and looked across the lawn to the Sound. Bill asked if I wanted to swim, but I browsed through his records while he did a few laps in the pool. He had the 1946 Serafin *Aïda,* which I had never heard; and I put on the Gigli "Celeste Aïda." Then his wife came in, as tall and as tanned as he, with the same etched precision of diction and wide voice swoops. They might have been twins, Bill the impish one, Pat more serious. When Bill went to the upright piano, Pat groaned and said she would look to the meal. We ate on the porch by candlelight, Pat apologizing for some concoction that seemed to waver up on the candle's flickers and waft itself into my mouth.

Bill had promised Fulton Lewis, Jr., to look in on his son, Buddy, who was playing piano in some Manhattan bar. So we dove into the little bucket seats and pelted back to town. Bill asked if I had been a long-time student of *Time* magazine. Quite the opposite, I said, we could not read secular publications in the seminary. But a year ago, when we went to our summer "villa," there was a stack of old *Times,* and I spent two nights slogging through them. After my abstinence, I was revolted by the righteous sleaziness of the thing. I wrote the piece, though I knew we could not submit articles for publication from the seminary. In fact, I had whole notebooks full of odd writings I had done in recent years. As soon as I left I typed up four of these articles and sent them off—one to *Commonweal* (on Chagall), one to *America* (on Gerard Manley Hopkins), one to *Thought* (on Dostoievski's *The Idiot*), and one to *NR*. Bill asked the results of my other three mailings, and I said there had been none— Bill answered first. (But there would be three rejection slips waiting for me when I got back to my parents' home in Michigan.)

Back in town, we drank beer at a little piano bar, talking to Buddy during his breaks. Bill wanted to know about the organ Lewis' father had just constructed. It was after midnight when Bill dropped me off at a hotel suite his own father kept for visiting business associates. Bill was expansive with his own brand of Irish blarney: "What a day for *National Review* when it gets both Whittaker Chambers and Garry Wills." At the hotel desk, he said, "You'll need an advance to buy some things," counting out five twenties. "Come into the office when you get up." He had that thirty miles to drive again, before ending a fairly typical day for him—a fairy-tale nine or ten hours for me. I woke my parents by phone, to see if they would believe my improbable tale. But I tried to hold onto reality. That footlocker of books I had just brought back from Xavier?—send it to me the quickest way you can. Forget the expense—I was a bit expansive myself, with that hundred dollars on the table. The trunk had my Aeschylus notes, and the books I was studying. I went into the suite's kitchenette, and mixed my very first gin and tonic—the only things left on the booze shelf. Even so, I didn't sleep.

I didn't read much Aeschylus in the following six weeks. The first thing I did, next day, was buy another suit—lighter material, but blue serge, so I could wear it year-round. When I went to the office, Bill told me Gertrude, his secretary, had already checked on available plays. "Not much in the summertime." But she had tickets for Rosalind Russell's *Auntie Mame* and Gwen Verdon's

New Girl in Town. Shakespeare in the park was free; I just had to show up at performance time. I saw *Two Gentlemen*—Lance and his dog were important to my theories of the fool. Later I reviewed Earle Hyman's impressive *Othello* at Stratford. New York was a dream world. Walking down the street, I heard Caruso's "Ingemisco" from the Verdi *Requiem* ringing through the air—it was part of the regular noon concert in Bryant Park, behind the Forty-second Street library. Soon I had found discount record stores, and laid in a supply of old Schipa arias I was aching to hear. Bill's sister Maureen let me use the phonograph in her apartment.

Life was even more exciting in the office than out on the street. *National Review*'s resident editors have, as I write this, shrunk to two. One of them, James Burnham, is semiretired, leaving the major editing to Jeffrey Hart, a full-time academic who flies in from Dartmouth every other week. Bill long ago drifted off from the magazine, whose name he uses while it uses his. He is absorbed in his own TV series and columns and books. But *NR* is now twenty-two years old. It is part of the landscape, a fixed thing by which other people steer. When I went there, it was not yet two years old. It was Bill's whole life, consuming his extraordinary energies. He was actively seeking new writers, some just as unlikely as I was, and all of them treated as well. A cranky band of bright editors taxed Bill's energy, fighting the world and each other, trying to use or help Bill, each intent on steering this new bark off in his own direction—which led to the Willi Schlamm showdown and exit. All five remaining editors attended office sessions regularly, even in the summer, since that was where Bill could be met and influenced. I got to know all these people, catching hints of the tempests brewed daily in editorial teapots. *NR* was founded at the end of 1955, just in time for its Republican ideologues to squabble over the '56 elections—purists saying Ike with Dick was a palliative at best, a distraction at worst; pragmatists saying one must maneuver in the real world. The lines drawn up in that election year survived for at least a decade.

I have no doubt, little journals being what they are, that *NR* is still a cat's cradle of schemes and crossing egos. But this is, surely, a pygmy war compared to what I saw, only partly comprehending, when Willmoore Kendall took elegant verbal swipes at his fellows. Brent Bozell and Frank Meyer formed an anti-Burnham faction, but then fell out themselves in theological wrangling. Burnham treated attacks on him as beneath response. Bill tried to stay above the conflict, half ignoring, half downplaying it. He alone was more intent on saving the ship than on steering it. I, as the "new boy" in Bill's tow, was only obliquely approached by most of these contestants—all but Frank, who was about as subtle as the farts he thought it *déclassé* to muffle or minimize.

Given the magazine's easygoing summer schedule, it was hard for Bill to scare up assignments I could work on. He responded in typical fashion. A *Times* item on the Hoffa hearings before a Senate committee caught his eye, and he said, "Why don't you go down and cover that?" I read the item more carefully, and pointed out that the hearings were expected to end the next day. But Bill is not to be deterred when in inspired mood. "It could stretch out. Go down and get a feel." I was off, early next morning, on my first reporting assignment, a fresh press card in my pocket. "Go see Sam Jones; he'll catch you up on the investigation." Jones was *NR*'s Washington correspondent. He was called, and he told me to meet him at the Press Club when my plane landed. Instead of taking me to the hearings, Jones took me to his table at the club—avid for an audience, even of one, that had not heard any of his stories even once. He was part of the pale crowd that lives at the Press Club to trade fading (and expanding) memories of past exploits. After a long lunch, during which he told me nothing of current interest, he deposited me at the hearing room. He could not even get me into the press section: I had to sit with the visitors. But I stood against the rail when Hoffa bounced in, to hear his banter with reporters. The notes I took were uninformative, since I knew little of the incidents he was being questioned on. Still, some exchanges were a joy: Asked if he realized what power he could wield as president of the Teamsters, for good or for evil, Hoffa pompously answered, "I will live up to *both* responsibilities." I saw two young faces—all teeth and bones, like handsomely grinning skulls, nodding together; but had no idea these were the Kennedy brothers till I saw the senator's picture shortly after in a Catholic journal.

Sure enough, fairly early in the afternoon, the hearings were concluded. Having rushed down to catch this tag end of ununderstandable conversation, I was surely not going to stick around for more Sam Jones stories. I called Bill at the office: What now? "Catch the shuttle back, and take the train to Stamford." That night Bill was holding the twice-yearly editorial conference at his home.

On the plane, the stewardess tried to take my heavy jacket and hang it up, but it was full of pens and notepads and paperbacks— I clung to my *vecchia zimarra.* Her big and mocking Italian eyes took in the book I was reading, Bergson's *Two Sources.* Later, when she sat down next to me for the landing, she said, "Aren't you a little young to be reading that?" She was reading Kaufmann's *Nietzsche,* which I knew; so I defensively quizzed her on it —she was too wise to resent that, though she had a right to. We had almost an hour to argue, since our plane was caught in the crunch over LaGuardia. I worried I would miss my train to Stamford. "I live in Wallingford, above Stamford. I'll give you a ride." Waiting outside the terminal, I almost didn't recognize her when the blue Alfa Romeo wheeled up.

I arrived late at Bill's house. Dinner was over; there were acrid afterfumes of explosion in the air. Frank, after taking the book section from Willmoore, had been forced to defend his turf against Kendall criticisms. Brent Bozell, Bill's brother-in-law up from Washington, introduced himself—lanky, all boxy chin and Adam's apple, he looked exactly as everyone had described him to me: young Lincoln, but with red hair and freckles. His voice made broad sweeps and veers—I was beginning to wonder if *everybody* around here talked like Bill.

Brent asked where I had been, and I told him. "Get anything from Sam?" No. He nodded with understanding. "From the committee sessions?" Not much. "Did you try to interview Hoffa?" No: I wouldn't have known what to ask him. I listened as others shot questions at him on the run from the committee room. "Sounds like a wasted trip." Sure was. (I didn't know it yet, but that day's was the most important trip of my life.)

"Bill may suggest you talk to Jonathan Mitchell. He's supposed to be our labor correspondent. Don't bother." Brent, who had hung around Capitol Hill writing what came to be known as Joe McCarthy's good speeches,* seemed the only person at *NR* who thought journalism had something to do with reporting. I remember, years later, a telephone call from Bill: "Do you know of a person named Joe Nu-*math?*" You mean Joe *Nay*-muth? "Is that how you pronounce it? Well, Harold Hayes of *Esquire* has asked me to do a piece on him. Is there enough there to bother?" I said I thought so; he could tell when he met him. "Oh, I don't have time to *meet* him." He wrote his article, a good one, from news clips, constructing it around his favorite story (often told) of Manolete's skill. Bill knows more about bullfighting than football.

National Review called itself "A Journal of Opinion," and the opinionizing was certainly fierce. But it lived on little nutriment of fact. Editorial conferences were, in the main, a dissection of the previous few days' issues of the New York *Times*. I was in the wrong place for learning how to be a journalist. But, of course, I never dreamed of being a journalist then. I was too busy becoming an ideologue.

But an ideologue of what ideology? There were several brands jostling each other at the magazine. Bill kept trying to play down difference (while Brent and Frank played it up). Conflicts were usually muted by Bill's ecumenical enthusiasms. Other young writers were found and invited aboard *National Review* with the same lax testing I received—John Leonard, Joan Didion, Arlene Croce, Renata Adler, Guy Davenport. I got an early taste of this nondogmatic side to Buckley when I asked him what would be a sensible next step on the Hoffa story: "Why not go see Murray Kempton? He was a labor reporter for years." Bill told me about Kempton, that first night at his home, when we talked of stylists we admired; so I had started reading his column in the New York *Post*. Now Bill, calling ahead, sent me over to the *Post*.

Kempton generously pulled out his clip file on Hoffa and loaned it to me. He also lent me his book *Part of Our Time,* with its sec-

---

* Cf. Richard Rovere, *Senator Joe McCarthy,* p. 241: "In one period, early in 1956 McCarthy had Bozell write some meaty speeches on foreign and military policy, and some of these were quite good. . . . But it all got him nowhere, and after a time he felt as silly as he looked in a toga."

tion on the Reuther brothers and the labor movement. (No one seemed to notice, when my *NR* piece appeared, that I said good things about Walter Reuther). We talked in his office for a while; he invited me to dinner; I began on the files while he finished his column for that day.

Dinner once again involved a ride from Manhattan—this time to Princeton by train. Murray's wife was away, visiting her mother; so he cooked while I changed sides for the Josef Krips *Don Giovanni*. Murray would stop stirring, at a cadence, hear it fall, and say: "What else? So inevitable!" Then he told me hilarious labor stories late into a boozy night. I slept (two hours or so) there, then we ran blearily for a morning train. I was just nimble and dumb enough to jump on, and found it an empty set of cars being trundled to a siding. Later that morning, I tottered into Bill's office, said I needed sleep, and went off to "80 Park" to read Murray's files on Hoffa. (By then, knowing I was going to stay for over a month, Bill had moved me into his father's double suite, complete with two kitchens, at 80 Park Avenue. At night, when I raised the blinds, I looked almost straight up at the Empire State Building's floodlit spire and spikes.)

Murray was as intrigued with Bill as I was, and we traded notes on the Buckley phenomenon, then entering its sixth year (if we date from the publication of *God and Man at Yale*). Only later did I come to think 1946 the real date of *NR*'s inception, the real launching of the political Buckley.

In 1946, Yale's freshman class was twice the normal size. The school had committed itself to receiving all those who successfully applied in earlier years but had to go off to war. Students were jammed into Quonset huts; but many had come there from barracks in any case. They were older than the normal freshmen, and more serious; competitive, with time to make up for—some of them used to command, young lieutenants demoted to "heeling" school activities.

One such, Brent Bozell, came from Omaha by way of the Navy. He had won his college scholarship by high-school oratory, and was eloquent for liberal causes. He soon led the campus chapter of United World Federalists—and got into trouble with the New Haven SPCA when he put tiny turtles in freshman mail boxes:

The slogan stuck on each turtle's back said, "Hurry World Government." But Brent was also anticommunist on religious grounds. His father, a Protestant flirting with the Catholic faith, sent him to Omaha's Jesuit school, Regis High, where (Father Lucius Cervantes tells me) Brent was very prayerful. He would be baptized a Catholic at Yale; but he had been putting this decision off for years. It was certainly not true that Bill "converted" Brent —though some at Yale saw him as a Buckley disciple or hanger-on. He drove one of the Buckley cars, dated one of the Buckley girls—he seemed to be wearing the Buckley religion as well.

But Brent did not just wear his religion. It wore at him, nagging and hardening. His smile, so skeptical it looked to some like an insult, was a kind of skeletal rictus at the world's perversions. It was a smile not to be trifled with, or blarneyed away, even by Bill, the world's greatest blarneyer.

Bill came to Yale from the infantry. His older brother Jim had been an immensely popular student there before the war, and had just returned to help start, over again, the suspended *Daily News* while beginning his own studies in the Law School. Jim told Bill to forget everything else and aim at being chairman of the *News,* the most influential and rewarding position on campus. So intent was Bill on this objective that he asked Jim, on the day when the staff had to vote for chairman, if it was ethical to vote for himself. Jim thought so—which became an embarrassing decision when Bill was elected unanimously.

Brent's sphere was the political Union, where he was considered a more eloquent speaker than his debate partner, Bill Buckley. The two waged holy war on communism, which involved hectoring Henry Wallace when he came to Yale. They were a very effective team, as Oxford's touring debaters learned. At graduation, Brent married Bill's sister Patricia; and he later collaborated with Bill on a book of collected debate cards called *McCarthy and His Enemies.*

Bill's pugnacious year as chairman of the *Daily News* has become that paper's most colorful legend of battles past. Not till the time of Black Panther trials in New Haven would controversy rage more noisily around the paper's daily appearance. Indeed, Yale philosopher Paul Weiss thought Bill an unwitting forerunner of campus dissidence and defiance of authority. When the administration censored his Faculty Day address, Bill "went public" with that backstage story and began his book attacking Yale's curriculum. By the time of his graduation, Bill ran an ideological salon of a pleasantly rowdy kind—witness the December "Messiah Party" at which a drunken professor fell, laughing, out of the window into the snow.

That professor could not enter this story more appropriately. His life was a dramatic series of fallings-out with virtually everyone he came to know well (and with some he hardly knew). But when his prize students first met him, he changed the Buckley-Bozell chemistry. Some might call it an act of alchemy in reverse. Did he turn the golden lads to lead? Without him, the combination would not have worked quite the way it did, nor have broken up so violently. It was never a light thing to join forces with Willmoore Kendall.

2 · *Kendall* Contra Mundum

*He had fine blue eyes, light-pained, direct, intelligent, dis-
believing; hair still thick, parted in the middle; and strong ver-
tical grooves between the brows, beneath the nostrils, and at
the back of the neck.*

—MM (*Mosby's Memoirs*)

Next to him, Thorstein Veblen was academically domesticated.
Willmoore was, for a start, vain, polished, awkward, honest, ruthless, kind, dignified, and comic—a walking sign of contradiction,
who lost no time, on a first meeting, contradicting you; everybody's enemy at some time, and always his own. In the words of
Saul Bellow, Willmoore Kendall *"had made some of the most interesting mistakes a man could make in the twentieth century."*
One measure of Willmoore's impact is the way Bellow took him,
as "Willis Mosby," into the title story of *Mosby's Memoirs*.

Willmoore seemed a walking code to be read, a cluster and
crackle of private signals—his green ink, the gray crew cut suc-
ceeding an earlier James Cagney hair style, his signature phrases
("off at the margin"), the muddy-purple plaid sportcoats (where
on earth did he find them?). Every private whim seemed to con-
vey some obscure public rebuke. But just when one thought he
had cracked the code, he read it and found an obscene message
addressed to him.

Bellow's Mosby sits in Mexico, drinking tequila and outlining his memoirs: *"Fundamentalist family in Missouri—Father the successful builder—Early schooling—The State University—Rhodes Scholarship—Intellectual friendships—What I learned from Professor Collingwood—Empire and the mental vigour of Britain—My unorthodox interpretation of John Locke—I work for William Randolph Hearst—Radical friendships in New York—Wartime service with the O.S.S.—The limited vision of Franklin D. Roosevelt—Comte, Proudhon, and Marx revisited—DeTocqueville once again."*

Change just a few things (like his native state, or his father's trade) and there you have Willmoore—late Willmoore, at least. Early Willmoore was a monster of a different order—monstrously bright and lovingly abused. His father, a mellifluous preacher, was blind from early youth. His scholarly yearnings baffled, this senior Willmoore Kendall conducted an itinerant ministry to Oklahoma's Methodists. Young Willmoore, a prodigy, learned to read at two. By five, he was reading to his father; shortly after, driving for him, seeing for him, playing flute to his father's piano. One man's acute ear trained the other's. So the foundation was laid—in Oklahoma accents, but with a preacher's emphases—of that extraordinary speaking and writing style, precise but also flamboyant, we hear refracted in Bill Buckley's tone and language.

I had thought everyone talked like Bill at *National Review*. But they were talking like Willmoore—like the Oklahoma boy whose diction had been sharpened by his years at Oxford and his doctoral studies in Romance languages. Willmoore wrote as he spoke, in long parentheses within parentheses, which were nonetheless easily grasped; in numbered clauses, with necessary disclaimers included (what he called "verbal parachutes"); in a pedantic framework enlivened by some inner heckling of colorful slang. Willmoore would at last perfect the character of learned hick, the Okie from Oxford, weaving professorial and hayseed phrases together. Only some of this was transferable to others. The barefoot-boy pose could not be used by Buckley; nor the sense of an argument going on with *himself* as Willmoore worked away at his interlocutor's defenses. But Bill and Brent, both his students at Yale, picked up what they could—a great deal. Jim Buckley, by preceding Bill at Yale, shows what the foreign-educated Buckleys sound like un-Willmoorized. Reid, who followed Bill, is more heavily dosed with Willmoorisms than Bill himself.

In Willmoore the barefoot memories were real. His father's work was in small towns, and Willmoore spent summers at the Oklahoma state prison where his grandmother was matron of women. He was fascinated by her black cook, serving a life sentence for murder. Because of his ability, Willmoore lost contact with other children (except for his bright and adoring sister); he moved in an adult world, flattered, overburdened. He skipped grades at school, or just stayed home and read. Not till a teacher of French and Spanish challenged his interest and concentration did he settle down to graduate from high school (at age thirteen). All this time he and his father were close enough, both bright, both "different," to hurt each other with daily love and acrimony. He read his father books that were over his own head—Willmoore senior correcting any sloppiness of diction, Willmoore junior correcting his father's whole view of the world.

When Willmoore was in his teens, he sent off a manuscript to Julius Haldeman, which came out as No. 440 in the Little Blue Book series. *Baseball: How to Play It and How to Watch It* by Alan Monk—his sister tells me the pseudonym was one of Willmoore's jokes, but she cannot remember the point. He knew how to affect a lofty tone: "A student of the new psychology, of course, finds it hard to agree with Mr. Huggins's truism to the effect that baseball players, like poets, are born and not made." His search for what he later called historical "derailments" had already begun: "The introduction of spiked shoes into baseball has revolutionized the slide . . . and the slight advantages of the head-first slide over the fall-away are now forgotten." In later years he would begin his list of scholarly publications with this title.

Through his teens Willmoore worked at reporting and other jobs while attending the University of Tulsa and the University of Oklahoma (where he got his bachelor's degree at age eighteen). School did not interest him, and relations with his father were at the regular shouting stage. At sixteen he ran away to New Orleans; but a relative let his father know where he was, and New

Orleans police were authorized to arrest him. His father went to
fetch him, and told the jail's warden to handcuff the boy to him
for the return trip—he could not, after all, "keep an eye on him."
Willmoore begged in tears to be spared that humiliation, promising not to run away. Yet when Willmoore finally left home, he
corresponded obsessively with his father—the two men trying
constantly, and failing, to explain themselves to each other.

In later years, Willmoore was convinced his father lost faith,
during his seminary years, in the gospel he had learned to preach.
But the preacher was about to marry, and his bride said he could
not make a living except in the ministry he was trained for. There
is no way of knowing whether Willmoore interpreted his father
(and his mother) correctly; but he thought he had—and his bitter violence against hypocrisy had its roots in the same experience
that made him seek a genuine authority all his life. The victim of a
blind but loving despotism, he both sought and fought a similar
power, puzzling himself and others in the role of authoritarian
rebel.

In graduate school at Northwestern, Willmoore got interested
again in his French and Spanish studies. He took a master's degree at age nineteen, and became a teaching assistant at the University of Illinois. He had completed all requirements for a
Romance-language doctorate, except for the dissertation, when he
went to Oxford as Rhodes scholar. There one of his tutors was
R. G. Collingwood, who stimulated an interest in political philosophy. Willmoore was also intrigued by the wit of a Catholic chap-
lain named Ronald Knox. In 1935, Willmoore received his M.A.
Oxon., married in England the girl he had left behind in America,
and went to Spain as a correspondent for United Press. He was a
sympathizer with the Republic, but disturbed by signs of Communist control; and his ache for authority responded to the Spanish
Church. (*MM:* "He admired Spanish masculinity—the varonil of
Lorca. The cavel varonil, the manly red carnation, the clear classic hardness of honorable control.")

Back in America, he gave up his graduate credits in Romance
languages at the University of Illinois and started doctoral work in
political science. After he received the Ph.D. he began teaching at
Louisiana State University, where he had a graduate student

named Hubert Humphrey, whom he considered lackluster. (*MM:* "And of the Vice President he said, 'I wouldn't trust him to make me a pill. A has-been druggist!'")

During the Second World War Willmoore used his fluent Spanish for intelligence work in South America, and left the Army a major. His expertise would be called on when the CIA set up its South American activities in 1947, but he was not a member of the OSS club—he had already moved to the right of his eastern establishment fellows. (*MM:* "He had expected a high postwar appointment, for which, as director of counterespionage in Latin America, he was ideally qualified. But . . . Mosby had sympathized with the Burnham position on managerialism, declaring, during the war, that the Nazis were winning because they had made their managerial revolution first.")

Willmoore went to Yale, in 1947, as associate professor in the political science department. He began as a campus "character" and quickly became a scandal. Recklessly eloquent, he became the scourge of what he called liberal hypocrisy—the liberal faculty veterans fighting a cold war while pretending not to. His pugnacity and panache attracted Bill and Brent, who could have been counted protégés if Willmoore had not been the one needing protection. They made a formidable trio—all three bright, handsome, Catholic (in varying degrees), Spanish-speaking, war veterans, glib, argumentative. Willmoore would debate a liberal like Tom Watson of the Law School, Bill would write that up in the *Daily News,* Brent would steer debate on the matter in the Political Union. Willmoore was invited to the elder Buckley's Sharon home, where he traded Mexican experiences with Buckley, Sr., the oil millionaire kicked out of Mexico by General Obregon. Bill's father had long wanted his son to do graduate work abroad, perhaps in Germany. But by 1950 he approved of Bill's staying on at Yale to take his doctorate from Willmoore. (That plan would be aborted when Willmoore decided the Korean engagement was a beginning for World War III and recruited Bill for the CIA; the first CIA man he introduced him to was James Burnham.)

Bill, Brent, and Willmoore were all diverted from their prior course and future expectations by the league they formed at Yale. At first their differences seemed to make them more effective.

When Bill wrote his postgraduate book attacking Yale's curriculum as antitheist and anticapitalist, he found Brent and Willmoore less interested than he in the glories of free enterprise. But Willmoore thought the school's authorities hypocritical because they pretended to alumni that they were inculcating the virtues of religion and of capitalism. Willmoore felt as strongly as Bill that the university should stand *in loco parentis*—he was always seeking a new *parens*. Brent, freshly baptized, was willing to go along with Bill's thesis in order to save the shakiest part of *God and Man at Yale*—the contention that the university should have an established religion. (Odd, that; since any establishment at Yale would certainly not be a Catholic one. Yet Brent would later argue that *America* should have an established religion—not reflecting, once again, that it would never be Catholicism.)

Willmoore later regretted the union forged at Yale with Brent and Bill. He told me, "Brent should never have got himself absorbed into the Buckley empire. If he had gone back to Nebraska he would have become a very distinguished United States senator." With Bill Willmoore was as bitter and obsessed as once he had been with his father. But Bill stayed his friend longer than most people could. When Brent and Bill wrote *McCarthy and His Enemies,* Willmoore closeted them in a hotel room to finish that dreary feat of dossier rummaging; Willmoore himself laid out the book's arguments on free speech and the need for social conformity. When the three men became founding editors of *National Review,* it was Willmoore's wit that rose above sophomoric level in the brief and deliberately outrageous opening paragraph of each issue. (*MM:* "Thousands of students and others would tell you, 'Mosby had a great sense of humor.' Would tell their children, 'This Mosby in the OSS,' or 'Willis Mosby, who was in Toledo with me when the Alcazar fell, made me die laughing.' 'I shall never forget Mosby's observations on Harold Laski.' 'On packing the Supreme Court.' 'On the Russian purge trials.' 'On Hitler.'")

Bill was greatly indebted to Willmoore; but he paid the debt back. To care about Kendall was to get on a breakneck emotional roller coaster, as various women (both wives and lovers) discovered. Bill tells the story of a Yale audience Willmoore stunned into grudging admiration at his defense of Senator McCarthy—

upon which Willmoore insulted the group for being so pliable, angering those he had wooed. He disarmed the pity he deserved by being still (marginally) dangerous, wounding as well as wounded, alternating charm and ferocity. In the course of a few weeks he (1) told me the very existence of *National Review* was justified by its "discovering" Garry Wills, (2) spent an entire dinner telling me I was not *sérieux,* wasting my time writing for *National Review* when I should be studying Plato, and (3) said I should write for *National Review,* but under a pseudonym, since the faculty at Yale (where I was then finishing my doctorate) would find a way to do me in for connection with the magazine. This last point reflected, of course, the refusal of Yale to give him a single promotion or raise in his fourteen years there. His department was wearing him down, to the point where he would let it buy out his tenure. (*MM:* "The real, the original Mosby approach brought Mosby hatred, got Mosby fired. Princeton University had offered Mosby a lump sum to retire seven years early. One hundred and forty thousand dollars. Because his mode of discourse was so upsetting to the academic community. Mosby was invited to no television programs. He was like the Guerilla Mosby of the Civil War. When he galloped in, all were slaughtered.")

It was a risky honor, always, and an education, to argue with Willmoore. The measure of his prickly integrity is that he never stopped arguing with himself. He was always moving backward from his last starting point, to hidden assumptions or previous questions evaded. When I reviewed his first collection of articles and reviews, I pointed out a series of contradictions in them, and expected him to "pull rank," at the very least, next time I saw him. Instead, he admitted the problems were there, and congratulated me on finding them. His mind was volatile despite his intellectual stubbornness—mainly, I think, because his skills and his needs were so deeply at odds: The former were skeptical, forever questioning, while the latter cried out for submission to some authority larger than he could find.

Later, when my book on Nixon was used as a textbook in various schools, I would be asked what training I had in political science—and I answered, at first, "The very best—not a single course in the subject." But that was cheating. Being grilled and guyed by Willmoore, hour after hour, was a course in political science as well as political Sade. We kept in touch, by mail and offprints, the latter all signed with a boyish bravado of penmanship in his favorite shade of "Quink." (*MM:* "Mosby, noting these reflections in a blue-green color of ink which might have been extracted from the landscape.") He put into his endless letters of personal accusation and explanation the energy that should have been saved for his books. He liked to talk at one person, to get a pained quick reaction. Publication was too slow a process—like drawing delayed blood on some other planet.

He never did complete a book after his 1940 dissertation on John Locke, though he was always telling others—including Bill —to stop messing with ephemera and get down to the "big book" each "serious" person should have in him. Willmoore's acute awareness of the claims of authority enabled him to look past the fashionable reading of Locke as a "possessive individualist" and weigh the real force of the democratic majority's "power to conclude." He arrived, by instinct and personal bent, at the kinds of questions raised by a later school of Locke scholars. Like them, he saw that society does not create law for Locke; it just changes the ways of administering God's laws of nature, which antecede the social contract. (*MM:* "Lectured on Locke to show them up. Except by the will of the majority, unambiguously expressed, there was no legitimate power. The only absolute democrat in America (perhaps in the world—although who can know what there is in the world, among so many billions of minds and souls) was Willis Mosby. Notwithstanding his terse, dry, intolerant style of conversation (more precisely, examination), his lank dignity of person, his aristocratic bones.")

Willmoore's "learned hick" pose was not just a façade. It expressed his basic position (and problem)—the combination of majoritarian populism with a more permanent need for authoritative guidance. He was the only anti-elitist at *National Review* in the 1950s. (Spiro Agnew's right-wing brand of populism was still off in the future.) His views should, of themselves, have led to a break from the magazine, apart from his difficult personality. But Bill defused philosophical debate so well that only a series of personal tantrums made Willmoore, finally, no more welcome at *NR* than in Yale's political science department. He drifted for a time from campus to campus, alienating colleagues with increasing efficiency. But his third marriage (blessed by the Catholic Church) and a job as head of the politics department at the University of Dallas gave him what little peace he could hope for in the last years before his death, at fifty-eight, in 1967.

Bellow's Mosby argues himself, with nihilistic brilliance, down into abysses: "I shall not cease from mental strife." But Willmoore did, in some measure, cease from strife. He learned to mute his rebelliousness and submit to a series of "masters" with almost childlike discipleship (at a distance)—John Courtney Murray, Eric Voegelin, Leo Strauss. Willmoore's student George Carey completed a posthumous Kendall book based on his 1964 lectures at Vanderbilt University. The book, *Basic Symbols of the American Political Tradition,* has weak foundations—in Voegelin's theocratic politics; in Strauss's belief that history is one long conversation in univocal terms, marred only by certain people's deliberate (though masked) use of equivocations. At his best Willmoore had been populist rather than theocratic, and acutely aware of historical milieux. But the intellect can only keep up so much self-heckling of Willmoore's violent kind. He found peace at last with his wife Nellie and a few disciples at his small department (autocratically run). He was back in a western family wrangling daily on fundamental matters around an eccentric father figure. Willmoore went back to that western region he considered pre-eminently American as a kind of blind preacher. His father used to say he was a "blackleg Democrat," with a stain of earth too deep to wash away. When the other Willmoore died, I learned that he too had been a registered Democrat all his life.

3 · *Nocks* Redevivi

I finished my first long commissioned piece for Bill, the one on Hoffa. Anything good in it was just recycled Kempton, which may be why Bill liked it (it was reprinted in one of the *NR* anthologies). He had not, after all, suggested that I talk to Jonathan Mitchell (who was already fading from the *NR* scene); but he did say "talk to Suzy"—Suzanne LaFollette, who was active in the thirties labor movement and had known an earlier Dave Beck than the one now sitting in jail, bloated and superannuated.

She told me labor stories. But one never talked to Suzanne long without hearing all about "the old *Freeman*." I did not even know about the newest *Freeman,* which had succeeded several other *Freemans,* including Suzanne's own *New Freeman* of 1930–33. They all looked back to the *Freeman* of the twenties, and to Albert Jay Nock.

When I later said to Bill that his style bore the mark of Willmoore's influence, he denied this (it was after the Buckley-Kendall break). He said the only stylistic influence he was conscious of was Nock's. I couldn't believe that at the time, and I believe it less now. Bill's style is oral, complex but always deliverable, arch but perfectly clear. Nock's style was fussed at, and static; a pretentious mosaic carefully laid, not a speaker's style at all.

Bill's admiration for Nock astounded me. But it is an admiration, verging on worship, that is widely shared. Perhaps you had to meet the man. He was clearly one of the century's great poseurs, a deliberate mystifier, a collector of wealthy patrons, a self-appointed guru to the world's distinguishing few. He is principally remembered now for his *Memoirs of a Superfluous Man* (1943), which tells little about his past, and that little false. The book even begins with a lie—that he had always resisted the urge to write an autobiography. He had energetically started one two decades earlier (*Selected Letters,* p. 65).

Nock was born (1870) in a midwestern Victorian rectory, and went to the Episcopal seminary in Middletown, Connecticut, where he was ordained. (*Memoirs:* "By the time I was thirty I had read quite a bit of theological literature by fits and starts, for no reason in particular . . .") After twelve years of the ministry, he deserted his wife (daughter of his church's warden) and two sons. (*Memoirs:* "I think it [borrowing rather than begetting children] is a sound precept, and one to be encouraged in all such circumstances. I would follow it myself if I liked children, but I have a great horror of them.") He went to New York and became a muckraking journalist for the *American Magazine*. He had become an ardent crusader for Henry George's "single tax." (*Memoirs:* "I did not follow George's campaign attentively, and was neither astonished nor disappointed when it came to nothing.") He dabbled in politics as the friend and promoter of the leading Georgist, Brand Whitlock. (*Memoirs:* "Suddenly he [Whitlock] stopped and faced me with the question, 'Have you any hope *at all* of the human race?' I replied cannily, 'As much as I ever had, no less, no more.'") Through Whitlock's friend in the British Parliament, Francis Neilson, Nock was taken onto the staff of Villard's radical *Nation;* but he was ambitious to form his own magazine, and got Neilson's wife, heiress to the Swift meat-packing fortune, to launch the *Freeman* in 1920. The magazine was Georgist in its politics. Its very title (spelling "freeman" as

one word) came from the motto prefixed to Book One of
George's *Progress and Poverty:* "He that is to follow philosophy
must be a freeman in mind.—Ptolemy." (*Memoirs:* The editorial
policy was apolitical, summed up in three maxims —namely, that:
"You must have a point. Second, you must make it out. The third
one is that you must make it out in eighteen-carat, impeccable, id-
iomatic English.")

An Anglophile, Nock gave his magazine the two-columed gravity of the *Spectator*. His own literary tastes were Victorian (with
Matthew Arnold superintending them), but he had the good sense
to put Van Wyck Brooks in charge of the reviews. The magazine
was anti-Wilsonian, opposed alike to the Red Raids and the
League of Nations. Wilson, it was thought, had sold out the radical dream, as Nock argued in *The Myth of a Guilty Nation* (that
nation being Germany). The view of an earlier Nock is best
recaptured in John Chamberlain's *Farewell to Reform* (1932),
which celebrates the Georgist tradition within populism and progressivism, and blames that tradition's demise on Wilson's "technique of liberal failure." Chamberlain was in 1932 supporting
Suzanne's effort to keep the *New Freeman* alive, since Nock's
journal had ceased publication in 1924 when the disputes between
Nock and Neilson became irresolvable. (*Memoirs:* "As soon as I
saw that the success of our experiment was certain and, if I may
say so, that it would be rather distinguished, my interest began to
dribble away.")

Nock, over the thirties, created a myth of himself as a gentle-
man scholar who had always been above anything so vulgar as
politics. (*Memoirs:* "Some years ago I was in company with half-
a-dozen men when the talk somehow turned on the odd question
of what are the three most degrading occupations open to man.
When the question got around to me, I said I thought the first was
holding office in a modern soi-disant republic. . . .") He was so
careful in building up his myth that his closest friends knew nothing of his priestly days, or marriage, or muckraking activism.
When Who's Who gave him an entry with just a few dates, he
threatened to sue the publication. His anti-Semitism became more
pronounced in the thirties. (*Memoirs:* "This principle [of equality
before the law for Jews] should be definitively understood as car-

rying no social implications of any kind whatsoever. 'I will buy with you, sell with you, talk with you, walk with you, and so following,' said Shylock; 'but I will not eat with you, drink with you, nor pray with you.'") In fact, guided by Ralph Adams Cram, Nock became a racist toward many inferior breeds (see Michael Wreszin, *The Superfluous Anarchist,* pp. 84–86, 114–17). Nock decided that the mass of humans did not and could not achieve the status of *homines sapientes.* It was the job of a true *homo sapiens* to recognize the fact and stop wasting his time on the mob. He should withdraw into leisure (made comfortable by various patrons) and write for the secret few able to grasp his message, the saving remnant.

One of Nock's final patrons was William F. Buckley, Sr. Nock dined at Sharon, comparing anti-Wilson notes with this rich oil man run out of Mexico as a result of Wilson's actions there. He thus became the first Thinker Bill knew familiarly (in his prep-school days). Nock was at the time a great enthusiast for Ortega y Gasset's *Revolt of the Masses*—and for over two decades Bill worked sporadically on what was to be his "big book," an application of Ortega to American politics, with the title *Revolt Against the Masses.* But Bill's antidemocratic animus, expressed as late as 1959 (*Up from Liberalism,* pp. 113ff.), had been partially suspended in the defense of Joe McCarthy on Kendallian grounds (as a voice of the people against the elite), and it seems to have been retired permanently in the celebration of Nixon's "Middle America" and the healthy "Trumanian" vulgarity of Spiro Agnew.

At *National Review* in the 1950s, John Chamberlain and Suzanne LaFollette remembered an earlier Nock than the one Bill had met at his father's table. But they, like Nock himself, had traveled some distance from their early radicalism. When I told John I admired his *Farewell to Reform* (which has, among other things, a fine survey of the political novel from Edward Bellamy to Jack London), he said he was embarrassed even to remember that book. This exemplified something that was borne in on me as I learned about the leftist background of many *NR* editors and contributors: that their work as leftists had been far superior to what they were doing now.

The large number of ex-leftists at the magazine has often been noticed in terms of ex-communists on the masthead. But the leftism represented there was mostly of a broader stripe, and drew especially on progressivism of the original *Freeman* sort. Indeed, the history of the *Freeman* and its imitators is really the prehistory of *National Review*. Turning the yellowed pages of Nock's journal now, I find it hard to see what impressed so many people in the twenties. Nock was only exaggerating a little when he said in his *Memoirs:* "We produced what was quite generally acknowledged to be the best paper published in our language." The "paper" (which Nock never names in his *Memoirs*) posed a problem to this man whose principal subject was himself. He could not disguise the existence of the paper, as he did his children and his Episcopal pastorate; but he subtly deradicalized it.

Some radicals wanted the *Freeman* to rise from its ashes in the twenties; they hoped Nock would try again with non-Neilson money. When it became obvious that he would not repeat the effort, his managing editor, Suzanne, founded the *New Freeman* in 1930. A pioneer feminist, she had been on John Dewey's committee to defend Trotsky from the Moscow trials. Many of the first *Freeman*'s writers clustered round her effort. Even Nock made an occasional contribution. But funds ran out in the Depression that Roosevelt was dealing with too timorously. George's antitax plan, meant to relieve the poor, was becoming an antigovernment program in his spiritual descendants. Frank Chodorov, after meeting Nock in 1936, became the director of New York's Henry George School of Economics, and renamed its newspaper *The Freeman* in Nock's honor. Latter-day Georgists like Chodorov and Murray Rothbard were still radical, but not militantly anticommunist. They resented any governmental interference in their lives, including Washington's.

The Freeman in its next form represented a different development of old Nockians. These were people who, having fought government regulation in its New Deal form, learned to like it in the much larger form of the warfare state. Radical energies faded into the fierce ecstasy of forties patriotism, and the *Freeman* stable of writers showed up (1946) in the anticommunist magazine financed by Alfred Kohler of the China lobby and edited by Isaac Don Levine, along with Ralph de Toledano. It was called *Plain*

Talk, and its first issue was addressed to "authentic liberals." But the journal's motto showed how the "freeman" motif had been put at the service of military preparedness in this first year of world peace: "A World of Free Men—America's Best Defense."

In 1950, *Plain Talk* was merged with an even more outspoken heir to the Nock tradition, a revived *Freeman,* which had for editors John Chamberlain, Henry Hazlitt, and Suzanne LaFollette. This new-old *Freeman/Plain Talk* pledged itself to the cause of "true liberalism" and called itself "A Fortnightly for Individualists." As such, it attracted some of the old Nock and LaFollette writers on cultural matters, Georgists still holding the progressive faith. But it also ran the work of militant anticommunists (who were often ex-communists). The latter writers, tired of debates over who were "true" liberals and who were not, began to cast liberalism as the immediate enemy of tough anti-Soviet foreign policy. The rise of Senator Joseph McCarthy put new strain on these opposed factions in the magazine, a strain that became unbearable when Forrest Davis, a genial and bearded veteran of *The Saturday Evening Post,* joined the editorial board. Davis had written McCarthy's speech against General Marshall. Henry Hazlitt resigned from the magazine, which caused the libertarians to rally against the foreign-policy "hard-liners." When Davis was pushed out in 1954, Chamberlain and LaFollette resigned in solidarity with him. The next year, Leonard Read of the Council for Economic Education bought the *Freeman* and installed Frank Chodorov as its new editor.

Chamberlain, Davis, and LaFollette were now three editors in search of a magazine. In some ways, they had more ties to the old *Freeman* than did Chodorov, though Read's group (especially Edmund Opitz) had stayed closer to the single-tax rationale of the twenties journal. But the three editors had a powerful new ally who was not interested in Nock or in sentimental recall of the twenties. This was Willi Schlamm, the Austrian *Wunderkind* who enjoyed a vivid communist career before blazing out of the Party in his midtwenties. He became an effective journalist, opposed to both the Communists and the Fascists, and had to run for America in 1938, where he began writing for the *New Leader.* Chamberlain, who was an editor at *Fortune,* met and admired

him, and introduced him to Henry Luce, who made him his expert
on world affairs. Luce was even preparing Schlamm his very own
magazine, on culture and the arts, when personal and financial
problems led Schlamm to resign from *Time-Life* in 1951. Then,
for a while, he tried to do, in a small *Freeman* column ("Arts and
Entertainment"), what he had planned to do in the Luce magazine (which had been tentatively named *Measure*).

Henry Luce was, especially in the Pacific theater, even more
militantly right-wing than he let his establishment journals appear.
This was the Luce of the China lobby (which backed *Plain Talk*)
and of Taft's support for MacArthur (Forrest Davis wrote
speeches for Taft on the China lobby line of "who lost China").
This was the Luce who backed Chambers, and made Schlamm his
adviser and employed John Chamberlain; the man whose wife
would later write regularly for *National Review*. But by the
midfifties Schlamm was disgusted with Luce's unwillingness to follow through on his "hard line" instincts, and especially with his
abandonment of Taft for the winner, Eisenhower. I suppose,
therefore, that Schlamm's history affected the first item I mailed
off to *NR* in a double way, since I made an attack on *Time* style
that he could praise just before he left.

By the midfifties Bill had finished his one-year Mexico stint for
the CIA (where he posed as a businessman) and completed his
book on McCarthy. He was working for the *American Mercury,*
though many of his friends wrote for the *Freeman*. He recalled his
Yale *Daily News* period with nostalgia, and the example of Nock
made him think that editing a journal could be a high calling.
Schlamm, done out of one journal by Luce, and prowling in the
company of ex-*Freeman* editors, had gone to the elder Buckley in
his quest for a patron. There was some talk of buying back the
Freeman for those editors who had left in protest, and who would
be joined by Bill. At the last minute this plan fell through, and the
Chodorov *Freeman* folded just in time for *National Review* to
start using the same type and layout from the same printer in Or-
ange, Connecticut.

The last copies of the *Freeman* and the first issues of *NR* were
so much alike, in appearance and personnel, that it would be easy
to confuse even participants in the transition if you handed them

single sheets from one or the other journal a few years later. Schlamm's "Arts and Entertainment" column in the *Freeman* was interchangeable with *NR*'s "Arts and Manners"—and not only in content. It was laid out in identical type, running down identical column widths. Burnham on books, Morrie Ryskind on movies, Frank Meyer on the learned journals—those were regular *Freeman* features, as was a report from England by V. A. Voight. Karl Hess and General Willoughby ran their work in both journals. Senior editors shared by the two journals were Chamberlain and LaFollette. Associate editors included Forrest Davis and C. Dickerman Williams.

In retrospect, the surprising thing is that *NR* was accepted as a brand-new magazine, not the *Freeman* under another of its many guises. Even a later editor of *National Review,* when listing the antecedents of the magazine, entirely overlooked the *Freeman* (Jeffrey Hart, *American Dissent,* pp. 24–28). The truth is that *NR* did strike off in a new direction, even while using much of the armament and personnel of the *Freeman*'s past. The *Freeman,* through all its changes, looked back to a "true" form of liberalism, one that had been radical enough in its day. This made it, paradoxically, conservative about a radical transition. But *NR* did not dream toward journals past. It offered a deliberately rootless kind of conservatism, one that would have no truck with liberals, "authentic" or otherwise. It, for the first time, made Liberalism (capitalized) the Enemy.

If *Freeman* types were uneasy about this, they could still talk about liberalism with a small "l" to old-fashioned Manchesterians; but Buckley knew Liberalism only as an object of attack.

In line with this offensive policy, Buckley gave the magazine a predominantly *monitoring* task. It came to accuse. This fit Buckley's conception of his own role. His first two books had been extended dossiers on the Enemy. *God and Man* listed the liberal textbooks used at Yale, and tried to document faculty attitudes toward religion and capitalism. It was presumed that the accusations, if substantiated, would automatically elicit a reaction in Buckley's audience. In the same way, the McCarthy book listed all the communist fronts belonged to by objects of McCarthy's accusations. Again there was a Kendallian assumption that "the people" would be set in angry motion if they could be brought to see what the liberal elite was up to.

Even at the outset of the magazine, this assumption of solidarity with the "silent majority" in America was held a bit shakily. An overhang of Nockian contempt for the people led Bill simultaneously to defend Joe McCarthy's populism and scorn the "demagogic" vulgarity of Harry Truman. But the inertia of Bill's first success made him cling to the strategy of his first two books (which had been, in part, that of his editing days at the Yale *Daily News*). If nothing else, this gave the magazine a personal stamp to differentiate it from its predecessors—not only from the *Freeman* but from *American Mercury* and *Human Events*. It would also keep it separate from Russell Kirk's *Modern Age,* which was being organized when *National Review* appeared.

The monitoring apparatus of the original *NR* quickly broke down. Bill did not know, yet, how hard it is to keep regular columnists all on schedule, and how boring their fairly narrow assignments would become if they did maintain their schedules. The magazine announced, at the outset, eleven ongoing features; and in each area the first task was to identify the Liberal initiative, chart its course, record its advances (or, rarely, its setbacks). The areas staked out were:

- the intelligentsia: Willmoore Kendall in "The Liberal Line";
- foreign policy: James Burnham in "The Third Cold War";
- Washington: Sam Jones in "From Washington Straight";
- other capitals: Willi Schlamm and five overseas correspondents in "Foreign Trends";
- Capitol Hill: Brent Bozell in "National Trends";
- the courts: C. Dickerman Williams in "The Law of the Land";
- unions: Jonathan Mitchell in "Labor";
- campuses: Bill Buckley in "The Ivory Tower";
- learned journals: Russell Kirk in "From the Academy";
- newspapers: Karl Hess and others in "The Press of Freedom";
- entertainment: Willi Schlamm in "Arts and Manners";
- front organizations: "C.R.B." in "On the Left."

There was a great deal of overlap in this layout. Bill's "Ivory Tower" was meant to do for campuses in general what he had done for Yale in *God and Man*. That intruded on Russell Kirk's assignment and—later—on Frank Meyer's. Willmoore's analysis of "The Liberal Line" often involved argument with the New York *Times* (whose drama critic was the principal target of Schlamm's "Arts and Manners"), and that made "The Press of Freedom" otiose. Sam Jones and Brent Bozell had fuzzily divided jurisdictions in Washington.

As I say, this elaborate scheme soon collapsed. Schlamm, who was editing both books and cultural matters, ranged over the political world as well. This made him, soon, drop the book section —which passed quickly through Willmoore's hands over to Frank Meyer—while retaining "Arts and Manners." (After Schlamm left, that passed to Frank, too.) Schlamm seems to have thought Bill would be a figurehead and money raiser, manipulable by the more experienced editors (principally himself). Perhaps Bill's courtesy and real deference toward colleagues helped mislead Schlamm. Bill was not only younger than all his editors except Brent; he was also less experienced as an editor than anyone but Willmoore. (Typically, Willmoore would be the next after Schlamm to chafe under the ignominy of taking direction from a former pupil.) Only Burnham, of those involved day to day in the magazine's direction, was secure enough not to challenge Bill's authority. But, of course, Burnham most completely shared Bill's concept of the journal's mission.

Burnham, the student of power, saw *National Review* as a particular pressure point meant to have some real impact on the overall strategic stance of America. The CIA had to work in secret with liberal "softies"; but a bright voice for the hard line could make even softies shift a decisive inch or two in the right direction. Pounding away at liberals was Burnham's game—as, in his Trotsky days, he had thought the way to move the revolution toward respectability was to pound away at Stalinism.

Surrounded by temperamental theorizers—by Willmoore and Brent and Frank—Bill relied much on the stability of Burnham, whose sense of priorities resembled his own. Neither man had come to explain the world, but to change it, the quicker the better; and to change it by unremitting attack. Internal questions are not welcome in an army; and Bill, for all his ecumenical instincts, had no talent (and little patience) for theory. That is why, despite years of sporadic effort, he could not complete his book on Ortega. He would, for the cause, make use of the Big Names revered by right-wing theorizers—Leo Strauss, say, or Eric Voegelin. He would endorse those he had no time to understand. Bill's admirable energy keeps him restless, unable to sit alone for a long time with a book. He learns on the run, expertly picking other people's brains; and his ecumenism is partly a real desire to learn from liberals because he is closer to them, day by day, than to the philosophers he invokes—as a general is often closer to the other side's generals than to the keepers of his country's hearth.

Morale at *NR* was kept up, in the early years, almost as an army's is. And the source of the unifying spirit was evident. Things lit or dimmed at *NR* with the coming or going of that pleasantest of neighs, Bill's laugh. His impact on others was summed up for me by Forrest Davis, who recalled his first meeting with him. Bill had come to Washington to recruit writers for his forthcoming magazine: "This positive *kid* came into the restaurant, with his tie half off, sat down, kicked off his shoes, and became the focus of the whole table's attention. By the time he left that restaurant, he had its staff almost fighting for the chance to serve him. I thought, 'Here's a man who's going somewhere!' "

Any threat to the magazine's early harmony got Bill's full attention, the deployment of his diplomatic powers. Though the most forceful person in *NR*'s office, he seemed to have less desire for egotistical display than all the others, not competing with editorial prima donnas; rather, flattering them all; baffling with kindness. I could see a man truly serving something outside himself when he did not (often) need to. It was odd that others sometimes thought the magazine a mere platform for Bill's performance.

But that seems to be the price of Bill's peculiar gifts, his strange power to ingratiate even on the attack. Laboring to achieve an effect beyond himself, he finds that he is his own most compelling subject. To please others, he must keep returning to himself. His best books are "performing versions" of his crowded diary—

Cruising Speed, United Nations Journal, Airborne. His spy tales celebrate his alter ego, Yale CIA man "Blackie" Oates. Just being Buckley is a daily spectacle and adventure. He has become unwillingly a dandy, a Nock, after all. He is the object of a personal cult subtly at odds with his own intentions. The very thing that charms even those on the left makes grimmer types on the right distrust him. Striving for objective results, he *seems* only interested in theatrical effects. What a curious trial for the aspiring ideologue: By restricting himself to combat, he floats above it—intending to strike blows, he is applauded for striking poses.

4 · Frank and Elsie

I spent six weeks in New York that summer of 1957, going back to school at the last possible moment, reluctantly. Aside from writing the piece on Hoffa, I had reviewed books and plays, and written a few paragraphs for the editorial section. Summer cut down on *NR*'s Tuesday luncheons; but the few I attended, with Willmoore and (sometimes) Brent in attendance, were crackling with the special fire of journalistic kids still new on the block, deliberately snotty (to each other and in print). Willmoore's friend Revilo Oliver was visiting from Illinois, and a new friend of Brent's, Fritz Wilhemsen from California. (Bill took Fritz and me on a hilarious sail one weekend. He had misplaced his boat and had to hire a plane to fly along the coast and look for it.)

Back at school in Cincinnati, and hard at work, I found my only continuing relationship with *NR* in long after-midnight calls, once or twice a week, from Frank Meyer (annoying my poor roommate). During these months Frank had absorbed "Arts and Manners" into his book section, so I sought out plays and movies

I could review from the Midwest; but mainly I reviewed books at a furious clip. I was his fastest and most frequent reviewer, begging for books. I even sent unsolicited reviews he did not use. Diana Trilling consulted the index to *NR* and discovered that I wrote about 150 pieces in the decade after meeting Bill in 1957. Far the greatest part of those were reviews, and most were not on political subjects (for a reason I'll go into later). After my seminary days, I was happy to have any outlet on matters I had been studying. Since I owned few books, even free review copies would have been pay enough (and Frank sent things he knew I would want, though he had no room to review them). The reward was even greater than that: *NR* tried to pay top money as a form of talent-hunting, and I got $50 for each 800-word review—good rates for a journal of opinion in the fifties.

I actually wrote a few more reviews than Mrs. Trilling knew. I was doing so much under my own name that I did some under a pseudonym (William Roman) to keep from clogging the pages too often. In the same way, Reid Buckley used the pseudonym Peter Crumpet to keep the magazine from looking like an exclusive Buckley preserve. Bill, I suppose for the same reason, used the pseudonym Aries when he wrote about sailing. I was also using a pseudonym for some of the children's Bible pamphlets I wrote at the time (part of a Doubleday series). I would write a pamphlet on the Catholic side under my own name, then change the Bible quotes and Church references for the Protestant one, written by "Lee Garland Stachen." I was also negotiating with Sheed and Ward for a book on Chesterton. In my first year out of the seminary I was making a fairly steady income as a free-lance writer while doing full course work at Xavier. I completed my master's thesis and received an offer of tuition and living expenses at Yale for the 1958–59 school year. Writing came easy—it would only get hard when I got better at it. I was anxious for some money to get back to New York—not because of *NR;* because of Natalie.

Natalie was the only name I had for that stewardess in the blue Alfa who drove me to the editorial conference at Bill's house in Stamford. I had expected her to come into the house when we got there. But she was wearing her uniform; she said she would feel uncomfortable—stewardesses were not supposed to meet passengers off the flight, anyway. In a naïve stammer of ineffectual arguments, I let her go, though I had forgotten her last name.

On the train back from Stamford that night, I told Priscilla (Bill's sister) and William Rusher (who had just joined *NR* as publisher) about the stewardess, and wondered if Eastern Air Lines gave out information on its stewardesses. When I didn't even know her name? Well, I thought it started with a C, and I knew it was Italian. They just laughed and told me, "Tough luck!" They were right, of course; but I was too dumb to know it.

I called the airline next morning, and got rejected. Thought a minute. Called again. No luck. Tried higher up. A story was forming. I finally got someone to listen: "I was given a ride by a stewardess named Natalie C. (an Italian name) who lives somewhere in Connecticut. I don't want to see her. I just want to know if I left a marked review copy of a book I desperately need, to finish an article today. Don't give me her number. Call her and give her mine; and tell her not to call me unless the book is in her car." He sounded very skeptical; but I sounded very sincere. By the time the story reached Natalie, it was so convincing she ran out to see if the fictitious book was in her car. Then she called.

We saw plays, went on picnics, and argued. She had been brought up a Catholic, but began to think while attending Sweetbriar that the Church was crazy on (among other things) contraceptives. I used my seminary arguments on her. She didn't believe I could believe them. "Come back in twenty years, and I bet you won't be saying that." She was right; but I didn't have to go back after twenty years. She was there all the time.

Eastern didn't fly to Cincinnati, but it did to Louisville. We met there when she could make it. By Thanksgiving break, I had enough money to fly to New York. On Thanksgiving Day we went to Frank and Elsie Meyer's home on a mountain above Woodstock, New York. I had already been there: I was sure that Natalie would love the Meyers at once, as she did. We went through late blaze of autumn in the Catskills up to a kind of book-lined elves' nook, with four small people in it—Frank, bent but with a large head, puffing about the room in a rumble of cigarette smoke and rhetoric; Elsie frail, her Virginia Woolf-pale features a lantern for quick fires within; and the two children, then very young—John with his father's features and mother's frame, and Gene who reversed that formula.

Frank had become, when we met him, the world's most gregarious eremite. He had been a sickly child, forced to withdraw from Princeton. His parents sent him to England, where he blossomed at Balliol. This was the high time of passion for the Spanish Republic; and Frank was a friend of John Cornford, son of the famous classics scholar, who led England's young men off to die in Spain. Frank came back to America a communist, and taught Party courses in Chicago, where he met a bored Radcliffe graduate married to a dilettante. Elsie Bown of St. Louis divorced her first husband to marry Frank and go wherever he went. In the Army, during World War II, Frank broke Party discipline in the agony of his separation from Elsie. After the war he went to his little Woodstock property to put his life together again, co-operated with the FBI in identifying midwestern communists, and began writing for the *Freeman*. Just down the hill lived Frank's best friend from boyhood days, Gene O'Neill, Jr., son of the dramatist. Frank and Gene argued and talked all night after the war about politics and art and religion. Gene was a natural actor who shunned the theater in flight from the ghosts of his father and grandfather; he and Frank divided up all the parts of a Shakespeare play and declaimed them at each other through the night.

Gene Meyer was named for this friend. But John was with his mother when she found Gene's body, naked at the bottom of the stairs in his own house. He had spent a long night of poetry and memories with Frank, went back to his home and brooded for hours, then opened his wrists in a hot tub and trailed blood around the house arguing with death.

O'Neill, who had studied in Germany and taught at Yale, was a pioneer in work on the Greek hexameter. Frank was delighted, when I first went up to see him, to know I was studying classics; he gave me Gene's note on Aristophanes and Horace. (The next year at Yale I studied hexameter theory with Howard Porter, Gene's friend and contemporary; Gene's 1942 article "Localization of Metrical Word-types" was assigned reading. Porter, one of my best teachers, later offered to get me a job at Columbia when Johns Hopkins fired me.)

Frank also learned, at our first meeting, that I formed play-

reading sessions in the seminary. He broke out the Shakespeare
texts Gene had used; and from that time on, every night when I
visited him, we read (or roared) a play of Shakespeare from midnight till two or three in the morning, with an audience of two
(Elsie and John) when others (like Natalie) were not present.
Frank had no ear for music, but he loved thumping oratory and
the muffled detonation of a drum. It is good his home was isolated, so no one could hear our ranting. We competed for the
juicier parts—I had to give up Hamlet to get Falstaff. The only
play he would not read was *The Merchant of Venice*. He admitted
that Shylock disturbed the carefully distant view he took of his
own Jewishness.

The problem he had with Judaism—its feel for supporting *community*—held him back, for ages, from the deathbed step that
made him a Catholic in 1972. St. Paul's talk of Christians as
members of one body struck him as "collectivist"—threatened to
suffocate that endangered individuality he kept asserting in eccentric ways. His bitterness against the Party was based on a feeling
that it had tried to cripple him by regimenting him. One can appreciate the depth of his reaction only if one knows that he came,
increasingly, to think that Area Codes and Zip Codes were a subtle assault on his very personhood. He was part cranky anarchist
—he educated both his sons at home rather than submit them to
the homogenizing school system. When a woman truant officer
came to the house and told Elsie she would need permission to
keep her children at home, Frank—awakened by the conversation
ahead of his noon rising—shouted from the next room: "You
need *my* permission to do anything with my children, I don't need
yours!"

But another part of Frank yearned back toward Balliol and European ceremony. He venerated Queen Elizabeth I, the King
James Bible, the Book of Common Prayer. He would have become an Anglican but for the "liberal" politics of America's Epis-
copalians. He was a snob when he was not deliberately playing the
bum. For an anarchist, he had a strange love of the British Empire and a distressing attitude toward all "wogs" outside the
civilized tradition where, alone, man could be trusted to go his
anarchic way benignly. Frank brought his children up on Tolkien,

C. S. Lewis, and Charles Williams, and only sent them to Yale because he could not afford Oxford. When Frank tried to reconcile the right wing's libertarians and traditionalists, he was adjudicating between his own head (symbolized by his "bohemian" ways, the utilitarian britches, the workmen's suspenders) and his heart (symbolized by his fussy grammar and Anglicisms).

Though he was nearing fifty when I met him, Frank had retained the enthusiasms and intolerances of youth. He was popular with right-wing campus groups in the fifties: wherever he went there was argument and laughter and mischief. I regret I did not tape some of his and Elsie's reminiscences of radical life in the thirties. Frank also filled me in on the background and prehistory of other editors at *National Review*. Between the long phone calls and frequent visits, I spent more time with him in the late fifties and early sixties than with anyone outside my own family.

The visits had a satisfying sameness. I arrived in the afternoon, late in a glorious bounce of sun off Catskill angularities, to find Elsie sorting mail, dictating to a typist, handling the dinner preliminaries. Frank emerged bearlike and growled his way back to life, checking the boys' Latin assignments; consuming endless cups of coffee. He would crash into his chair, lie there in a humorous frog-slump, fix me with his bleary yet acute eyes, a hooded stare —then leap to a bookcase, shouting for his glasses, to find a quote refuting me. He had purplish lips, a mottled underground look; he truly hated the sun. Elsie had to sneak out to her garden while he slept—Frank thought her daylight love of flowers an aberration or weakness. All good things got done at night.

Dinner was fresh from the garden, or from things frozen as Elsie had picked them. Frank rumbled his brief blessing, *"Benedictus benedicat."* Then argument and phone calls, Shakespeare and more argument; till dawn, when Elsie made eggs and her special blend of coffee. I would stick my head out, a minute, at the sun, which seemed always "rosy-fingered" there (not fingering *rays,* of course, but a red glow where dawn "touched" the mountains). Then off to bed for the day.

Frank's isolation on his mountaintop was a way of protecting an individuality he felt "they" were assailing, everywhere, in modern society. But once he had withdrawn to his own turf, he wanted the whole world—or as much of it as he could lure there—present and arguing with him in the living room. To talk with Frank was to be plugged into a network of constant interchange with dozens of people. He was often shouting from his phone to his dining room, making one large conversation of his evening's visits and the steady stream of phone calls. He kept in touch with all his reviewers, with a large group of politicians and educators, with the *NR* office and its scattered editors.

I was involved in a typical Frank interchange in 1961. Pope John's social encyclical *Mater et Magistra* had just appeared, and Castro's slogan was still vivid in American minds (*"Cuba, sí; Yanquí, no"*). Frank called to tell me he was writing a column that would brand the encyclical "ridiculous" (he later softened this to say that some *interpretations* were ridiculous). I thought he was being imprudent, but told Frank his argument could be put in four words: *"Mater, sí; Magistra, no."* Frank liked the crack, and repeated it to several *NR* editors over the next few days. It showed up as one of the magazine's smart-aleck opening "paragraphs": "Going the rounds in Catholic conservative circles: *'Mater, sí; Magistra, no.'*" This caused an outcry against Bill as a "false Catholic." But the distributor of the phrase was, as so often, Frank. My life has been regrettably duller without him.

Frank and Elsie became our best friends. When, two years after we met, Natalie and I were married, Frank got a small grant (two thousand dollars) to take us to England for our honeymoon, where I worked on Chesterton's private papers at Beaconsfield. Later that same year, I ran out of money while finishing my doctoral dissertation, and Frank got me a job writing editorials for Jack Kilpatrick at the Richmond *News Leader* during a crucial seven months. Meanwhile, Frank and Elsie changed their wills to make us guardians of their sons if the parents should die together in an accident. The saddest thing about my break with *NR* would be the fact that Frank helped precipitate it (to Elsie's distress).

But in those first years, some of the funniest and happiest nights I spent were euphoric with polemical wraths, feigned and real, as Frank argued in and out of his small living room, dining room, kitchen, and study. Elsie punctuated the discussion with cries of "Oh *Frank!*" (eyes rolled up) or "Oh *Garry!*" (her schoolmarm asperity heart-stopping in its underlying warmth). Elsie was a gardener of genius, one the very plants seemed to love—as animals certainly did. A mother raccoon used to shepherd her offspring—under the watchful eyes of cats and a dog—into Elsie's kitchen for a nightly snack.

Frank's first *NR* columns—on the learned journals—quickly went the way of Bill's other monitoring schemes. After that Frank wrote a political feature called "Principles and Heresies." But most of his energy went into the book section, which many readers thought was the best part of the magazine. The first time I went up to see the Meyers (during my six weeks at the office), I told them my favorite *NR* reviewer—after Schlamm, my favorite *NR* writer—was Robert Phelps. Frank was instantly on the phone, inviting Robert up—he lived in Woodstock, much of whose art-colony gossip would go into the Phelps novel *Heroes and Orators*. Early in the fifties, when Robert was just getting his start as a writer, the promise of a job made him yearn to attend a particular writers' conference. But he had no money for the trip, and neither did the Meyers. So Elsie went around the village asking for money to help a local artist. Robert attended.

I think of that as a symbol of the way Frank and Elsie cared for their young reviewers. A good anthology could be made of the reviews Frank got from Robert, from Guy Davenport, from Joan Didion, John Leonard, Arlene Croce, Francis Russell, Hugh Kenner, and others. Frank once told me to keep an eye out for a good Manhattan movie reviewer. I had just read a stunning review in *Commonweal* by one Arlene Croce. Frank called her at once, found she needed a job, and had *NR* hire her as copy editor. She was senior editor when she left to become America's best dance critic. Frank's love of the telephone gave him an advantage many editors lack: He was indefatigable in pursuit of reviewers, prodding them with frequent telephone requests, reminders, demands. He would call England as easily as California, leading Willmoore to claim that Bill paid him his salary or his phone bill, whichever was higher. The Anglophilia imbibed at Balliol led Frank to coax reviews from Auden, both Waugh brothers, Arnold Lunn, Shane Leslie. Poor Frank apologized to me when he got Evelyn Waugh to review my 1961 book on Chesterton. Frank had given Waugh the (false) impression my book was the reworking of a doctoral dissertation, and Waugh dismissed it with an expression of his distaste for that genre and the comment that criticism of contemporaries is a waste of time. (Bill offered to kill the review, but I said that was unthinkable. Actually, I tend to agree with both Waugh's positions; but I did not consider Chesterton, born sixty years before I was, a contemporary.)

Frank had a consuming interest in *NR*'s office politics, though he rarely saw the office. His feuds with Jim Burnham and Russell Kirk were famous—long-standing arguments he interrupted only to argue with other foes and his own allies. The war on Burnham was frustrating for the same reason that it was endless: Burnham would not deign to notice it. Frank thought Burnham's pragmatism unprincipled, and Frank seriously entertained, now and then, the belief that Burnham was running *NR* as a CIA operation. (Not only Burnham and Willmoore but Bill and Bill's sister Priscilla had been in the CIA.)

There was also a personal reason for Frank's resentment of Burnham. He described to me one night how he had watched Burnham, as a Princeton senior, preside over a table of the most admired students, just at the time when Frank, an underclassman, was about to withdraw from school. Then, when he went to Balliol, he again faced the legend of Burnham's brilliance and popularity. It must have seemed the work of some malicious historical imp for him to find Burnham at Bill's elbow just when Frank was trying to join the inner circle of *NR* editors. When Frank was feeling particularly exercised over some policy of Burnham's, he would take off the shelf Orwell's *Shooting an Elephant* and read to visitors its attack on Burnham's "power worship."

If Frank could not get a rise from Burnham, he worked Russell Kirk into very satisfying frenzies. Frank had rightly dismissed Kirk as a sentimental vaporizer in a *Freeman* review. Kirk waited years to return the favor when Frank's first book appeared. Kirk never had a close connection with *NR;* one reason was his unwillingness to share editorial rank with Frank Meyer. If he had known what Willmoore thought of his scholarship, he might very well have broken off his one continuing tie—the columns written on his alma mater, Michigan State, as "Behemoth U."

Frank was understandably amused when I told him how I met Kirk. Kirk's journal *Modern Age* came out about the time I first went to New York. After he read some of my reviews, Kirk invited me to write for him and suggested I come see him in Mecosta, Michigan. During a Christmas break from graduate school, I borrowed my father's car in Lansing and drove over to Mecosta with a friend, a fellow student.

Kirk was then living alone in a barn behind the house he later inherited from relatives. The barn was unheated, so he told us to keep our overcoats on while he bustled us over to a fireplace. His reviewing policy was simple. Books sent to the journal were piled haphazard in a corner; he told me to go over and pick out any I wanted to review. Kirk was determined to show us his summer cottage on a nearby lake, where he dreamed his dreams and viewed his visions. But this was Michigan, in winter. Even the main roads were icy. When I saw the snow-choked back road he wanted us to travel (in my father's car, for Kirk had none), I suggested we save the cottage for another visit. He would not hear of it, and we were soon wedged in a trough of snow, unbudgeable. Kirk could neither push the car nor manage its wheel, so my friend and I tried what we could, unsuccessfully. We were for going back, to find help. Kirk insisted we see the cottage first. It was obviously a shrine in his own eyes, the lair of a wizard. So, after a long walk farther into the woods, we saw it. But not much of it. He had forgotten the key.

By that time, walking over the frozen lake seemed a quicker way back to town than rethreading the snowy trail. When we got out on the lake, my friend saw a light in another cottage: "Let's go there." Kirk was against the idea: He did not know the owner of the cottage. "What does that matter? If someone got in over a road, he must have a Jeep or truck, enough to pull us out—or take us to a garage." Kirk followed us, protesting.

The cottage held a father and son who had been out duck hunting. They were friendly; fixed us drinks while we described our plight. Kirk had withdrawn into a corner without a word. When his drink was ready, and the man held it out, Kirk advanced slowly, drew his card case; picked one, presented it; and told the man he was an author. (Kirk's essays about his European wanderings make them sound like a combination of Hilaire Belloc's and Roy Campbell's boisterous travels into the past from one inn to another.)

I saw Kirk just one more time, years later, at a meeting of the right-wing Philadelphia Society. (As I say, he was never to be found at *NR* affairs.) By then Kirk had married; his wife came up after Kirk's lecture, carrying their newborn child in a loose woven sling with two handles. She went off to get diapers and, when she came back with her hands full, asked Russell to pick up the baby. He puzzled a while at the task, found one handle, and jerked it up. The baby rolled with a thump onto the floor. Frank was not surprised when he heard.

Frank's spirits were sapped in his (and the century's) sixties. His prolonged youth ended in a prolonged bout with cancer; he could not read the changed mood on campuses, and became obsessed with "barbarians" destroying "our" civilization. As sometimes happens, the prospect of a man's own death became a portent of the world's end. Elsie could no longer argue and laugh him out of his antiblack outbursts. The long phone calls became repetitive harangues. But on occasion Frank's old love of life would bubble up, and the postmidnight call became a delight again instead of an ordeal.

When he died, so did Elsie, though she went through the motions of life. She too became a Catholic, but still argued with me about the Church's condemnation of suicide. She would not hear *anyone* condemn her beloved Gene O'Neill. Besides, a few years earlier she had come to visit Natalie and me, seeking help to talk her out of suicide. After Frank's death, she talked of him nonstop whenever we met. Her great love for others had always played around and through her total love for him. Two years after his death, she killed herself—and killed something in all of us whose lives she touched and brightened.

5 · Communism and "Convenience"

Frank Meyer was open and ecumenical in his editing canons, but increasingly closed and fanatical in his politics. I did not write much about politics at *National Review* because I flunked Frank's first test. After our opening phone conversation, he had sent me Frederick Schuman's *Russia Since 1917*. The book seemed learned, thorough, and compassionate—the things I called it in my review. I did not realize that Schuman was one of the *NR* editors' favorite devils of the period—Willmoore called him, in an upcoming issue, an "arch Soviet apologist."

Frank cheerfully told me it was a terrible review, which he could not run. He would protect me from such blunders in the future—so most of my assignments were literary. And even then I did not pass muster at times. When O'Neill's *Touch of the Poet* was first published, I thought of my Collins grandfather—like the hero, he was named "Con"—and reflected on Irish problems with drink and matriarchy. Frank delicately told me that "many of our readers are Irish Catholics"—he later admitted that meant the *Buckleys* are Irish Catholic. He would have to kill all that section of the review. Later, harsh comments about Reid Buckley were excised from a public exchange I had with him.

Killing entire reviews was not uncommon at *NR*—as I say, Bill even offered to suppress Evelyn Waugh for having the temerity to dislike my first book. Since Bill knew I admired Chambers' *Witness* in the seminary, he asked Frank to give me Whittaker's *Cold Friday* when it appeared. The review praised the Witness but not his writings: "In this collection of works-not-in-progress, all the man's failings are unredeemed . . . the faltering attempts at poetry, the retailing of all the subsidiary points of Dostoevsky as if they were something new, the crushing insights into evil that come to every precocious adolescent." The superficiality of Chambers' "mature" reflections made me go back and read *Witness* for the third time—where I now saw the same faults I had described in reviewing *Cold Friday*. How different were these pretentious musings from the wit and constant laughter of the Chambers I met in *NR*'s office and had lunch with. Bill was (with Mrs. Chambers) a keeper of the flame for "Whit." He apologized, but said he could not run my review. (I sent it to Russell Kirk's *Modern Age,* which ran it.)

Bill justified his review policy by saying the magazine played frankly the advocate's role. (I thought of that in later years when "advocacy journalism" became a target of Richard Nixon's defenders, including *National Review*.) Frank sometimes chafed at Bill's rules in these matters, and did his best to circumvent them— reducing books by Bill's friends to "briefs" or giving them to predictably dull reviewers, so he could cut the copy down if not entirely out. Once he called me and said, "Can you think of anything nice to say of Taylor Caldwell?" I said no. "I haven't been able to find anybody who can. But Bill wants it." Bill's sister Priscilla finally bit that bullet. Bill's service to others gave him freedom to treat his own books in the same handsome way. Each as it came out was given a long lead review in the magazine, invariably written by a personal friend.

Frank's ideological distrust of me, born of the Schuman review, had no warrant so far as the Soviet Union was concerned. I had

grown up a Catholic cold warrior, praying after Mass every day
for the conversion of Russia, rallying to anticommunism around
that cold-war icon, the statue of "Our Lady of Fatima." I went to
high school in Wisconsin, where two of my best friends were sons
of Congressman Charles Kersten, one of Joe McCarthy's closest
Wisconsin allies. In my senior year, I cheered General MacArthur
when he rode through his hero's welcome in Milwaukee. I did not
have much chance (which I surely would have taken) to cheer
McCarthy, since I went into the newspaperless seminary just six
months after he made his opening charges at Wheeling. I would
not begin to question my own cold-war mentality till the sixties,
when the Indochina engagement looked not so much "imperial" to
me as dumb.

In 1959, on my honeymoon in England, I wrote the most political of my *NR* pieces. Bill had planned an "under thirty" issue of
NR to show off the magazine's young writers. John Leonard did
Bill's column of that period ("The Ivory Tower"). I wrote in
Frank Meyer's place ("Principles and Heresies"), and sounded
much like Frank. He and Brent had planned protests and demonstrations against the Khrushchev visit to Camp David, and I
cheered along their effort, calling the Camp David meeting "Nero
in our Camp." Eighteen years later Diana Trilling resurrected that
horror to prove (in *We Must March, My Darlings*) that I wrote
even sillier anticommunist stuff than she had. Which is true, with
this minor difference: I quit.

Glib anticommunist editorials about "foreign policy" were all I
could contribute to the Richmond *News Leader* when I went there
in February of 1961. Local news, soothing or abrading to the
publisher's friends, had to be left to more practiced hands, those
of Jack Kilpatrick. I came early into the office, damned Russia
and/or China in heightened rhetoric (read, alas, by *News Leader*
regulars as if they had never heard such things), and was home by
lunch to start typing on my dissertation. I saw little of Richmond
in the process, though I liked what I saw. But when I finished the
dissertation in May, I had to plunge into another kind of study.

My graduate work had left me no time to read the political classics, and a try or two at Aristotle's *Politics* had not encouraged me
to go further. My political ideas—or, better, prejudices—had

been picked up from literary sources, and never questioned much: I swore by Dr. Johnson and John Ruskin, Cardinal Newman and Gilbert Chesterton. All I could answer, when Bill first asked after my politics, was "distributist" (that is, Chestertonian). Bill rightly took Philip Burnham's word that distributism is not "conservative" in the Buckley sense, since Chesterton was a scathing critic of capitalism. But I also fit into another characterization of the distributist—as merely sentimental medievalizer. I had made no serious effort to connect the stray political opinions picked up in my reading. I found this embarrassing when I came to write editorials daily, and determined to remedy the situation as soon as I crossed the hurdle of my dissertation.

I had only read two of the political classics, and not read them well, by 1961. Plato's *Republic,* at both the graduate and undergraduate levels, was required reading, but more for its language and imagery than its politics (or even its philosophy). Augustine's *City of God* had become a favorite when it shone out from the severely restricted list of things we could read in the novitiate —though again I had read it more as an allegory of the soul's pilgrimage than as a political book.

That left me with a long reading list for the summer of 1961— Aristotle, Hooker, Locke, Burke, Rousseau, Jefferson, Adams, Mill, Tocqueville, Calhoun. I went at them with the energy of starting something fresh; and Frank Meyer gave me a deadline to meet in reporting my results. Frank had some grant money to publish an anthology called *What Is Conservatism?* Behind schedule as usual (along with most of his contributors), he needed another essay after several writers did not produce what they promised. Frank was following the course of my political self-schooling with interest, doubt, and suggestions.(He brought up Bagehot and Shaw, but I had no time left; they would have to come later.) Frank wanted a quick job—done by September; and that suited me, since I would be entering the Center for Hellenic Studies that month (as a Fellow in its first year of existence), when Greek studies would reclaim my attention.

I finished on time, though Frank still had to wrestle with the book for another year or two. My essay "The Convenient State" has been anthologized three times—four if you count as two books Bill's trade volume *Did You Ever See a Dream Walking?* and his school text *American Conservative Thought in the Twentieth Century.* It was my first serious effort at reflection on politics, and despite its errors of historical judgment it contains the germ of everything else I have had to say or explore in the area. I would not regret it much, despite its mistakes, if it were written less turgidly. I still agree with its main points, inchoate as they are and showing still my half-digested reading in so many sources. But *NR,* in its many ads for Buckley's anthology, later removed all mention of my essay, which comes first in the volume. One of the two, *NR* or I, was wrong (then or now) in how we understood that 1961 essay. Or both were. The latter, I guess.

My starting point, in 1961, was influenced by Frank's and Brent's endless arguments over the relative importance of freedom and order in the history of Western culture—Frank standing for the individual's autonomy, Brent for a state-supported "virtue." I thought the argument needed recasting. Willmoore asked the right question: What *kind* of order is there to be, not how *much?* And based on what *authority?* But I thought he gave the wrong answers. I was lucky to witness the squabbling of these doctrinaire friends. They put the challenge of my study in a vivid and personal form. So I began my essay with the emphasis on individualism that marks Europe's culture and seems to run wild in America's nineteenth-century cult of "frontier" self-reliance. What order would Faustian, would Promethean man submit to? Nothing, said one form of liberalism, except rational persuasion. But I argued: "Any attempt to base political freedom on the claims of man's intellect makes the state the center of truth—in Plato, truth as moral enlightenment; in Aristotle, truth as a set of logical imperatives—and nothing is more absolute than the claim of truth upon man" (*Did You Ever See a Dream Walking?* p. 14).

Having escaped the religious authority of the East (this was Eric Voegelin talk), Western man tried to erect a secular absolutism. Here I cited Acton: "In the Jewish as in the Gentile world, political and theological obligations were made to coincide; in both, therefore—in the theocracy of the Jews as in the politeia of the Greeks—the State was absolute" (ibid., p. 35). Free pursuit of the truth is a noble ideal; but what if one should have the bad

luck (bad in terms of liberal ideals) to *catch* it? What then? "Man
can refuse to think, or think confusedly; but once the evidences of
reality are received within the intellect, it is not free to think anything it pleases" (ibid., p. 14). Despite my classicist's bent and
training, I could not see how a free society could be based on
reason. (This was not the same thing as saying the state must be
irrational, though Frank's young libertarian friends said that
about my essay.) Even when I thought I *should* submit to Plato
and Aristotle, I kept resisting them—and found, as I tackled the
City of God again, that Augustine had rebelled against their authority.

As early as Book Two (Chap. 21), Augustine said he felt he
must argue with the classical assumption that the state is founded
on justice. This was an astonishing assertion for a man whose
background was Neoplatonic. Only years later, when he reached
Book Nineteen (Chap. 24), would he face the challenge he
had set himself at the outset of his long work. I have come to
think that insight the great breakthrough in Western political
thought, though I could not give an adequate account of it in
1961. But I already realized that the Lincolnian ideal of a state
"dedicated to a proposition" was a kind of masked theocracy.
Augustine was not, as so many had assumed, a theocrat. He was
the greatest critic of theocracy. Indeed, he was accused of taking
such a gloomy view of the state that he made it almost impossible
for God to have anything to do with his creation on its political
side. Yet the man who made *love* the basis of the state cannot be
called merely negative or pessimistic about man's political capaci-
ties.

Those who recognize that Augustine refused to ground the state
on justice accused him of condoning injustice. The same thing has
happened to Newman and to Johnson, both antitheocrats in their
own day. I quoted Newman in my essay: "Satisfaction, peace, liberty, conservative interests [are] the supreme end of the law, not
mere raw justice as such" (ibid., p. 20). That quote came from a
tract *Who's to Blame?* made up of eight public letters of "war protest" written by Newman in 1855. He argued that the genius of
the British Constitution was compromise, which sat ill with the
crusading attitude of war. One or the other must "give"—the

Constitution or the Crimean War effort; Newman hoped it would be the latter.

Newman placed such emphasis on the government as pragmatic accommodation that he defended even England's "paragovernment" (as Bernard Bailyn calls it) of "bribes" involving placemen and titles. After I had finished my essay, but before it was delivered, I was invited to give a paper at a right-wing academic gathing in California's Pepperdine College. The group was made up of young college teachers and graduate students—for example, an anticommunist assistant professor who later went to Congress, Philip Crane. But most of the participants were "libertarians" of the semi-anarchist kind. They thought my paper an attack on the very ideal of justice, and focused especially on the defense of bribes. Even today I run across people, students of those professors, who think of me as an apologist for organized crime.

I had already taken sides in the little intramural dispute between libertarians and authoritarians—not that, given the sides, I had much choice in the matter. There was an almost *religious* test involved. Libertarians, purists of the free market, hated to see any market of ideas closed up by doctrine. The authoritarians, the only obvious alternative, were largely Catholic in the broad sense. Frank's principles were libertarian, but his sentiments were Anglo-Catholic; so he presented himself as a "fusion" of the two sides, walking proof that it could be done. Bill, with his inherited devotion to both capitalism and Catholicism, made a similar claim.

But the fact that men can live with contradiction does not remove the contradiction—it just makes the contradiction go philosophically "underground" and play funny games there. Individualist and Catholic are night and day, since *kath-holou* means permeating (literally, "through the entirety"). The isolated and the integrated, the singular and the communal, are opposed at their deepest level of meaning. Bill Buckley can be a laissez-faire businessman and a communal believer only by the same train of historical accidents that brought different types together at that Pepperdine College conference. The right wing in America is an alliance caused by a common bugaboo: "statism" (whether communist, socialist, or welfare-supplying). Insofar as the welfare state was the current expression of American liberalism, and liberalism was the American tradition, these "conservatives" could not even claim a living tradition. They were rebels against the present order—which is not a bad thing in itself, though it is an odd position for those calling themselves conservatives.

In the early sixties, Goldwaterism attracted authoritarians calling for state censorship of pornography, for state-instilled morality on matters like abortion, and for local power to enforce Jim Crow laws. It also attracted libertarians who thought all those things infringements on the free choice of the individual. Strom Thurmond and Milton Friedman marched together, odd Mutt and Jeff, behind the senator's unfocused ramble.

Neither side could be happy with the alliance. The libertarians, nineteenth-century Manchesterians, were not happy with an electoral necessity of calling themselves "conservatives." Polls show that, in defiance of logic, Americans think of conservatives and liberals as, respectively, calling for less or more government spending on social needs—as opposed to defense spending, where the terms reverse themselves. Authoritarians, on the other hand, professing a love for tradition, were unhappy at the "rootless" rationalism and laissez-faire morals of libertarians. (Even authoritarians like Russell Kirk, another Goldwater speechwriter, adopted one part of nineteenth-century liberalism—laissez-faire economics —while denying its rationale and original matrix.)

I, of course, was unhappy along with the rest. I did not like to be lumped with Brent as a theocrat or with Kirk as a sap; yet Chesterton had made me anti-individualist. He put the absurdity of free-market thought in a single sentence: "It is as if ten mine workers ran a foot race, and the winner got to be Lord Northumberland." Catholic social thought began not with the individual but with the family as the basis and model for society (a starting point I would later find in Francis Hutcheson and all his eighteenth-century disciples, including Hume and Jefferson). So I ended my essay with a rejection of libertarianism as in any sense conservative. Since Frank was arguing for "fusion" in this and all his books, he asked me to delete or dilute that ending, but said he would run it if I insisted. I diluted it. But I gave the original ending at Pepperdine, where the libertarians confirmed my instinctive resistance to them. Though I differed from authoritarians on many points, we at least had some common ground. I felt sure, now, that I had nothing to learn from the libertarians at all.

I was wrong. Certain of them, from their suspicion of the state in general, thought creation of America's own warfare state to oppose communism had gone too far—had, in fact, just given us *two* statist superpowers. Though not pacifists, they were not crusaders either. They could criticize communism without feeling an instant duty to destroy it. That was not an attitude restricted, by any logical necessity, to the libertarians. It was, in fact, one that should have flowed from my own first "solution" to the right-wing dilemma; but I was too dense to see that.

My attempted solution was to avoid the patriarchal conclusion from society-as-family by arguing, in effect, for brotherhood without fatherhood: for political society above the family level as a matter of mutual deference rather than submission to one patriarchal source of authority. This was what Willmoore seemed to be aiming at in his majoritarianism. I thought I could see a better way of putting it in terms of a commonalty of interests (Johnson), "property" in the large sense (Newman), or overlapping loves (Augustine). I was approximating, though I did not know it then, Hutcheson's concept of benevolence as the basis of the social contract. The point was not, as Willmoore thought, to find and assert the binding authority, Locke's "power to conclude," to which all must defer, but to find an ethic of deferrals, putting off conflict in the name of common good things held.

I took a word used in passing by both Hooker and Newman—convenience ("coming together")—to express the goals of this political society. This does not acquit men of their accountability to justice—though it admits that men, if pushed, will have very different ideas about what justice is. It simply says that finding justice and enacting it are not the first reasons for the state's existence: "The state, like the family, like the corporation, like the labor union, is bound by laws of morality that are incumbent on all human endeavor, corporate as well as individual. In carrying out its function, the state must act with justice. But its specific aim is not to enforce justice as such" (ibid., p. 21). Basketball teams should not cheat. They must be just in that sense. But they exist to play and win ball games, not to bring down justice upon earth. In the same way, the state exists to hold people together in peace, not to enunciate "raw justice." I chose the term "convenience" for its inviting etymology, and to escape the moral disfavor belonging to other appropriate terms like "expediency" or "compromise." The nation should be a human "convention." In a 1971 essay on Jefferson, I appealed to eighteenth-century usage:

> To speak of "convention" in our day—to speak of it conventionally—is to risk misunderstanding. The word suggests to us formality, a matter of empty forms—yet the "forms" of society were ceremonies then. "Convention" was a lively matter, as lively as the constitutional convention in Philadelphia. It is not mere punning to link such uses of a word. The active note of con-vening still animated words that seem placid to us —as when John Adams called a good wine and his constitution "convenient." . . . By reactivating the root sense of words, men were led to think in etymological clusters—like convening, convenience, convention. To accept a convention was to come together in conscious agreement on its observation and significance. It was a great time of congress and convenings; of public business, carried on in public by conferrings and consent. "Convention" was just consent put in more lasting form—the word still meant certain kinds of written laws, as well as unwritten usage.

Insofar as my first guesses and hints in this matter are defensible, they must be given a grounding I understood better (and will talk of) later. But even then I should have seen how at odds with the essentially compromising ideal of "convenience" was any absolute crusade for "liberation" of the world from communism. Our very fear of the Soviet Union arose from a certitude that, in war, Russians would fight us—and do it very well. How could that be true if they were only slaves or helots yearning to escape their masters? How, for that matter, did a nation ravaged by war, incompletely industrialized even before the war, reach so quickly a level to challenge America at her historic peak of power? Celebrators of the "free market" should have been the first to see that such efforts were not made by the use of grudging labor, by the compulsion of "inefficient" slaves. Admittedly, there were injustices in Russia and China, massive and terrible—as there had been slavery, the genocide of Indians, the seizure of territories, in America's rise to power. One does not have to condone communism in order to condemn the kind of crusade America mounted against communism in the 1940s and 1950s. Yet I still applauded that crusade, even while advancing "convenience" as a means of escape from ideological constraints I could see in others.

I used to tease Frank about the way he opposed the state while becoming obsessed with it. He thought of nothing else, day or night. It had even greater power over him than he thought it was *trying* to get. Once one defines oneself primarily by opposition to one other thing, the essential surrender is made. One resembles those Christians who defined themselves in terms of opposition to the devil. The devil became their operative god, the thing that filled their thoughts and limited their actions. The obsessed person longs for some Ahab showdown with his own white whale. He grows to resemble the cruel thing he opposes, becomes its antitype or photographic negative—as America's secret police and internal surveillance began to resemble the Soviet Union's in the time of our obsession with Russia. The only way to fulfill that obsession is "fusion" indeed, the nuclear fusion of an ultimate showdown, Ahab flinging himself on the whale.

Fear as the operative element in self-definition reached a pitch in 1961 that forms a kind of parable. An offshoot of the Kennedy administration's early civil-defense program was heated public debate over the morality of shooting one's own neighbors if they tried to overcrowd one's bomb shelter. Obsession with an enemy almost always makes one's neighbors become the enemy—hence our vast "internal-security system." Frank, a friend of Herman Kahn who admired his effort to make nuclear war "thinkable," argued stoutly for the shootout at the shelter, and I bought his argument. It was hard to hold an ideal of "convening" in such an atmosphere of excluding, of segregating in the largest sense—the ultimate "isolationism" and individualism of solipsism. I only held to the convenient ideal by failing to see how little I acted in accord with it.

6 · Catholic Politics

If my reviews for Frank were mainly literary, what *NR* writing I did directly for Bill dealt with Catholicism. When I entered Yale's graduate program in 1958, I was just up the road from Bill's Stamford home. I saw him often, and sailed with him—one of life's great experiences, which can be vicariously enjoyed now by readers of his book *Airborne*. Bill was then engaged in an odd war with his coreligionists, and anxious to recruit allies. He had been forced, by the debate, to form a kind of informal Catholic "brain trust." The principal figures in this group were a teacher in the New York seminary system and three of his old pupils. The teacher was Monsignor Florence Cohallen. The pupils were Monsignor Eugene Clark (later the press officer of the New York Archdiocese), Monsignor Roger Pryor (later director of schools in the New York Archdiocese), and Neil McCaffrey. Neil had left the seminary years before, and was working for Doubleday—it was he who arranged for me to do children's pamphlets on the

Bible. Something of a genius at direct-mail selling, he later founded the Conservative Book Club and began publishing his own line of books under the Arlington House imprint.

Because of my seminary background, Bill included me in this group; and because of my greater availability, I soon found myself answering his questions about papal authority, encyclicals, Catholic social teaching, etc. He assumed I knew more about such questions than I did in fact—a flattering assumption that made me do some of the homework I should have done earlier. When Bill engaged in a much-publicized series of debates with *Commonweal* editor William Clancy, he tried to make it a four-way exchange, with me questioning Clancy while some ally of Clancy's choosing questioned Bill. Nothing came of that, though Bill drove up to New Haven to go over likely subjects of debate before the series began.

In the wake of the flap over *"Mater, sí; Magistra, no,"* Neil McCaffrey had one of his constantly fizzing ideas for a book. Neil keeps files on everything, and had all the Catholic attacks on Bill, along with the answers Bill had made to them. He planned to publish that record, with a supplement of essays commenting on the exchange. Half a dozen or so people were asked to contribute essays—as one of them, I was to write on the binding force of papal encyclicals. As often happens with such projects, some of the essays Neil most wanted were not produced, and some of those that came in were unsatisfactory. About the only things usable, by the project's deadline, were Neil's Introduction and my essay—which, even with the "documents" included, made for a very short book. It threatened to get shorter when Neil ran into trouble about getting reprint rights for some of the attacks on Bill. At that point, Bill suggested I summarize the controversy and comment on it; so Neil turned the whole thing over to me.

That involved me in a much more ambitious statement than my original essay had contained. My "homework" done for Bill over the past four years had made me realize that, despite constant Catholic babbling on the subject of encyclicals, no book in English had dealt with their doctrinal force. I set out to write a short book in the summer of 1962, and wrote a long one instead. (I was developing a pattern of summer productivity, in reaction to the scattered labors of the school year: in 1959 I wrote my Chesterton book in England, in 1960 I did most of the work for my Aeschylus dissertation, in 1961 "The Convenient State." After *Politics and Catholic Freedom* in 1962, I did *Roman Culture* in 1963.)

Will Herberg, who had become *NR*'s religion editor and another of my teachers at the magazine, wrote an Introduction for my book. (One of those newspaper reviewers who never gets beyond the first few pages said it was surprising to find a long book on papal statements written by a Jew.) Since the book appeared while the Second Vatican Council was still in session, it became an instant anachronism. It was not simply a matter of everybody changing sides—"liberals" now denouncing encyclicals rather than using encyclicals to denounce others, "conservatives" sticking with the Pope even when he issued his disastrous encyclical on contraceptives. Rather, the "sides" faded or were effaced. The old arguments, good or bad, no longer had any audience. When later I wrote another book on the Catholic Church (*Bare Ruined Choirs*), Bill said on his TV show that he found the two books inconsistent. Yet I still think the basic argument of *Politics and Catholic Freedom* was sound; it had just become irrelevant.

I argued, back then, that Catholic encyclical letters on social problems did not impose, by papal authority, a specifically Catholic politics on all Catholics around the world. Now that point goes without saying; my thesis becomes irrelevant by having no one who opposes it. One would think the only people claiming there *is* a mandated papal politics, back in the 1950s, would be critics of the Church like Paul Blanshard, predicting a return to the Inquisition. Blanshard had more of a point than he knew, since the silencing of Father John Courtney Murray was kept a secret when it occurred in the 1950s—and Rome silenced him precisely for saying that there should be no Church-established politics. But Rome was aberrant, not Murray, as Vatican II would make clear.

The astonishing thing is that Catholic liberals, for shortsighted gains, called for a specifically Catholic politics all through the forties and fifties of this century. The allies of Father Murray were themselves claiming that the "social encyclicals" boiled down, in effect, to the Democratic platform of the last election year, and that Catholics who did not adhere to it had departed from their faith and defied the Pope. People who deplored the Pope's condemnations in his more proper realm of *theology,* made him an oracle in *politics.* The game was an odd one, though understandable. Some Catholics wanted to prove they not only *could* be democratic with a small "d," but *had to* be Democrats in the party sense. Older liberals remembered the Al Smith campaign, and charges that a Catholic could not be a true American. In the general superpatriotism of the cold-war years, they started saying only "true Americans" could be Catholic! And that left out Buckley. When Bill said he intended to oppose the welfare state in America despite the social welfarism of Pope John's *Mater et Magistra,* he was accused by assorted priests and lay theologians of schism, heresy, defection from the faith. One priest trotted out the European tag of the old temporal-power days, *Qui Mange du Pape, en meurt* (biters of the Pope die of bellyache). For a heady moment, the victims of heresy hunts like that directed against Father Murray became heresy hunters themselves—as, they say, beaten children grow up to be child-beaters.

This was such a delightful game that even non-Catholics wanted to get in on it. Gore Vidal, who would write the Introduction to a 1977 book calling Christ a fraud, professed shock on "The Tonight Show" that Buckley would defy the Vicar of that Fraud. Murray Kempton, in a very kind review of my book, did comic penance for his fellow liberals:

> Now I can find every reason except a personal one to quarrel with Mr. Buckley, but my own soul is hardly so permeated by grace as to entitle me to question the state of his. So, being an American, I automatically whistle up a priest. That is a polite form of that special sort of Americanism which leads Mrs. Madalyn Murray's enemies to write her notes like "Jesus Christ will fix you." The wrath which fell upon Mr. Buckley after his comments on *Mater et Magistra* came quite often from men in orders, and the possession of orders gave them an authority which should have been the more carefully rationed, not just for the disproportionate weight it has upon the saved, but because of the undeserved comfort it extends to the unsaved. Many of those who are in the field against

Mr. Buckley would never think to bow our heads to the Cross except when it is withdrawn from him.

Murray went on to make the point I should have, but didn't, because what I condemned in the libertarians I still condoned in Bill: There *is* something about laissez-faire individualism that is historically at odds with Catholic tradition—but this is a matter not reachable by papal fiat or by those who challenge the sincerity of their fellow believer's religion. It is one thing to challenge another's historical interpretations; it is another to deny that person's faith or good intentions.

I wrote to show there were severe limits to the Pope's teaching authority even under the old "legalistic" view of that power. This was something Newman had demonstrated in Victorian England (when he was accused of being a papal "minimalist") and something that twentieth-century conditions made more explicit. But to engage in that kind of analysis is a waste of time when Catholic subservience to papal statements has almost evaporated, even on the far right (where Catholics have supported Bishop Lefebvre's defiance of the papal ban on "Tridentine" Masses).

What made the book worth doing for me was the amount of reading it entailed in the works of Cardinal Newman. His emphasis on the need for continuity within development helped me escape the sterile definition of conservatism as somehow opposed to change. Opposition to change is like denying gravity—you can try it; but the first cliff you walk off will be your last. Change is inevitable. The question is how one changes—as a tree does in growing, or as a corpse does in decomposing. One does no terminological service, either, in trying to contrast "true" conservatism with mere "reactionary" tendencies. The tree *reacts* as a unit to wind and nurture; the corpse no longer reacts as a whole, though it is chemically very active and "innovative." In his lifelong reflection on the development of Christian doctrine—which, more and more, meant to him the life experience of the Church—Newman did not talk so much of change or changelessness as of identity within change. To have an identity is not to be fixed at one stage of learning; it is, rather, to have a capacity to integrate new experience within a self-correcting continuum. One is never more oneself than in the extension of the self. To cease extending is to begin decomposing, losing identity as a living unit. Newman made the test of life a power to assimilate, to be fed by multiple experience, not baffled or isolated by it:

> The development then of an idea is not like an investigation worked out on paper, in which each successive advance is a pure evolution from a foregoing, but it is carried on through and by means of communities of men and their leaders and guides; and it employs their minds as its instruments, and depends upon them while it uses them. And so, as regards existing opinions, principles, measures, and institutions of the community which it has invaded; it develops by establishing relations between itself and them; it employs itself, in giving them a new meaning and direction, in creating what may be called a jurisdiction over them, in throwing off whatever in them it cannot assimilate. It grows when it incorporates, and its identity is found not in isolation, but in continuity and sovereignty. . . . It changes with them in order to remain the same. In a higher world it is otherwise, but here below to live is to change, and to be perfect is to have changed often (*Development*, 1 i 2).

Furthermore, Newman made the seat of social identity for the Church the whole body of the faithful, not just the hierarchy or the priesthood. He got into his trouble with Roman authorities by writing that, during the Arian period, the Church at large preserved the faith when bishops and priests strayed into heresy. Of course, in more normal times, Newman admits a governing task to the bishops; but his extreme case shows that experienced continuity with the Gospel rests in the Christian community at large, not in a private revelation to Popes or the teaching sector (*Magisterium*) of the Church.

That argument remains important for me in two ways—one narrowly theological, one generally political. It seemed to me, as I read Newman, that the contraception controversy among Catholics was another example of the phenomenon Newman connected with the Arian period—a case where the body of the faithful lived truer to the Gospel tradition than did its formal teachers. The

sensus fidelium saw no Gospel warrant for that "natural law" condemnation of contraceptives the Pope continued to uphold. When
I made this point on Bill's TV show, "Firing Line," in 1973, he
thought I had gone too far:

> BUCKLEY: There is a sense in which the Catholic Church's
> brightest moments have been when standing athwart the
> spirit of the age.
> WILLS: Ah, but see, you have made a jump which is terribly
> significant. All of a sudden the Pope, standing against his
> own people, his own priests and nuns and laity and theo-
> logians, has become the Catholic Church standing
> athwart the age. . . . Now he is not a spokesman for
> them; he's a spokesman against them. That's the situation
> he has put himself in.

Newman's treatment of the Arian experience had another
meaning for me—it approached, in political terms, that "brotherhood without a father" I was trying to perceive in the "convenient" origins of the state. Some leaders must be chosen at intervals, by election or other means; but their power is delegated, and
is a symbol of the community's own sense of itself as a corporate
body. It is said, in derogation of democracy, that the followers
lead and the leaders follow. Just so. Both should do that. "Compromise" is not a fault but the characteristic virtue of a democratic statesman, who must try to represent the community as a
whole. Newman's treatment of the development of doctrine in the
body of the Church explained the way he reached the politics of
Who's to Blame? The discussion of papal encyclicals might cease
to be a Catholic parlor game, but my obsolete book taught one
person something more about politics—me.

Though the book disappeared as soon as it was published, it
was the occasion for large changes in my life. A young Catholic
editor in Iowa, John Leo, gave it a favorable review in Bob Hoyt's
Kansas City paper *The Catholic Reporter*. Shortly after that, Hoyt
started his *National Catholic Reporter,* and asked John and me to
be, respectively, his liberal and conservative columnists. We became sparring partners and good friends—some readers were disappointed or felt cheated when they learned that we were friends.
As Pegler said, a grudge match always increases the gate.

Hoyt, who was second in a line of great editors I have worked for, wanted more fight than he got; he asked me to choose more clearly identifiable "conservative" positions to write on, because my book's argument put me on the "free speech" side of things in the Church. Some officious priests and editors were trying to silence John Leo with the weapons they had used on Bill. The monsignor who edited Camden's Catholic paper publicly demanded that Hoyt stop "allowing his newspaper to become a platform" for John Leo. So I had to go to the defense of my sparring partner. (If they silenced him, whom would I have to fight with?) The occasion of that outburst was Leo's denunciation of Cardinal Spellman for exiling Daniel Berrigan to Mexico. John had sent me the letter of protest to be published in the New York *Times,* and I signed it for the same reason that I had opposed the attempt to impose a Catholic ban on Bill's politics. Yet Bill criticized my signing the letter, and we had our first serious argument on this matter.

Another matter on which Leo and I agreed was the contraceptive debate that filled much of the Catholic press in those days —had done so since Dr. John Rock, a Catholic, not only helped develop "the pill" but advocated its use. Hoyt's paper was the first to get and publish the majority report of the Pope's own commission advocating the acceptance of contraceptive methods by Catholics. I wrote in favor of that not only for the *NCR* but for *NR*— much to Brent Bozell's horror. Bill was on my side in this matter; my homework in the encyclicals had borne some fruit. When the Pope's new encyclical reaffirming the ban on contraceptives appeared, Bill asked me to write *NR*'s editorials disputing its claims. Later, when some *NR* person drew up a collection of Bill's aphorisms (*Quotations from Chairman Bill*), I found some phrases from those editorials attributed to him.

The strange thing about my time as an *NCR* columnist is that I earned my conservative reputation mainly by taking a liberal position on civil disobedience in the antiwar and civil-rights movements: I said one should "work within the system" of elections and electoral pressures—a stand I would soon regret, and one that was inconsistent with my own "convenient state" arguments on the limits of the electoral system. Though I criticized the first antiwar protests in California, I never wrote directly on the growing

Vietnam War (my column appeared in the years 1964–66), because I did not know what to make of it. Considered purely as an anticommunist venture (the only justification that would have occurred to me then), it seemed to me rather dumb, the wrong kind of war waged the wrong way in the wrong place. Besides, my wife was and is a pacifist, and her arguments had already helped change my mind on capital punishment. But like too many other Americans, I assumed the experts knew something I did not about Indochina's importance in the struggle against communism; so I neither criticized nor supported the war in my columns. I ducked. I evaded.

The *NCR* column was also the occasion for my being fired by Johns Hopkins. In order to pay us a little more, Bob Hoyt syndicated Leo's and my columns out to Catholic papers—ten picked up mine, including Baltimore's arch-diocesan paper. (It was there I had the misfortune to advocate Spiro Agnew's election for governor in 1966, over George Mahoney, who ran a racist campaign on the slogan "Your Home Is Your Castle.") The chairman of my department resented the fact that I wrote occasional reviews for *NR* (he was an "Old Blue" Yalie who despised Bill), but he could not do much about that. My "regular journalism" in the Baltimore *Catholic Review* was another matter, he said. He demanded that I stop it, or he would oppose my getting tenure. I resented the implication that I was neglecting my teaching or study of the classics to write about seven hundred words once a week. I refused, and said I had published as many articles in learned journals as others at my level. He also knew I had a book on Sophocles' *Antigone* half finished, and had seen praise for the completed portions from Bernard Knox of the Center for Hellenic Studies. He answered that I could have done even more learned articles if I stuck to my field. Our parting was unpleasant in a comic way. He said anyone who wrote for *National Review* would doubtless be more comfortable not working for an institution that had an open hiring policy—a ludicrous comment, since the Hopkins record on racial hiring was, at that point, not something to take pride in.

The man, now dead, was a fine scholar, and had always been gentlemanly to that point. But I clearly bothered him. He ran his department in a mode he had picked up from the military, and had for years refused to hire anyone new. I was hired while he was away one year. The youngest man in the department at that point was twenty years my senior; the other three members were entering their sixties. Later, the campus prediction that the department would fall apart when everyone retired at once came true. A new chairman brought in asked me back, but by that time I was teaching as much time as I could spare in the Hopkins Humanities Center.

Back in 1966, I had a year of teaching to complete, during which I could look for a job. Some academic friends made offers, but I thought I would see if I could make a living with my pen. I had been tempted to stay on a year at the Richmond *News Leader* and start writing articles and books for money—my predecessor there had been Richard Whalen, who went to *Fortune* and was working on his life of President Kennedy's father. But wiser heads told me "free-lance writer" was another name for the unemployed. I thought now I might defy the wiser heads, at least for a year or so.

Neil McCaffrey came to my rescue, as he had when I needed money in graduate school. Then I wrote children's Bible pamphlets for him. Now he gave me seven thousand dollars as an advance on a biography of Bill, to be put out by Arlington House. Bill, like most famous people, was glad to have an acknowledged biographer, as his excuse for turning away time-consuming interviews with aspiring biographers whose work would never see print. When Neil later demanded his advance back, Bill gave the biographer's role to Larry Dubois, who had done research on him for a *Time* cover; and later the designation went to an *NR* staffer. My rules when working with Bill were that I could use anything I got first elsewhere, and only things I got first from him with any restrictions. The restrictions, so far as I had time to test them, were in effect nonexistent. He is, if he will excuse the term, "liberal" in such matters.

I wrote the first chapter of that Buckley book—picking him up at a Yale debate with William Sloane Coffin—and Bill suggested I send it to his friend Harold Hayes, the editor of *Esquire*. Harold ran it and offered me a contract writer's job as "Contributing Editor" at the magazine. The pay beat my academic salary, and the work looked easier (four articles a year)—but I was wrong about that. Harold has all kinds of editorial skills, including the ability to get lots of work from his writers.

I did no more on the Bill book. Almost immediately after giving me the advance, Neil McCaffrey was angered by my attacks on George Wallace in the *NCR*. That paper's "conservative columnist" was not conservative enough for him—he thought I had been corrupted by John Leo, and asked for his advance back. Just as well, since I had no time for other projects in my first months at *Esquire*. Since I had been fired for being a journalist, I thought I might as well learn how to be one. I was in the right place for it, at Harold's *Esquire*. And that was the right time for it, the late sixties.

PART TWO

THE LIBERAL SYSTEM

7 · Esquire *Days*

My first assignment for Harold was in December of 1966. Jack Ruby was dying of cancer. Harold wanted me to interview him, but it would be hard (perhaps impossible) to get to him. Harold had just found an investigative reporter with some of a private eye's skills, Ovid Demaris. Ovid got to U-2 pilot Gary Powers when no one else could. Harold would later give him the hopeless task of getting to Howard Hughes. Besides, Ovid knew Dallas well, and had been in the police garage when Ruby shot Oswald. (I'm surprised no conspiracy theorists have, yet, woven Demaris into their skein of plots.) Harold wanted Ovid to open doors so I could do the interviewing. No doubt he also wanted me to pick up some of Ovid's skills, which I tried (not very successfully) to do. Ovid, with a kind of nagging naïveté, wears people down, makes them talk longer than they meant to and say more than they realize. We literally laid siege to Oswald's boardinghouse and George Kennan's farm (while Svetlana Alilluyeva was hiding there) together. Ovid was also good at getting information from police, something I tried to imitate when writing on riot plans in the major cities for Harold. There is a touch of the con man in Ovid, redeemed by his vain candor. He *tells* you how good he is, before he *proves* it. I like him immensely.

Ovid demanded that he be listed as co-author of the Ruby piece, though I was to do all the writing. Fair enough. I was still teaching my final year at Hopkins, and could not go to Dallas until the Christmas break. Ovid went there ten days earlier to open doors and get Ruby's family or lawyer to let us in. But the Dallas police, stung by the loss of Oswald, were letting no one near their other "Kennedy prisoner." Ovid was still trying when I got to Dallas—he never gives up. But I saw it was hopeless. I had just caught the flu from my children, and was ready to turn around and go home. Ovid told me to take aspirin, go to bed, and listen to a batch of tapes he had made with Dallas policemen and officials, with Ruby's friends and nightclub employees. I heard Ovid's questioning technique used on the most astonishing collection of vivid characters. I listened to the tapes over and over, dozing and waking again, and decided I wanted to meet these people —especially Bill Willis, the drummer in Ruby's club and a close friend of Jack's.

I called Harold to tell him I thought there was a story there even though we could not get to Ruby. The call went through to Harold's empty office, where Noel Parmentel (a sometime contributor to *NR*) picked up the phone and accepted the charges: "What the hell are you doing in Dallas, Garry?" I asked what the hell he was doing in Harold's office—he went and got Harold. I spent three weeks in Dallas, and wrote an article on Ruby's motive for killing Oswald. We had turned up so much material that I convinced Harold I should do a second article, on Ruby's trial. Bob Gutwillig, an editor at New American Library, liked the articles and said they could be published as a book if I added just a bit on Ruby's death, which had occurred by then. I had become fascinated with Ruby, and read all the parts devoted to him in the Warren volumes; so I had Ovid make more tapes with lawyers and people interviewed by the Warren investigators (I would play the tapes going to and from class that last spring of my full-time teaching) and added two sections as long as the original articles themselves. The book was little noticed, because it came out quickly in the spate of New American Library books flooding the market those years, and was lumped with other late riders on the stream of assassination books. But I retain a special fondness for the book, in which I was learning as much as I could of the reporter's and the investigator's craft. And I still think it shows that Ruby was involved in no conspiracy.

Harold teamed me with Ovid once more—this time to get to Stalin's daughter in her first months of hiding in America. Again we failed to get the interview, but I wrote an article anyway about the whole Svetlana operation; it was my first look at the way the CIA works. After that Harold came up with one of those schemes that drove his contract writers to near breakdown. In the wake of the Watts and Detroit riots, police forces were gearing up for urban war. Some ambitious riot plans had been reported; others were presumed to exist. Harold told me to go to the major cities and see if I could turn up more of those plans. The project deepened and broadened, and took two months of intense travel and interviewing, with Harold on the phone encouraging, making suggestions, authorizing more expense money. When it ran, it was the longest article *Esquire* had ever published. (But the only riot plan I ever got hold of, after stealing it when a National Guard officer left the room, was such an omelette of acronyms as to be of no journalistic interest.) Bob Gutwillig snatched this up for another New American Library book, under the title *The Second Civil War*.

The book attracted little notice, that little of a recondite sort. Chemical MACE was just being put to use by police, and I had a long interview with its inventor just before he stopped talking to newsmen; so law reviews discussing various suits involving MACE had no other source to cite on the inventor's claims for his product. I tried MACE on myself, and praised it as a safe and effective control device. One of the people who sang its praises to me was Joseph Woods, sheriff of Cook County. When next I met him, he was picking up his sister Rose Mary and her boss, Richard Nixon, during the 1968 presidential campaign.

I met others I would run into after doing the article, like the

officers of the Chicago police force who rioted themselves during
the Democratic convention in 1968, or "Red Squad" men who
observed later demonstrations. I found great stupidity in the military, as one would expect. One of the greatest fools I talked with,
General Carl C. Turner, was the liaison man for all military assist-
ance to cities threatened with riots. I was not surprised, later, to
find him in trouble with authority for taking confiscated weapons
home to his private collection.

The article (and book) made Frank Meyer furious, since I took
seriously the grievances of black militants. I sent the book to Neil
McCaffrey, whom I still considered a friend despite our disa-
greements. He wrote back that he would hang it on his door when
my rioting black friends came to burn him out; maybe it would
deter them. Even Bill told Larry Dubois, when he took over as
designated biographer, that I had "gone over to the militants"
when writing *The Second Civil War. NR* would later run a long
attack on me, and put on the cover Huey Newton's famous picture
in a fan chair, with my head on Newton's body. The magazine's
gift for spotting "black militants" was about on a par with its
identification of "communists" in the fifties.

Yet I was conscious of no change on the matter of race. At the
Richmond *News Leader,* when Jack Kilpatrick was away in the
Soviet Union and I took over as editor, I wrote a long attack on
Carlton Putnam's *Race and Reason,* which the publisher refused
to print because the editor of our sister paper, the supposedly
more liberal *Times Dispatch,* had written a favorable Introduction
to that racist tract. I wrote for *NR* a long and favorable review of
James Baldwin's *The Fire Next Time,* which Jeffrey Hart, in his
book on the magazine's history, would cite to show that *NR* had
an "enlightened" position on black problems (though Willmoore
Kendall wrote me at the time that the review showed I had "gone
liberal"). In 1964 I wrote for *NR* that blacks should be recom-
pensed for historic grievances by a policy of preferential hiring
(and when Bill repeated that in a column he was attacked in one
of Neil McCaffrey's books for selling out to liberalism). Both in
NR and in the *NCR* I argued that conservatives are bound to the
concept of "historic guilt" for racial wrongs, since those who glory
in inherited values and traditions must admit accountability for

historic wrongs. Guilt for the past is the other side of gratitude for the past. "The 'new Negro' . . . would rather be feared than patronized; and he is getting his way. And he should."

In the seminary I had taught catechism at black schools and hospitals with my black friend Ted Cunningham, whose resentment at the Jesuits' stalling of his entry into the order I shared. I was often reminded of him when talking to black community-relations officers on police forces, who had to suppress resentment at their white brother-officers' stupidity and tactlessness in dealing with the black community. It is certainly true that the misery of black ghettos was struck in on me with new force by my interviews and travels for *The Second Civil War*. But my basic attitude had not shifted. I had not even changed my opposition to civil disobedience as a tactic in the struggle for black rights (I now wish I had).

I had some later dealings with black militants, but not of the sort to disturb even the most nervous *NR* reader. In covering Martin Luther King's funeral, I heard the Reverend James Bevel give, in Memphis, the most searing and effective sermon I have ever experienced. I tried to talk with him afterward, but he refused to be bothered. After my article describing his sermon appeared in *Esquire,* he started calling me, trying to set up an appointment. I was busy on something else, but he asked to come visit. He came into the house, hugged me as his "brother," stunned my wife with his eloquence and cordiality, then gave me The Pitch. He would march from Washington to the UN demanding deliverance for the "captive nation" of American blacks; I would travel along recording his triumphs; and we would split the proceeds from the resulting book. I wasn't interested. He grew more eloquent, and also said I could have three quarters of the profits. When he finally turned over 100 per cent of the profits to me and I still said no, he got up without a word of good-bye to his "brother" or that brother's wife, and stalked out. Now, *there* was the Jim Bevel I had met in Memphis.

Another militant I met through Duke Hunter, one of the black police officers I had dedicated my book to. Duke, later fired by Joe Woods as too militant for the Cook County police force, went to the District of Columbia and fell in with a wild man who had a scheme to deliver the black vote to Republicans for a price. A secret meeting was set up for me; the con man checked the hotel room for bugs, put his back to a corner, and pulled out his gun. He said I must never tell a soul of his great scheme—but if I told the world in a book, he wanted half the profits. I later wrote this incident up for Harold, to show the crazy side of the sixties.

Another time I saw a gun drawn, but in anger—at John Lewis' apartment. Ivanhoe Donaldson got into an argument over South Africa, and I was happy to escape along with Donaldson, whose house guest I was. As a militant I made a very devout coward. I am still not an absolute pacifist (like my wife); but what militancy I saw made me a great deal more pacific.

As I say, I had not changed my view on civil disobedience when I wrote *The Second Civil War*. I understood better the grievances of the blacks, but I still thought civil disobedience a tactic that would not work in practice. In the same way, I blamed riots on police "toughness" simply from a tactical viewpoint, and thought containment of riots (as opposed to mass arrests or instant retaliation) the only policy that would make the policemen themselves safe. To my surprise, one of the advocates of a containment policy, Ray Girardin of the Detroit police force, denied he had said what I reported, or even that he had talked to me for more than a couple of minutes. I had a half-hour tape of my conversation with him, containing all the quotes I used in the article, which I produced on the same TV show where he had denied his quotes. He was feeling the political pressure to be "tough," against his own best judgment about his men's safety; so he had to deny that he said anything as "soft" as my article indicated. When Mayor Daley came out with his "shoot to kill" prescription for rioters, I wrote that such self-defeating "toughness" was a prescription for riot—which effectively broke off my relations with Frank Meyer.

When Frank learned that Bill was going to let me cover the Democratic National Convention in Chicago for *NR,* he tried to block the assignment. When I turned in that article, so critical of Daley, there was a great silence around it in the office until one young staffer smirked to me, "So at last Wills has struck out." Bill ran the piece, to other people's displeasure; but he rejected the next article I sent him, criticizing the Vietnam War on what I thought (and still think) very conservative grounds. The piece appeared as a chapter called "Our Country" in my Nixon book. I argued from Stephen Decatur's famous maxim, from the example of Robert E. Lee and George Washington, that self-defense is the only justification for war, that Vietnam did not involve our defense, that pre-emptive strikes were not normally justifiable. Bill said he would run the piece only if I would preface it with an explanation of how I got from my former position to my present one—the first of many such requests, which I am finally heeding. I thought the article itself showed how a conservative could conclude to the Vietnam War's immorality. I had earlier told Bill I thought the war dumb as an anticommunist matter. If I now thought it immoral, I could give no better explanation than the one I wrote.

Bill was right, of course, to see that I was no longer an anticommunist crusader. The article I sent him condemned wars for the truth and killing men for their own good: "Most discussion of our policy is a debate between rival Causes, not an attempt to move away from the concept of holy war." But in the terms I proposed in the piece itself, that was not a defection from conservatism but the elimination of a stand inconsistent with my own "convenient state" rationale for politics. I had argued that politics should not be based on a universalist claim for justice imposing "the good society."

Bill and I parted amicably—which is more than I can say of some young *NR* staffers, who had apparently been nursing a resentment at my retention in the magazine's pages for so long. One of these people, who went to work in Richard Nixon's victorious 1968 campaign, told me on that campaign's travels that he was happy to see I was "expelled" by the right before it came to power, so I could not share in the spoils.

On the other hand, the FBI called me after Nixon's election, spurred by knowledge that I had once started a biography of Bill. Did I know anything that would disqualify him for appointment to federal office? (Nixon had put him up for the USIA.) I vouched for his Americanism; but he was approved anyway.

8 · *Observing the System*

I wrote at a feverish pace for Harold Hayes—just as I had, ten years earlier, when entering a "new world" after the seminary. Harold complained about the length of my articles. Noting that it took me two long pieces to cover Ruby's death, and I never even reached his death, he told me on the Svetlana assignment, "At least get her out of India, if not actually to America." But he liked the thoroughness of the articles he was midwiving, too. When he put together his own *Esquire* anthologies, mine were the longest pieces in *Smiling Through the Apocalypse,* and I did the only original article for the *Fortieth Anniversary Celebration.* While nodding to a certain prior claim by Bill, Harold justly wrote that I began to be a journalist under his tutelage.

Two books grew out of my early work for *Esquire,* almost by accident. And then I was launched on a third one, entirely by accident. Murray Kempton had agreed to do a piece on Richard Nixon's newest try to be President, but found he could not get the time for it. Harold called me in Michigan, where I was visiting my parents, and asked if I could get straight to New Hampshire and pick up this assignment. I went without enthusiasm—Nixon bored me. I had missed most of his vice-presidential years by being in the seminary, but I tended to believe people who assured me I had not missed a thing.

I found what any national reporter could have told me—that the best time for getting to know a politician is early in a presidential race, when his staff is open, his first moves ill covered, his crowds small and well worked-over. Richard Nixon could never be really accessible; I think he is inaccessible to himself. But he was a lot closer to accessibility in January and February of 1968 than ever before or after. The same was true of his family, friends, and supporters. Because of *Esquire*'s lead time (a perpetual problem in the fast-moving sixties) my article had to be written before the Wisconsin primary, though it would appear after it, so I had to take the broadest possible view of the man and his career. I checked back with early friends of Nixon, interviewing Ralph de Toledano, an acquaintance from *NR* days. I called the father of my high-school friends, Charles Kersten, who had been Nixon's colleague in the House. Both Kersten and de Toledano told me to see Father John Cronin, who had been a secret speechwriter for Nixon in both his Senate and vice-presidential days, a good friend of Rose Woods, and an honest man.

Cronin gave me lots of solid gossip about the Nixons (most of which I could not use) and one "hard news" item of the sort Harold loved: Nixon, despite what he wrote in *Six Crises,* had heard about Hiss from the FBI before Chambers ever named him, and was given information leaked by the FBI all during the Hiss investigation. I went back over the Hiss-Chambers affair and, despite my diminished regard for Chambers' mind and style, concluded (what I still believe) that Hiss did lie under oath. I wrote my piece and hoped it would stand up even if Nixon lost in Wisconsin.

The article was out in mid-April, and Dorothy de Santillana of Houghton Mifflin—another in my pantheon of editors—asked me to lunch. She wanted a book on Nixon. I asked her, What if he loses? "No matter. What you saw in that article is worth explain-

ing, even if we never hear about Nixon again." I had alternative
ideas to suggest—a book on Dr. Johnson, or on Shakespeare, pet
projects long put off for want of any publisher's interest. She kept
up the record of noninterest in those ideas, and said she could
promise a decent advance only for the Nixon. She has a wonderful
gift for getting her way, and every writer who worked for her
loved her.

I talked to Harold. I could only cover the rest of the campaign
if he would let me do at least two of my four annual articles on
some aspect of it. He thought that was possible—and took my
chapters on the Checkers speech and on Spiro Agnew. He also let
me out of my exclusivity arrangement, saying I could peddle
Nixon material elsewhere (one chapter went to *The Saturday
Evening Post,* and the convention chapters to *NR*). I signed
Dorothy's contract.

The Vietnam War could no longer be evaded. It split the
Democrats as Gene McCarthy and Bobby Kennedy challenged
Johnson while Humphrey waffled. The level of protest picked up
at election gatherings, and George Wallace was leading a coun-
tercharge. The advice that protesters should work within the system—so easily given in my *NCR* columns—began to sound hollow as I observed the system for the first time close up, trying to
describe it. "The system" was an important part of the political
vocabulary in 1968. People were trying to change, oppose, uphold, wreck or work within "the system." The term's use arose
in reaction to Dr. King's ideal of "direct action." Indirect action—
through the courts (the old NAACP strategy) and by changing
elected officials—was praised or blamed as the system. For the
"kids" (another political term that came into general use in
1968), working within the system meant going "clean for Gene"
—shaving off beards and joining the Eugene McCarthy campaign.

The aim of the kids was to end the war. But what has electoral
politics ever had to do with war decisions? The iron rule of twentieth-century American politics is this: To get the nation into war,
first get elected by promising not to get it into war. That happened
with Wilson in 1916, with Roosevelt in 1940, with Johnson in
1964. When the Vietnam War ended, it would not be because of
any election. The "mandate" of Nixon's landslide re-election in

1972 (against the "peacenik" McGovern campaign) would have given Nixon freedom to prolong the war even further if Watergate revelations had not weakened his standing. Only then did Congress refuse Kissinger's request for more aid to the Thieu regime.

Elections actually prolonged hostilities. In 1964 Johnson said that our aid to allies would not lead us into war. In 1966, he was still pretending that the engagement was limited and would not spread. In 1968 he went through elaborate peace negotiations in Paris, while candidate Nixon said he would not disturb that process by saying anything about the war. In 1970, casualties went down and missions were infrequent. In 1972, peace was around the corner. A rhythm emerges. Every even-numbered year, around September, the war was heavily sedated. Things looked better as we did less, and a bright face was put on things. Then, to make up for "lost time," to regain our posture of bargaining from strength, the bombing built up again in late November toward an even-year climax in December. The 1972 Christmas bombing was just the last and worst of what had become a biennial destructive feast at the winter equinox.

The off-year elections of 1970 were the supreme test of the electoral system's ability to come to grips with an ongoing dubious war. The issue seemed inescapable. In the spring of 1970, when Nixon invaded Cambodia, campuses erupted, classes were suspended. Some colleges closed early, neglecting final examinations and grades. The mood hardened after students were killed at Kent State. That summer the Calley trial led to a conviction and to strong public reaction. It was widely believed that violence would attend the fall campaigns, that some schools might not be able to reopen or maintain a regular schedule.

Never was the cry to "work within the system" stronger. As a kind of bribe to encourage this, schools adopted the Princeton Plan—students would be let out of class to work for peace candidates. But when students went to the training center for this plan, the first thing they were told was, "Don't argue about the war; it just turns people off." Then what could they do? Canvass to find favorable areas and turn out the vote—that is, conventional politics. But candidates did not *want* peacenik kids wandering around their district asking questions to test each area's "liberalism." Paul Sarbanes, running in Baltimore, complained to me: "They asked questions like, 'Do you support open housing?' I had constituents calling up, worried, to ask what bill I had in mind. We've *got* an open-housing bill. I didn't want them stirring people up on irrelevant issues." Or on any issues. Candidate after candidate said there was not much he could do about the war, but he would try to cut taxes. The kids went back to school and ignored the Princeton Plan. The war went on.

There was nothing anomalous about this. Our electoral system is simply not an instrument for making decisions. Americans are always discovering that truth, then letting it slip through their fingers. At every election we are told this is the time to discuss "the issues." And in every election we are told that the issues are being evaded. Of course they are. That is what elections are meant to accomplish. Issues divide people, and getting elected depends on an ability to unite voters in a broad coalition. Hard decisions on prickly matters get made *between* elections—preferably well before the next one. It is a commonplace that not much serious decision-making is done in the fourth year of a President's term, since he is trying to coast through the re-election time riling as few people as he can. President Kennedy told senators that the growing Vietnam problem would have to be coped with—*after* his re-election.

Some might argue that war is a bad sample to use when talking about the decisive quality of elections, since Americans feel less informed and concerned about foreign affairs than about domestic ones. The time-honored maxim is that domestic issues, and especially the economy, decide elections. That is probably true in one sense. The economy affects elections. But do elections *decide* anything about the economy? The 1932 election is considered a great turning point in our politics. It ended the long party dominance of Republicans (essentially uninterrupted since the Civil War) and made possible the New Deal. But what rational debate or choice was involved in that election? The people could not choose the New Deal, since it was not a program formulated yet, even in Roosevelt's mind; and certainly not one offered to public inspection and debate. Far from it. Roosevelt ran on a promise to bal-

ance the budget and end Hoover's wasteful spending. Only when
he had been elected on the standard campaign slogans could
Roosevelt afford to make any decisions to cope with the reality of
the Depression. Even then, his first moves were to strengthen the
economy by bailing out big corporations and the larger farms with
the NRA and the AAA. Only as re-election time came near did he
spread around some of the money thus pumped into businessmen's coffers with the WPA, NLRA, and Social Security Act
of 1935. By 1936 Roosevelt had balanced his hard and popular
decisions in such a way that the electorate did choose the New
Deal—*after* it was a *fait accompli*. This retrospective sanctioning
occurs in elections. But decision-making, to be a real act of self-
governance, should be prospective. We call our nation self-
governing because we *decide* on our course, and the decision
takes place at election time. Approving a completed journey is not
deciding on a course.

I should have been in a position to know these simple facts
about our elections—I should not have talked nonsense about
making decisions "through the system"—because I was not a liberal; and it is the liberal myth of a free intellectual market that
makes us think of elections as times of great debate and decisions,
times when all issues get discussed and we choose the best
policies, just as we choose the best men. So dear is this theory that
most Americans manage to maintain it against the evidence of
every election they take part in. That is why the pattern—evasion
of issues—is always greeted with surprise and called an aberration. The permanent reality is considered a permanent *departure*
from reality.

What actually happens in an American presidential election? (I
deal mainly with presidential elections, as those attracting most attention and turnout, greatest prior discussion and subsequent
analysis. If the "debate model" of elections is not vindicated here,
where could it be?) Each party puts up a candidate, by a process
of prior compromise, who can speak for that party's natural constituency (or for most of it—why, otherwise, put him up in the
first place?). This natural constituency must be given certain conventional assurances and recognition, in platform, staff, scheduling, etc.—after which it can be taken largely for granted. There

were no more votes—or very few more—for a Democrat to get in
the South when it was "Solid," so the party made its ritual appointment of a Southerner as vice-presidential candidate, and then
went hunting "where the ducks are" (as Senator Goldwater put it
with his customary risky candor).

The strictly partisan vote is assured from the outset—Democrats
who always vote Democratic, Republicans who always vote Republican. The trick is to woo the independents or undecided,
those who would not otherwise turn up at the polls, those not
clearly affiliated with either party, new arrivals on the voting
scene, or even the shakably loose-hanging members of the other
party. The task of going after these voters is made easier by the
rational model of debate that most voters wish to see in a campaign. After all, if one is to judge each issue and each candidate
"on the merits," one should begin with a certain neutrality. Jurors
should not be prejudiced, but open to all evidence, from whichever side. That is why, even when party enrollment was high,
voters approached by pollsters represented themselves as still
deliberating, open-minded, waiting to see what the arguments are
on either side (which candidate is the "better man"). No one likes
to be considered blindly partisan.

Though this debate imagery is still popular, voter analysis long
ago established that the truly issue-oriented people are the frank-
est partisans. Since our parties are not ideological, but constellations of interests, the more educated and active people look to
the long-term impact of these constellated groups on the values
they cherish, not to frothy campaign rhetoric. This, of course,
helps the candidate focus his campaign efforts "outside the fold."
The blind partisans will vote for their mama's and papa's party,
no matter what; shrewder partisans, *because* they are not blind,
will look past the exigencies of vote-getting season to the long
trends of party support and obligation. The candidate is freed to
flirt elsewhere, since most of those "at home" will count him basically faithful.

In order to woo those not permanently fixed in one cluster of
interests, one tradition of party, the candidate takes soundings to
find out what "independents" most want to hear. The aim is to
identify concerns, trends, fears, and hopes that can be played on
without any great specificity of program. Even the few specifics

that may have emerged in a primary, or in the party's platform, are notoriously neglected as the candidate takes his national stance for the final weeks of campaign. It is easy to see why. Even if it were certain that 55 per cent of the people favor all the specifics of Plan Alpha, it would not be clear that the *swayable* part of the electorate, that still up for grabs, conformed to such a division. Yet, having pledged himself to the specifics of Plan Alpha, the candidate could be expected to support, as well, Plan Beta, since it too is popular with 55 per cent of the people. The trouble is that these two majorities do not have an identical constitution. Perhaps 20 per cent of those supporting Plan Alpha are violently opposed to Plan Beta. The urge to vote *against* is, in most cases, stronger than that to vote *for*. So the net effect of supporting two majority proposals would be the achievement of a minority supporting the candidate in *both* matters—35 per cent. And that may understate the problem. The intensity factor is higher on negative votes—the opponents of Plan Beta may go out and bring in new voters not originally figured in. Also, in partisan politics, there is a special animus reserved for "traitors" on one's own side—for example, the feeling Taft supporters always reserved for Nelson Rockefeller. Thus the opponent of Plan Beta may be *specially* mobilized against the candidate *because* he supported Plan Alpha. There is angry disappointment that one who was on the right side should now desert to the other side.

If these possibilities arise in the case of two clear positions, where we have assumed full knowledge of the support being given them, you can imagine the complications when a whole *range* of vaguer yet interlocking issues comes into view. The size and makeup of the support for many of these will be unclear; the impact of such new programs on a candidate's natural constituency is unforeseeable. To take concrete stands on a large number of issues would suicidally entangle the loyalties of people who do not agree with *all* of the candidate's stands. Even if a voter agrees with most of a candidate's stands, the position on just *one* matter closer to that voter's heart may cancel the accumulated support on matters considered more apathetically. Taking too detailed positions will not only make it harder to woo the available undecideds; it can even dislodge parts of the candidate's first constituency. That loyal "hard core" was formed by the convergence of interests and traditions in the party—a general and overall support. But a key segment of such loyalists can be offended by just one issue too vividly put forward. The more detailed a candidate's stance, the harder it becomes for voters to put favorable interpretations on that stand.

So the candidate must deal with a twofold problem. He must tailor his approach to the moods and hopes and fears of the specific election, the sentiments that move and tell and count at the moment; yet he must keep his appeals to this populace suitably vague. This is made easier for him by the fact that voters who will respond to one vivid advertisement, or well-staged rally, or shrewdly crafted slogan, are by definition rather impressionable. A campaign, as it comes down to the last stroke or two of publicity, oratory, and shows of confidence, must seek the broadest common denominator in voter manipulability. Those still undecided at the last minute tend to be unconvincible or unconcerned. There is no sense trying to affect the former; and the latter, short of flipping a coin, can be won simply by catching their attention before the other man does. It would not do to offend them by imposing unaccustomed agonies of thought.

Thus the dynamics of an election compel a candidate, as he nears the end, to leave serious people alone (as already committed, or as needing efforts of discussion, debate, and reflection, that no harried candidate has time for) and to court the fickle. Who, after all, is going to be won in the last days' flurry of instant rallies (repeating all the best slogans developed in the race), expensive TV shows, telephone calls? Not the philosophers among us.

We must remember, too, that all candidates, after targeting the swayable undecided, are sending out roughly the same signals. They have employed pollsters of comparable technique. These have polled comparable segments of the population. Their findings are not going to be very far apart. They have found out what the people want to hear, and told their respective candidates. What candidate will, at that point, go out and tell them what they do *not* want to hear? So the campaign becomes an interesting exercise, one that might best be called: Tell me what to tell you.

In the course of his campaign, each candidate feels fewer and fewer constraints from his original base of support. Party faithfuls tell each other that the candidate "has" to say whatever he is saying while he runs. Once in office, he will revert to form. And, after all, the vague formulae of the campaign's later stages are hardly challenging to the party's orthodoxy, or to any clear position. Thus there is no reason for the candidate to deprive himself of the fruits of the polls that he has paid for. He will try to say what people want to hear, just hoping that he says it a shade better than the other candidate can manage to.

The importance of these pressures is reflected in the growth of the pollster's role in most elections. Joe McGinnis would have come much closer to the "selling" of Presidents if he had followed a Pat Caddell around, instead of a Harry Treleaven. Name recognition, public "image," the tags and loaded terms that show what impresses a voter in the candidates—all these things are measured, now, before a man can launch an expensive national candidacy. And his "pitch," once the race is begun, must be calibrated to any perceived shift in response to his "image." Scheduling, targeting, associating, dissociating, repetition, omission—all must be judged by the response they elicit from the public; and if the election itself is the *final* poll, the candidate is always taking the temperature of crowds—his campaign is a walking poll. What lines go over? Which ones flop? Things are added, tried, rejected, based on the popular response. He is a walking gauge of what will "sell," a litmus test of crowds, himself responding to each group's responses.

It is often noticed that candidates say almost exactly the same things in the last stages of their race. They have "middled in" toward that central group of waverers each still hopes to win. But I noticed something even more surprising as I followed Nixon— what I described in my book on him as "compensatory counterstress." The candidates middle in toward each other so energetically that they tend to pass each other and fall, rhetorically, into the opposite camp. They fear that the indeterminate middle may see them as bound by the extreme form of their natural party's stance, so they *over*emphasize ancillary considerations. In the 1960 debates, Kennedy was more anticommunist in his rhetoric, Nixon more civil-libertarian. Each leaned against a presumed caricature, and leaned so far that he fell across the middle point, away from his "home" position.

One might think these rhetorical antics are bound to cease after the election, each candidate snapping back to his true form. But a funny thing happens to officeholders. Even after the election they find their greatest freedom of movement is *out* from their constituency. They can *presume* on people the other candidate, had he won, would still have to woo. Thus, since every politician wants to leave his mark—to achieve *something,* at least—the most spectacularly achievable things stand some way off from his own origin. Nixon could go to China; Humphrey would not have been able to. On the other hand, a Johnson could lead us gradually into large-scale war over Indochina, but Congress would have balked at Goldwater's first move in that direction. The one thing Kennedy could not support was aid to Catholic schools—since too much favor to "one's own" stirs resentment in the larger community. In the same way, Johnson had to be fervid for civil-rights bills *because* he was a Southerner. Every President who is active at all will be accused at times of "betrayal" by his first supporters. It was predictable that Southerners would soon be grumbling that Carter "sold them out" after the 1976 election.

Of course, this is only part of the picture, and one cannot predict just where an officeholder will be tempted to move off from his constituency—otherwise cynics could rightly advise us to vote against our preferred candidate and let the dialectic of events force his opponent to do his work for him. What I am stressing is precisely the unpredictability of electoral outcome. Even those who complain of "broken campaign promises" have often construed too narrowly the hedged or ambiguous campaign statements. The candidate has *labored* to be imprecise, and only loses when he gets pinned to specifics. It would be hard to make rational predictions on the basis of campaign rhetoric, even if that rhetoric could be made binding on the candidate after the election. The officeholder will betray many false expectations, but also many reasonable ones. Franklin Roosevelt was "a traitor to his class," but also to those voters who believed him when he said he would cut spending. The fact that most people were happy to be betrayed later on is comforting. But it makes working "within the system" look more like playing the lottery than like rational debate and decision "on the issues."

9 · "Good Elections"

The previous chapter roughly summarizes what I had to say about elections, about decision-making through "the system," in *Nixon Agonistes*. Once that book was used in political-science courses, both teachers and students criticized my chapter "A Good Election" in ways that made me reconsider and develop my first impressions. But their arguments did not lead me to their conclusions.

Some endorsed V. O. Key's efforts to prove elections meaningful in the choice of policy. In *The Responsible Electorate* (1966), Key used polls to show that apparently "stable" majorities are really in flux. People do move, change, die, switch. That seems to be true, but not very important. A stable neighborhood is not one where no one moves in or out, dies or grows up; but where values and ethos are sustained at the same level *despite* comings and goings. If a majority holds the same lead over decades, it does not matter that the majority is not repeated, at each election, in each of its integers.

Key also claimed that voters are not responsive to shallow election showmanship; many have made up their minds before the campaign begins. He used polls to show that there was solid and growing approval of the New Deal even before Republicans chose an inept candidate in 1936, and that there was solid and growing disapproval of Truman even before Republicans chose a glamorous hero in 1952. (Key wrote in the period of liberal trauma after voters were so benighted, in liberal terms, as to choose an Ike over an Adlai.)

I think Key undermines his position with his own argument. He makes it sound as if there is a rolling approval (for example, of Roosevelt) or disapproval (for example, of Truman) that will decide the election no matter what the other side does. If so, then the election is not a debate between equals presenting alternatives to an impartial judge (the electorate). It is a contest between incumbents and their public, with challengers reduced to the role of feckless speculators or accidental beneficiaries. In other words, Key supports the view that voters sanction or approve change retrospectively. In 1936 they ratify, as it were, the choice not put before them in 1932. New choices were not signaled to them in 1936—Roosevelt would spring the court-packing plan after reelection, as he sprang the New Deal after election. His popularity declined, but he recovered by 1940, when the voters got their chance to sanction his overall performance—once again, in retrospect. The voters seem to get their elections after the fact, which means (among other things) that the remnant of any term must run its course even if they disapprove of what has been sprung on them. Then their only means of punishment is to take the alternative candidate, no matter how little they can surmise about his future performance.

There is great inertia in the American political system. Evidences of this are the advantage incumbents have, the long periods of one-party dominance, the difficulty of dislodging even controversial programs once they are funded. The incumbent is a known quantity, with experience. Even those who voted against war when there was peace tend to rally patriotically behind war when there is war; and acquiescing in a war, once under way, is obviously quite different from choosing to go to war in the first place. Wars are not easily stopped in any case; and neither are giant government programs. (Eisenhower could not have "repealed the New Deal" after 1952, even if he had wanted to.) Most people prefer what they have, once they have it, to risky political change; they choose the safe over the flashy. There must be widespread and sharp discontent to reject the incumbent of a theretofore majority party (for example, Herbert Hoover).

There is much to recommend this cautious approach. But it makes liberal shibboleths ring hollow—those that talk of rational debate, and setting new courses, and deciding issues on their merits, and letting the best man win. Is the *incumbent* certifiably the best man in most cases? He *must* be, since he wins. These facts make it especially hard to tell the disaffected that they should bring about change only within the system. The system is geared to prevent change, to mute issues, to defuse trouble, to sedate wars rather than debate them; to glide through an election, not battle it out with logical rigor.

In a sense Key admitted that elections were meaningless on the way to defending them as meaningful. He began the search for "critical elections" that so busied political scientists in the later fifties and early sixties. It was granted that your run-of-the-mill election did not matter much; but when events called for vigorous response, a critical election could change events. Most elections are not critical, but any election might be; and that potential for meaning redeems the process. "Critical elections"—normally defined as the transfer of power from one clearly defined party to another party with a policy alternative—understandably fascinated people in the 1950s. Sociologists were describing Americans as gray-flannel conformists, students as a silent generation, and business as Madison Avenue drill. Eisenhower was, for academics, a synonym for apathy. Politics seemed all a matter of drift; election analysis, just getting on a solid mathematical footing, seemed to confirm the power of political inertia. With the force almost of nostalgia, students of politics harked back to the one (or two, or three) elections they had always thought of as having made a difference. Woodrow Wilson said that he would teach South America to hold good elections. Scholars in the fifties wanted to find, again, the time when Americans held good elections—good in terms of liberal theory—elections that presented clear matters of choice which the people then judged. To their great relief they came up with five or so such good elections.

Key first suggested the critical-election theory in 1955, and offered a sample, just to get things started. He proposed 1928 as a year that realigned party bases, though it did not make for immediate change in the White House. He was trying to avoid the anomaly of 1932 as a critical election when the New Deal was *not* offered to the people for their judgment. Later, in *The Responsible Voter,* he would avoid the problem in the opposite direction, as it were, by stressing 1936 as the time when a real decision was made in favor of the New Deal. Others soon joined in the hunt for our good elections; different candidates were offered, different categories used to qualify them. Angus Campbell thought it safe to count three elections critical—though James Sundquist preferred to deal with three critical *periods* rather than elections. Robert Dahl and Harry Jaffa counted four such elections. Gerald Pomper came up with five—but only two of his five were on most other people's lists. The variations in the lists might hint at illusory qualities in the concept. But there seemed a psychic need for it, a need to "save" the reality of our politics by preserving the phenomena that reflect our political Idea. So a consensus formed around the five favorite contenders, those still listed at the outset of Walter Dean Burnham's *Critical Elections* (1970):

1. *1800.* Jefferson's Republicans overthrew and—as events were to prove—destroyed the Federalist Party.
2. *1828.* Jackson's Republican-Democrats ended the reign of the Jeffersonians and the Era of Good Feelings.
3. *1860.* Lincoln brought the new Republican Party into power, reducing the Democrats to minority-party status and the Whigs to nonexistence.
4. *1896.* The Republicans beat the combined forces of the Democrats and the populists (People's Party) to establish a large margin of superiority for the next 3½ decades.
5. *1932.* Franklin Roosevelt began a Democratic reign that lasted at least until 1952, and perhaps to this day—so that Democrats continue to hold majority-party status in voter registration and in legislative elections to this day.

It is an interesting list, on several counts. Though the aim of most theorists in creating the list was to vindicate elections in general, they could only come up with five cases that command any wide assent. More to the point, the list included only one example of a critical election in our century—indeed, on the face of it, the space between critical elections seems to have been widening: There were three in the first seventy years of the republic, and only two in the last one hundred and fifteen years. It has, on this showing, been almost half a century since our last critical election. Is there something in the process that has made elections less and less critical—that is, on the theorists' own assumptions, less and less meaningful—as the nation grew? A finding of that sort could dismay the students of democracy who note that, in the course of these developments, the franchise has been extended, popular education raised to new levels, the means of communication improved. People are presumably better equipped to make intelligent choices as a whole—yet they seem to be given fewer and fewer opportunities for choosing. The last critical election took place almost half a century ago. This does not encourage respect for voting as a general exercise. If one is lucky, one *might* get a chance to participate in one critical election during his or her lifetime.

I repeat, these are reflections on the list as given—yet even these five are open to objection, and different scholars reduce the number to four or three; or they admit some examples only with strict provisos. Each case labors under its special difficulty. And the closer one looks at each, the less does it resemble any other in the list. Take them one by one:

1. *1800*. This is the one most frequently dropped from the list. Robert Dahl says it should be called an "aligning" rather than a "realigning" election. For him, it marks the beginning of a formed two-party system, rather than overthrow within such a system (the only thing that would give us a parallel to later "revolutions"). I would go further and say that the 1800 election just supplied us with one precondition for the party system as we understand that term today.

The 1800 contest was barely an election in our sense of the word. The electoral college was still functioning as more than a vestige of its original self—though this time there were pledged electors (the precondition for popular voting). The method of drawing up tickets was still rudimentary, which is what threw the election into the House. The basis of party structure was still the congressional caucus, which was unofficial verging on conspiratorial. The partisan press was secretly hired, and traces of "faction" were covered over. Where public discipline could not be imposed, bribes and deals were swift to breed in the dark (for example, the attempt to throw the election to Burr). Outside this barely respectable network of party scheming, men were identified as Federalist or Republican because of shared sentiment and volatile alliances. Even Paul Goodman, the defender of this situation as "a first party system," admits: "It is often difficult to fix clearly a politician's partisan identity in the 1790s and early 1800s, and shifts from one party to another occurred frequently."

The pledged electors and inchoate coalitions of 1800 were not the result of party competition; rather, they established one precondition for such competition. Yet even that precondition was not sufficient. Most men were still trying to avoid party. Jefferson, in his famous statement "We are all Republicans, we are all Federalists," was saying that Washington's partyless system had degenerated into an unrepresentative faction. Jefferson was restoring the *true* partyless system. And, sure enough, the Federalists rapidly declined, then more gradually disappeared, after the 1800 election. The party died away to long but low New England mutterings. Even in the two decades preceding the partyless Era of Good Feelings, Jeffersonian Republicans made up three quarters of the presidential electors and four fifths of the Senate. Thus the 1800 election was not the overthrow of one party by another, but of one attempt at a partyless system by another such attempt. The Jeffersonians supplied a transition from the "national" administration of Washington to that of Monroe.

Jefferson's election brought about no deep change in policy—as Henry Adams demonstrated in his great study of that Administration. How could it? The new President had already held the nation's high offices—minister, Secretary of State, Vice President—in the "Federalist" years. A critic of Washington's neutrality policy, Jefferson affirmed it in stronger terms than ever at his inauguration. A critic of Hamilton's federal finance policy, he took more highhanded steps in gathering funds to purchase Louisiana than Hamilton had ever done. A critic of Adams' Alien and Sedition Acts, he committed more autocratic acts in enforcing the embargo than Adams ever got away with. The bank was not dissolved. The federal government did not surrender any powers, but added some.

Modern scholars generally grant the lack of a *policy* turnabout in 1800, but hail the event because (as Richard Hofstadter put it), 1800 "gave the world its first example of the peaceful transit of a government from the control of one popular party to another." One must stretch pretty energetically the definition of "popular party" to validate that claim. Jefferson's struggle with the Hamiltonians was a squabble of factions within a ruling order, adjudicated by an ad hoc council (the electoral college). It is true that Washington presided, by his awesome authority, over an unusually (perhaps uniquely) peaceful aftermath to revolution. *That* was the achievement that made minor conflicts possible— clashes more of personality than of doctrine; certainly not, yet, the formed contest of two "popular parties." The late Morton Grodzins made a good case that it was the moderation of John Adams, exercised against party pressure, that made for the peaceful transit in 1800—Adams distrusted the Hamiltonians more than he did Jefferson. He precipitated, in this preparty situation, the analogue of later party splits, so that Hamiltonians threw their weight to "Republican" Aaron Burr. This loose analogy is not enough to make 1800 a true parallel to later displacements of a majority party.

2. *1828:* How, in a comparatively "partyless" system, were candidates nominated? Through the first quarter of the nineteenth century, legislative caucuses held that power. When, in 1825, the House added the electing power itself to its repertoire, there was popular revulsion against this clubbish autonomy. Martin Van Buren organized what Walter Dean Burnham called "an extremely heterogeneous opposition to 'insider' politics," and put up Andrew Jackson, the loser in 1825, as an anticaucus candidate. This was a first step toward the convention system for nominating candidates, a stage that was reached in 1832. Thus the 1828 election supplied

us with a second precondition for party competition at the popular level. But a *precondition* cannot be a *result* of the thing it prepares. The 1828 election, even when confirmed by the 1832 results, "had remarkably little effect on party formation." The words are those of the principal student of this "second-party system," Richard P. McCormick, who contends: "It is common, in describing American politics in this era, to assert that by 1828 or by 1832 a functioning party system existed; but it would be my contention that in many states the crucial stage of party *formation* had not yet been reached" (italics added). Only after the Whig Party was founded in 1834 were two truly national parties in the field—and they did not meet in entirely competitive form until 1840. The second party system, according to McCormick, had a sixteen-year gestation period (1824–40), a developed period of twelve years (1840–52), and a decline of eight years (1852–60). The year 1828 is not the critical one, even in this cycle of growing and dissolving party alignments—much less in the whole course of American politics. Gerald Pomper's computer study shows that the major aligning movement of the period took place in the 1836 election, making the competitive system possible. So 1828 does not furnish us with an example of a minority party's growth within a two-party system. It marked another stage in the development of such a system.

3. *1860:* I have argued that political parties in America tend to mute differences, making them manageable. But the "second-party system" of Jacksonians vs. Whigs took this tendency to a ridiculous extreme—it *ignored* differences, leaving them unmanaged. This was the only period in our history when the two parties had no distinct regional bases at all; yet it was just the time when the worst sectional differences were developing. "The Senate's role during this period," Walter Dean Burnham says, "was that of a congress of ambassadors concerned with working out the terms of intersectional compromise." Yet presidential races were never emptier of content, never more focused on mere entertainment, than during this time. It was the age of electoral log cabins and canoes, of Whig generals and Democratic inoffensives, of nostalgia and escapism. It is not surprising that this was the only period in our history when incumbency proved no advantage to a Presi-

dent. The itch for novelty put men into office and took them out with equal levity.

As this game grew emptier, "causes" formed and made raids upon the electoral charade. Minor parties multiplied, for those who cared about other things than torchlight parades. As early as 1840, the Liberty Party was in the field, and it played a part in Clay's 1844 defeat. In 1848, both major parties lost principled minorities to a walkout at their conventions—"Conscience" men leaving the Whigs, and "Barnburners" the Democrats. That was the election in which the Free Soil Party adopted and spread the doctrines of the Liberty Party. By 1850 the Free Soilers embarked on a series of artful mergers with winnable elements of either party—with middle-western Whigs and New England Democrats. In 1854, the American Party (Know Nothings) played the same game, and a rash of new parties sprang up in protest at the Nebraska Act. The results were so confusing that in 1855 the *Congressional Globe* (predecessor to the *Congressional Record*) had to give up its practice of identifying speakers by party—the variety was too confusing. In 1856, the nascent Republican Party, picking up support from some Free Soilers and Know Nothings, reflected the growing sectional split in the nation by winning eleven of the sixteen northern states. In the next year, Republicans in some areas fused with Know Nothings to form the Union Party. By 1858, the Republicans had a congressional majority in the North.

The chaos of 1860 can be measured from the fact that eight national conventions were held. First the Democrats, assembled in Charleston, fought a ruinous platform battle pitting North against South; they had to adjourn without choosing a candidate after fifty-seven ballots produced no winner. Southerners who withdrew from this meeting held their own convention as Constitutional Democrats. The remnant of the Whigs tried a new coalition as the Constitutional Union Party and nominated John Bell. The Democrats reassembled in Baltimore, nominated Stephen Douglas, and drove out the remaining Southerners. This group met with those who had walked out earlier and, in the fourth and fifth Democratic conventions of the year, chose John Breckinridge.

While Democrats tore themselves apart, Republicans resisted

raids on their members by other minor parties, making party unity their highest norm. The man backed by most delegates, William Seward, was rejected because of his uncompromising stand on slavery. In the 1970s right-wing elements in the modern Republican Party, speaking for Ronald Reagan, accused Gerald Ford's people of making the party "go the way of Whigs, defeated because we don't *stand* for anything." In 1860, the Whig candidates, John Bell and Edward Everett, took a much more forthright stand than the Republicans did. While Bell was addressing the danger of secession, Lincoln made the most astonishing campaign pledge in the history of our politics. He said he would not discuss divisive issues until after the election—and he stuck to that pledge. He did not give a single campaign speech, or answer a single substantive question, from the people or from the press. Yet this election is offered to redeem the debate model of our liberal theory!

The Democratic and Whig parties broke down because the country was breaking down. Lincoln's election said, in effect, that the nation was now two countries. He did not get a single electoral vote in the South. Our elections are meant to compromise differences. When they run up against a difference that cannot be compromised, they lose their function. This "critical election" did not decide the whole nation's course; it merely showed that conventional political decisions could no longer bind the whole nation. One can hardly redeem the electoral system by pointing to the single time when the whole system broke down. It was because the election could resolve nothing that resolution went to the arbitrament of arms.

Even so, it is interesting to see how electoral politics in the North returned to its ameliorative role once the secessionists were removed from the picture. The Republicans were moderate in their first war aims, expressly excluding emancipation as one of them. In 1864 Lincoln's party changed its name to bring in old Union Party members, and he ran with a southern Democrat to distinguish himself from the radical Republicans. The Democrats, for their part, ran a general and a colonel as their candidates in 1864 and 1868, stressing their loyalty in wartime. (McClellan actually repudiated the 1864 platform for showing too "copperhead" an influence.) Despite the fact that five conventions were held in 1868, the parties showed a return to ticket balancing and compromise.

4. *1896:* Harry Jaffa, who calls his four deciding races electoral "revolutions" and says they have all brought in change "from the left," has to exclude 1896. It was, rather, a counterrevolutionary effort that meant there would be no revolution. It beat off the Populist challenge in a reaffirmation of the hard-money and high-tariff principles that had been upheld by the presidential Republicans and the Cleveland Democrats. The 1896 campaign, far from bringing in change, signaled that no major change was going to take place, despite premonitory rumblings from the West. The Cleveland irruption into the Republican period of hegemony was illusory; while capitalizing on Republican divisions (Halfbreeds vs. Stalwarts) and the "corruption issue," it divided the Democrats on a longer-term basis and assured their loss of the West. Even Sundquist, who puts this election at the center of his first "critical period," admits: "Those who did change their party loyalty were for the most part voters whose shift in attachment was in the direction of conformity with the regional party system established before and during the Cvil War." In 1896 normal ties were restored after being abnormally stretched under Cleveland.

5. *1932:* So we return to the starting point of it all, to the fondly remembered election of Franklin Roosevelt. Most critical election theorists seem to have begun with an emotional certitude about 1932, then looked for other examples of electoral "overturn" to show that this was not just a splendid exception. (No one has yet found a generally acceptable post-1932 critical election.) Yet, since they found all their other critical elections in the nineteenth century, the theorists went back to conditions very different from those prevailing in 1932—to times when a two-party system in our sense did not exist (1800, 1828), or when the system entirely broke down (1860), or when sectionalism failed to overturn the major party (1896). Besides, those were periods of a comparatively small electorate (no women, blacks, transients), with restrictive poll tests and poll taxes. It seems a bit desperate to "save" 1932 as a critical election by going back to such different conditions.

And there is the troublesome fact, implicitly recognized in Professor Key's veer off to either 1928 or 1936, that 1932 offered no choice between debated alternatives but simply a revulsion against the inactivity of Hoover. Roosevelt did not promise to *do* anything different, just to *be* different, which was enough. Indeed, a good deal of New Deal mythology overstressed the kind and quality of change between Hoover's and Roosevelt's administrations. Hoover had initiated the RFC, but with no time for it to show results. He wanted to close the banks, and asked Roosevelt to back his move during the then much longer interregnum of almost five months—but Roosevelt would not bail out his predecessor. Roosevelt's own first moves, admittedly done with greater vigor, were on lines already traced out by Hoover. The same electoral pressures that would prolong the Vietnam War had prolonged response to the Depression in 1932: Hoover felt the normal instinct toward caution moving toward a re-election fight. He tried (like all candidates) to give his own term a flattering interpretation—a thing that made him sound silly by November of '32. Roosevelt, on the other hand, benefited from the freedom to move out from one's constituents once he came into office. He bailed out the corporations, using the RFC with greater freedom than could any Republican considered an apologist for "big business." Nor did the Depression finally abate, despite all the activism of the New Deal, until World War II sent our economy skyrocketing.

Admittedly, a great change took place in 1932, one that made the minority party become the majority party. But that brings up the real limits on any critical election approach to our politics. Handed the book of American history, professors try to read the margin as if it were the text. The striking thing about our politics is not scattered turning points (if that is what they were), but long periods of party dominance. Inertia rather than energy marks the large picture; continuity, not reversal; contentment, not rejection. When something invades that contentment, the minority party gets a shot at the election. Otherwise, not.

As late as 1964, V. O. Key wrote: "In about only a third of the states do the two major parties compete on a fairly even basis. The remainder of the states diverge in varying degrees from the two-party system" (in favor of one-party dominance). The net effect of the overwhelming attachment of many states to one or the other of the national parties means that, in reality, no "party system" exists within such states for state purposes. And even in states not dominated by one party, there are districts, municipal fiefs, or belts of single-party dominance, raising the percentage of the citizenry that lives, in effect, under one-party rule. In states dominated by one party, the minority party manages to survive. But it does so, not as a chemical diffused through liquid; more like marbling in a cake—in enclaves where *it* dominates.

It is not surprising that Americans should vote so heavily from one-party bastions of varied sizes and sorts. Surveys by Paul Lazarsfeld and others long ago established that the main source of political information is word of mouth from peers. Social environment shapes voting practice. Family, status, profession, job, and residence are the key factors. If a "lifelong" Republican is sent into a heavily Democratic environment, the odds favor that person's becoming, eventually, a Democrat or ceasing to vote—and the odds are even higher for his or her children acting that way. This is not a matter of accommodation, simply, or weakness of individual view. It soon becomes obvious to the "immigrant" into a heavily Democratic district that his or her vote will not normally count if it is cast for losers. One can have more effect on the kind of rulers one gets by voting for the least undesirable Democrat in a primary. And activists find a majority party opening the way to actual office-holding, where one can have an effect.

These single-party pressures are not merely geographical. Within certain professions, career and advancement depend in some measure on shared sympathies with one's peers. An Ivy League academician will experience as many subtle pressures toward Democratic candidates as country-club businessmen have felt toward Republicans. Despite the decline in actual party registration, these pressures still form coherent interest blocs with inertial stability. The southern "conservative" vote has stayed fairly stable in the white community whether it went to the Democrats, Dixiecrats, George Wallace's American Party, Republicans, or (partly) back to Democrats. When the group "shifted," it did so corporately, to prevent change rather than initiate or symbolize it. One of the strongest correlations throughout our history has been of Church membership and party allegiance—see, for instance, Paul Kleppner's *The Cross of Culture* (1970).

These pressures have given us the long Republican dominance from 1860 to 1932 and the long Democratic dominance from 1932 on. During the Republicans' time of power, the only Democrats elected were Cleveland and Wilson. During the Democrats' period, the only Republicans elected have been Eisenhower and Nixon (with Ford filling out the latter's term). In two cases, those of Wilson and Nixon, the majority party split into two competing factions and let the minority in by a mere plurality. Some kind of breakdown seems necessary for the minority to have a chance. In the protoparty situations of 1800 and 1828, the partyless system itself broke down. In 1860 the entire national life was split apart. In 1932 the economy broke down. In 1952 the coldwar system (symbolized by the Korean War abroad and McCarthyism at home) broke down, and Eisenhower restored a spirit of compromise, infuriating those (on both sides) who wanted decision.

The dominant party has suffered shocks when whole new electorates have been added at once to the system—those from new western states in 1828 and the 1880s, women in 1928 (the first year they turned out in large numbers, accounting for some of the shift noticed that year by Key), blacks and young voters in 1968 (precipitating the Democratic split that gave the South to Wallace). These shocks are to be expected *precisely* in nonideological parties that represent group identity and sectional interests in a stable way. They have little to do with rational debate on policy alternatives.

Emphasis on change rather than continuity in our politics reflects political scientists' own values rather than response to evidence. Even when the "outside" party comes into office, the changes in policy are less than people expected. Eisenhower did not repeal the New Deal. The welfare state continued at much the same rate under him and under Nixon. Even a radical budget-cutter in principle, Ronald Reagan, did not make a significant break in California's fiscal policies. The cold war did not return with Nixon—he broadened peaceful coexistence to détente. The continuity of policy is symbolized in the Vietnam War's long nurturing under Eisenhower, Kennedy, Johnson, and Nixon—as well as by the interchangeability of senior advisers to the foreign-policy and economic establishments. In the circumstances, evidence (even misread evidence) of change becomes a novelty and a relief —as if, by shifting one's focus, one made the small letters of a book's text blur into neutral gray and the margins stand out with great visual simplicity. But the messy everyday business of our electoral politics has more to do with preservation than with departures. The trouble with reading a margin is that it leaves the mind with nothing much else to do after the eye takes its visual bath in the clarity of white space.

10 · Settling for Less

I was surprised to find that, after *Nixon Agonistes* came out, I was no longer considered (by those who noticed me at all) a conservative. Richard Nixon was thought of as conservative, and I wound up on his White House "enemies list." But I could hardly be considered a liberal, either. My book was as critical of the liberal approach to electoral politics as a "free market" of ideas as it was of the economic free market. Covering the 1972 and 1976 campaigns as a columnist (and for various magazines, principally *The New York Review of Books*) convinced me, all over again, that elections just do not *do* what people have assumed they do. I tried out my analysis in several seminars at Johns Hopkins and found great resistance in the students. They kept saying that elections *must* offer rational choice, or how are we self-governing? What, otherwise, makes those nations that follow our system "the free world" and those nations that lack elections "captive" ones?

But when I could not convince my students, Kenneth Arrow

could. That is both odd and natural. Odd, because I merely argued from observation that elections do not normally decide policy matters by a process of conscious reflection and choice, while Arrow proves that they *cannot* do any such thing. It is natural, however, that students should be impressed by Arrow's thesis, since they were better scientists than I am. They were studying things like statistics, which has become part of the political scientist's repertoire. (Willmoore hated this development, and insisted on calling his discipline political philosophy rather than political science—not reflecting that Plato was a mathematical theorist and Aristotle based much of his method on the laboratory analysis of animals.) I welcomed analytic support for my admittedly impressionistic conclusions.

Arrow rediscovered "the paradox of voting" that eighteenth-century students of probability had first detected. The Marquis de Condorcet noticed it in studying the efforts of juries to reach a conclusion, and Jean-Charles de Borda in trying to create rules for election to learned societies. It occurred to "Lewis Carroll" in the nineteenth century, when he tried to correct the inadequacy of voting methods at Oxford's faculty meetings. In the 1940s Duncan Black turned it up again. But by an accident an economist's work (Arrow's *Social Choice and Individual Values*, 1963) first brought the matter to wide notice in political-science circles. The independent rediscovery of the problem attests to its reality and persistence under a wide variety of approaches.

Here is Arrow's statement of the paradox of voting (or the Condorcet effect):

Let A, B, and C be the three alternatives, and 1, 2, and 3 the three individuals [choosing]. Suppose individual 1 prefers A to B and B to C (and therefore A to C), individual 2 prefers B to C and C to A (and therefore B to A), and individual 3 prefers C to A and A to B (and therefore C to B). Then a majority prefer A to B, and a majority prefer B to C. We may therefore say that the community prefers A to B and B to C. If the community is to be regarded as behaving rationally, we are forced to say that A is preferred to C. But in fact a majority of the community prefer C to A.

Put concretely: If two voters out of three prefer, say, Reagan to Ford and Ford to Carter, then the majority should prefer Reagan to Carter; but in Arrow's model a majority prefers Carter to Reagan. Put another way: The winner will depend on the order in which one individual is matched against another. Put another way: Any winner will be at the bottom of one person's scale, in the middle of another's, and only at the top of one voter's range of choices. Thus the paradox—a "majority" for everyone and for no one.

The model does not falsify what happens in our elections, except in one way: It understates the problem. The more alternatives there are, and the more choosers, the more anomalous the results become. And remember that Arrow is not considering here the "intensity factor" of people's real preferences. That is: If a winner in the model is only mildly preferred by one voter, leaves another voter indifferent, and is heatedly resented by the third, social dissatisfaction will be increased by his winning, even though it was legitimately arrived at by majority vote.

Ingenious people have tried to disprove Arrow's analysis by challenging its conditions or inventing mechanisms to circumvent the outcome; but more ingenious people have shown that these evasions do more to disguise the problem than to solve it—see, for instance, Niemi and Riker in *American Political Science Review* (1961). The paradox is insoluble because the reduction of triadic choice to dyadic decision-making is of necessity circular— "voting mechanisms allowing one unweighted vote per person cannot take into account all the relations among three or more alternatives." As Riker put it, "One feels the same sort of retrospective pity for the arithmeticians of proportional representation as for the geometers who tried to square the circle until it was discovered that π was a transcendental number."

Borda tried to evade the paradox by a weighed point system for expressing preference. But any usable point system misrepresents the scale and intensity of preference by reduction, suggesting equal intervals between the points and a point spread along the same parts of a scale. It tends, that is, to approximate the vote of a man who likes all the choices but mildly prefers one to others, and the vote of a man who despises all the choices except one.

Also, in politics, multiple winners with a plurality leader tend to be unmanageable. Besides, as Black and Riker both point out, even Borda's scheme does not preclude the paradox.

Black points out that the paradox is precluded if the choice is restricted to "single peak" preferences on a graph—for example, in "single issue" elections, where there are only two clear alternatives. But that can rarely express the range of opinion on any one complex problem, and certainly not the range of issues involved in most political elections. In fact, the *appearance* of single issue elections is usually given, when it occurs, because of arbitrary exclusions in a primary process that limits the matters for choice. We are told, for instance, that only two candidates are viable—take your pick between them, though your real preference lies elsewhere. The attempt to have runoff elections just extends this problem after the "real" election and brings us back to the fact that, in pairwise voting, the outcome will depend on the sequence of votes. This has long been recognized in committee procedure, where the later a motion is introduced the better are its chances of adoption. It is not tested against all the other motions, only against the remaining one or two. Borda expressed the principle this way: "One may compare [the outcome] exactly to two athletes who, after having exhausted themselves against each other, are subsequently vanquished by a third who is weaker than either of them."

Black, following Lewis Carroll, saw the possibility of evading the paradox by "sophisticated" or strategic voting—that is, one can look down the cycle of pairwise matches and make one's real choice win by signaling a *different* choice in some earlier matchup —which means that the only way to gain real preference is to express false preference. Riker phrases it this way:

In a society of two people, if person 1 orders the alternatives *a b c,* while person 2 orders them *b a c,* the best person 2 can do if he tells the truth is a tie between *a* and *b*. If, however, person 2 misrepresents the position of an irrelevant alternative *c* and reports his ordering as *b c a* . . . the society adopts the order *b a c*. . . . In fact, *a* and *b* tie if both persons lie or both tell the truth; but if only one lies, the liar wins. . . .

There may be nothing wrong with lying as a political strategy, but one would not, I assume, wish to give a systematic advantage to liars.

Some people, like Gordon Tullock, think congressional "log-rolling" is a sophistication that, through a sequence of trade-offs, leads to a "calculus of consent" expressing real preference in correct gradations. But Riker has shown, in concrete instances, that this bargaining process lends itself disproportionately to obstructionists. Besides, in order to play the game intelligently, one must know all the alternatives beforehand and know how other players are going to act. This leads, in practice, to the kind of "second guessing" and imputed motive that Keynes saw in the "voting" on stocks' market value:

> Professional investment may be likened to those newspaper competitions in which the competitors have to pick out the six prettiest faces from a hundred photographs, the prize being awarded to the competitor whose choice most nearly corresponds to the average preferences of the competitors as a whole; so that each competitor has to pick, not those faces which he himself finds prettiest, but those which he thinks likeliest to catch the fancy of the other competitors, all of whom are looking at the problem from the same point of view. It is not a case of choosing those which, to the best of one's judgment, are really the prettiest, nor even those which average opinion genuinely thinks the prettiest. We have reached the third degree, where we devote our intelligences to anticipating what average opinion expects the average opinion to be. And there are some, I believe, who practise the fourth, fifth, and higher degrees [*General Theory of Unemployment*, p. 156].

Sophistication just leads deeper into paradox.

I experienced the difficulty of expressing preference by vote in a situation that should have made the problem easier than it is in mass elections. A group of putatively knowledgeable people, on friendly terms and with some shared values, was asked to judge the finalists in a film festival. The winnowing out of the finalists had arbitrary aspects; but one could at least hope for fair treatment of those finalists once they were chosen. Any amount of discussion was allowed, and any procedure or rule change that was generally agreed on. The results, as I remember, went something like this:

There were eight judges and just over twenty films. In a straight vote for first, only one film was liked by more than one judge; so it only got two votes (one fourth of those cast). They tried a one-two-three rating: The favored film picked up a second and a third, increasing its claim to win, but still leaving a majority of judges dissatisfied. (One asked: "Can you cast a negative vote if you give up your positive one?" Blocking the leader had become important.) They tried a weighted system—each judge given five points to distribute at will. This only gave the leader fourteen out of forty points (ten from those who voted it first and gave it all their points, and four points from two other judges).

The panel was still not satisfied, and those resisting the lead film asked that the money be split up and each judge give his share as he wished. That was an unpopular move with some, who wanted the cash to go in one block (fifteen hundred dollars) or as a graded first, second, third (one thousand dollars, three hundred dollars, two hundred dollars). But the opponents of the lead film had a majority to get recognition for other films. The lead film received seven hundred dollars, and ten other films were given varying amounts. The result was anomalous in many ways (besides being hard to explain to the newspapers). The film that came in second by ranking vote (first, second, third) came in fifth for the money. Enthusiasm and ingenuity finally collapsed, early in the morning, into sullen resignation. Some intelligence and much goodwill, given not only free reign but enlightened encouragement, could not come up with a result very rational.

Election theorists, for all their skills and effort, have not been more successful in coming up with a "fail-proof" system for avoiding the paradox (or the other inequities of rating systems in general). They cannot do this even when, for the sake of the intellectual game, they try out processes complex, lengthy, and expensive—and therefore unlikely to be used in the real political arena. Most, indeed, admit that their "reforms" would backfire in actual practice, would introduce new elements of doubt, new awareness of inequities, in the voters' minds. Better let voters think that elections *are* doing what they fail to do than disillusion them. The immediate practical test of the rules is, after all, a willingness to abide by them.

Should we leave it at that—*say* the process concludes because we *want* it to conclude? Conclusion for its own sake becomes the supreme norm. Our system "works" for no other reason than that it *is* our system. Falling back to that last rather thin defense is not necessarily ignoble. After midnight, the film board I described would accept any of several arrangements just to get home, away from the endless bargains and bickering. Professional negotiators insist on nonstop bargaining because willingness to accept less than satisfactory contracts grows toward the end of any fatiguing process.

Perhaps, with a kind of blind luck, we do escape the paradox after all. The rational effort described by theorists from Condorcet to Arrow involves clear alternatives clearly presented, then ranked in clear order by rational choosers. Obviously, these are factors missing from our elections. "Reforms" of the system are meant to extend and clarify the options, equalize opportunities for their exposure, increase participation by the voter, remove distractions and extraneous factors (for example, unequal use of money by different candidates). Yet even if all these reforms succeeded— even if every American voted and voted wisely, among candidates speaking clearly and on equal terms, in great detail about their real view—even then we could not avoid the paradox. Then, indeed, the force of the paradox would strike home at us most clearly. Remember that people first became aware of the paradox in situations of high-level involvement and awareness—in juries, learned-society votes, and faculty meetings.

The genius of our system is to make the paradox irrelevant because we are so clearly *not* making choices among clear-cut alternatives, not expressing clear gradations of preference, not approving plans prospectively. The politicians labor long and well, and successfully, to make all this impossible, to sound much the same as each other, to mute or hide or fuzz divisive matters, to tell as many voters as possible what they want to hear.

We put up with the system because it *does* say what we will put up with, what we agree to agree on. That boils down, clearly, to a decision to keep putting up with what we have—the incumbent party and programs and spokesmen—or to stop putting up with them. What we are willing to settle for, at the end of the process, is partly arbitrary and partly meaningless; but our willingness to settle is the minimal goal we had to propose for ourselves. A refusal to settle would deadlock or sour the process. Suppose I favor A, will settle for B, and cannot abide C. You, by contrast, love C, hate A, and know nothing about B. If I rate the alternatives three points for A, two for B, and one for C, and you rank them three for C, two for B, and one for A, the result is a three-way tie, with each option getting four points each. That would better express one aspect of our choice, since neither of us is satisfied with or really wants B—who is, nonetheless, the only candidate absolutely revolting to no one. We will settle for B, but only to prevent the worst from happening (the worst being in my eyes C, and in your eyes A). That is why Americans normally vote *against* in an election. The probability that any one of us will get our very favorite person is small; that we could all get our very favorite is impossible. But we can eliminate the generally unacceptable.

The choice of political candidates and issues is subject to an elaborate if informal system of *vetoes* implied or expressed, of maneuvers to make sure "the other side" does not get its most objectionable views approved. This kind of veto can only be exercised if people agree, in effect, not to get their own most distinctive views accepted, either. The result is not a positive expression of anybody's will, but an agreement by most people not to *impose* their will. That is why divisive things get tacitly excluded from the discussion—religious differences, an ongoing war, slavery in the first half of the nineteenth century. That is why there is such emphasis on the *procedure* of voting as opposed to the substance of things being voted on. Richard Nixon did many things illegal and immoral—the secret bombing of Cambodia, the violation of Geneva rules on weaponry, the intervention in the Calley and Manson trials, the mass arrests of May Day. But none of these things could be made to matter when the House drew up its impeachment counts. The minor burglary of a rival party's headquarters was seen as an attempt to interfere with the electoral process; and to violate the system is to poison the springs of our democratic confidence that we are governing ourselves. We would rather talk about that than about wartime criminality Procedural matters are less personal and moral, and therefore less divisive.

A kind of delayed Victorianism once claimed that "polite" society does not discuss anything so ruffling to the sensibilities as religion or politics. One might say that elections, too, are not the time to talk religion or politics. Senator McGovern claimed, after his 1972 race, that he could have convinced people that the Vietnam War was immoral if there had not been an election going on at the time.

The voting process succeeds—it expresses a consensus; but only by stripping away the debatable, the new, the risky, the different. It returns people to the safe few things they agree on. The election returns people to the obvious, even when the obvious has become the threadbare—for example, Roosevelt's pledge of devotion to a balanced budget. It has been the custom for Americans to claim that, through competition of the fittest men in our politics, the "best man" prevails—so much so that we hear "the system has failed" when it can only present us with "the lesser of two evils" for our vote. But "best" and "evil" miss the point. We are muddled by our mutual vetoes and blocking maneuvers in toward the less questionable of two platitudes—the less questionable one being the more platitudinous platitude, which deserves to win. If the game is walking backward, the quickest walker backward is the best at the game. Elections sift men in order to find the safest, least abrasive, least original man—the man minimally objectionable to a maximum number of groups.

This returns us to a point made earlier—that elections settle questions of legitimacy, not policy. They tell us who will govern, not how they will govern. They settle the rotation order among our rulers. And they do this with extraordinary success. In theory, the transition from one regime to another might be thought the most unstable and precarious time for a political system. Wide and heated debate should divide. Yet our nation is never more united than at the close of an election. The campaigns have celebrated our togetherness, the things we agree on. The candidates' middling in toward each others' positions is structurally very important to the success of an election—not only to victory for one or other candidate, but also to satisfaction and acquiescence in the voters. The losing side does not feel total rebuff. The victors have not "eliminated" the opposition. Since differences were finally seen as marginal, almost everyone can live with the result. That thought transforms overnight the candidate who gets, say, 43 per cent of the people's vote (Nixon's plurality) or 42 per cent (Wilson's plurality) into "the President of all the people." Not everyone will agree with what he does; but everyone agrees that he *is* the President, and should be—his inauguration is a matter of national (not merely party) celebration, and traditionally ushers in a "honeymoon" period the President tries to extend. One reason so many people favor retention of the electoral-vote count for Presidents is that, even though it *may* overturn the popular vote, it *normally* exaggerates the victor's margin, making a plurality look like a majority, making a narrow majority look like a wide one. This increases the appearance of legitimacy. It makes it easier for us to want what we get—and we want to want that. We'll settle for less; but we'll call it more.

After an election, the losing candidates' advocates feel disappointed, as anyone must at losing after great effort. But they can look forward to a rematch precisely because the game is a stable and recurring one, with agreement to abide by the settlement as a condition for participating in the first place. This would not be the case if life-and-death issues had been clearly defined and debated toward a decision. People who insist on the purity of the debate process cannot understand the amicable nature of politicians toward their rivals. Noticing the long periods of one-party dominance, Walter Karp argued (in *Indispensable Enemies*) that minority parties could not lose so consistently unless they agreed to lose. He felt the show of competition just covered up conspiracy. Party bosses set up the minority candidates as evil boxing promoters might, for a price, set up endless patsies to make the champ look good. His argument had been made earlier, and more elegantly, in an English context. Hilaire Belloc and Cecil Chesterton, in *The Party System* (1911), described elections as fake battles staged to distract the populace while their pockets were being picked:

Now, if we were soldiers in an army subjected to a system of military law of unusual severity, we should perhaps submit cheerfully to our lot so long as we believed in the vital reality and value of the cause for which we were fighting. But if we found that all the time that we were being flogged and/or shot for the smallest infraction of discipline, our chief officers were continually conferring with the officers of the enemy, were on the best of terms with them, concocted their plan of campaign in concert with them, always carefully avoided every occasion of decisive engagement between the two armies, and generally treated the whole war as a friendly game of mixed chance and skill between themselves and their friends and relations on the other side—then I think our floggings and shootings would justly become a matter for complaint and even for mutiny.

The misleading note struck in that passage—typically, for the two men—is the trumpeting note of war. Politics is, like sports, a *substitute* for war. It tames and controls animosity. It does not fight to destroy, to eliminate the opposition. That is why the Darwinian parallel so often used—that campaigns give us the best leaders by putting them through a "survival of the fittest" test—is mistaken. We do not eliminate the inferior species, as natural selection must do, to re-engage the survival issue with new rivals. We just give the loser a rematch. "Wait till next time" is the perennial cry of the losing candidate as well as the losing baseball team. In fact, in sports there have been long periods of dominance by certain teams simply because the best players all want to get onto the best teams. This would insure almost permanent supremacy to certain teams if elaborate recruiting and drafting rules were not set up by sports commissions to make for more competitiveness. There is no commissioner of politics to reassign candidates in the parties; but fans root for minority parties through long periods out of office, much as fans stuck by the losing New York Mets for years. Parties build up interest in their cause by presenting each election as an apocalyptic showdown; but then they settle for calling it Apocalypse No. Three-hundred-and-something, and look forward to dozens of apocalypses down the road. This should come as no surprise to people who can work up frenzies of delight or anguish over the contact of bat with baseball, depending on whether the man at bat wore a blue uniform or a buff one. And if it is said that this reduces electoral politics to the level of baseball, well, what's the matter with baseball?

PART THREE

ELITES

11 · Business

Well, one thing that's wrong with political "baseball" is that it is played with bombs and young boys, not bats and balls. Decisions get made in politics that have life-or-death effect. It is not like being called out by an umpire. Does that mean Chesterton and Belloc were right in saying that others bleed because politicians play games?

Decisions, admittedly, get made in politics; but what has that to do with elections? The decision to make war having been made, some protesters in the late sixties were looking for ways to unmake that decision through an election. They could find no way. More important, they could find no election that decided we should go to war in the first place. No wonder they felt a certain disappointment in the electoral process.

Political decision-making of a serious sort tends to isolate itself from elections. That is why war comes more easily in the first year of a President's term—in 1917, 1941, 1965. I am not accepting the Charles Beard thesis that Roosevelt created the occasion for

World War II. But there is a general tendency for Presidents to be more "activist," more risk-taking, when they realize they do not have to face the electorate for a while. The Bay of Pigs invasion came during Kennedy's first year in office. I think President Nixon would have responded more combatively when North Korea shot down an American plane, just after his inauguration, if he did not have his hands already full in Vietnam. He *inherited* his war—and prosecuted it actively from the outset. President Ford was new in office when he experienced the euphoria of command over the *Mayaguez* affair.

Running for office and ruling are quite different disciplines. Once Roosevelt is elected, he does not have to keep repeating campaign slogans. He can try to address the real challenge of the Depression. Then he no longer "consults" the electorate. He calls in the experts—in his case, the "Brain Trust." He asks economists how to deal with the economy. He asks the elite to help him lead.

We can see a general rhythm in presidential terms, action occurring to the extent that it is buffered from any chance of electoral rebuff—a first year of initiative, followed by relative placation during the off-year elections; a third year of "chores," getting hard things out of the way so that the fourth year can be spent loosening up the economy, ameliorating problems or hiding them. But when the President *does* feel free to take serious thought and action on problems, he turns to those who have the time and requisite skills to give the matter serious thought, or those who have the influence to help turn thoughts into action. We are, in that sense, governed by an elite. The electorate can, retrospectively, "grade" the elite by passing or failing the politicians who employed it. But voters take little part in the planning of serious actions. Politicians like to say they learn what to do from their constituents; but the more serious the politicians, the less is that true. The people did not tell Roosevelt how to cope with the Depression, any more than they told Lyndon Johnson to step up the war in Indochina. The future response may inhibit a President in doing what he would like to do. But he would like to do, normally, what he takes on the best advice of the best students dealing with any subject.

Experts err. The "best and brightest" can mislead us, and often have. But they are going to lead us, nonetheless. They represent political "intelligence agents" in the broad sense—not as spies or CIA spooks, but as informed people passing on the best information they can ferret out for government use. If they err, we must try to get better experts. But we cannot do without experts, any more than we can do without brains in order to avoid erroneous thinking. The risks of being led by the best and the brightest are not avoided by looking, for guidance, to the worst and the dumbest. We have not progressed much if we trade in the misinformed for the uninformed. At least the misinformed know what the subject is. In baseball, bad players are traded, if possible, for good ones. Bad players are not traded for nonplayers.

Everyone in our society seems to resent elites—but only certain elites. We are all elitists; we are all anti-elitists. The right wing resents pointy-head professors and smart-aleck commentators; but it likes corporation heads. Businessmen resent academic economists and labor union hierarchs, but they tend to like generals and admirals. The left resents "the power elite," but likes academic socialists. Goo-goo types resent the lobbies, but like civic-minded philanthropists. Everybody resents one or other aspect of the managerial bureaucracy.

I started covering politics just when the New Left was determined to remain absolutely pure of elites. There was to be no "cult of personality" in the Movement. Media freaks were disowned by the serious left, and some leaders deposed themselves for the sin of leadership (Robert Moses of the Mississippi Freedom Democratic Party was the most famous and admired example). SNCC types mocked Dr. King as "De Lawd" because he would not "let the movement speak for itself." "Spokesman"—even "spokesperson"—became a bad word. Communes fell apart (even faster than they might have) because the only way to become a leader was to forfeit respect. Everyone had to perform every function, highest and lowest, turn and turn again.

When the right wing decided I was no longer one of them, some *NR* writers started calling me a liberal, despite my sustained criticism of the liberal system, as best symbolized in our electoral politics. But Bill Buckley introduced me on his TV show as a radical. That is as misleading as most of our political labels, since Bill sometimes calls himself "a conservative radical" (as does Norman Mailer). Yet I was certainly not at one with the radicals in their anti-elitism. One of the principal sources of New Left thought (to the extent that there was such a thing), and one of its links to the old left, was C. Wright Mills' *Power Elite.* He thought America's power structure had to be *dismantled* because it did not act the way its defenders claimed. I think it should be retained for the same reason. I was more set against the ideal of businessmen than against their practice.

The myth of the free market, the cult of the self-made man, social Darwinism—all these deadened the spirit, even to the extent that businessmen pretended to believe in them. But, luckily, they had little to do with what businessmen actually did in the real world. The last thing they want is competition or a truly free market (if such a miracle could be momentarily contrived for them). In *Nixon Agonistes,* I attacked the splintered legacy of nineteenth-century liberalism as it had been enunciated by men like William Graham Sumner, who believed in the free market of ideas *and* dollars. Since Nixon, with that time lag characteristic of him, tried to embrace this old system in its entirety, I referred to him (too hopefully) as the last of the true liberals, a displaced and dimmer-witted mini-Sumner. It is interesting that some people criticized my book because they felt I had to be *praising* Nixon when I called him a liberal. "Liberal" and "virtuous" were interchangeable terms in our centers of education.

The liberal is in theory opposed to elitism because a good system should work, as it were, by itself. We are not to trust to good rulers, but to a *system* that keeps *all* rulers in check. If we cannot have literal equality, every person can have an equal wariness for his or her own interests, and trust the machinery to turn out a balanced product. Stephen Spender put it this way in *Forward from Liberalism:*

> Socially, liberal thinkers such as Godwin or Mill regard democracy as a kind of laboratory in which everyone by expressing himself freely is submitting his life to a process of experiment. Godwin believed that from the more successful experiments happy examples of life will emerge for the ma-

> jority. . . . As Godwin pointed out, "The true object to be kept in view is to extirpate all ideas of condescension and superiority, to oblige every man to feel that the kindness he exerts is what he is bound to perform, and the assistance he asks is what he has a right to claim."

To get rid of all ideas of superiority is to get rid of elites. I can understand people wanting that in some of their wilder moments. But I don't see how they can believe in its accomplishment.

I define an elite simply as any group having privilege it can turn to influence. Privilege I define as exemption from the expenditure of energy to gain the bare necessities of life. Insofar as we are, any of us, exempted from that form of necessity we have a certain privilege, or free space. The signally exempted, able to turn that privilege into power, are "elect," the chosen-out or elite, who exercise actual power. Only they have the leisure to acquire skills and goods for the swaying of others. A man or woman whose bread-winning job leaves no time (or who thinks it leaves no time) for study, argument, observation, speaking, writing, volunteering, lobbying, organizing, dunning, protesting, or whatever, is obviously limited in the impact he or she can have on the political system in the large sense. (Liberal theory would like to restrict politics to elections, since *everyone* can in theory vote).

Martin Luther King, given the means to travel, acquire a doctorate, study the Gospel, perfect his sermon style, write, correspond, make influential acquaintances, was part of an elite. He had exemptions he could and did turn into instruments of powerful influence for the service of others. Privilege is not good or bad of itself, in Dr. King or in Nelson Rockefeller. It can be used well or ill. It is the sword given not for ornament but use. All those with privilege should turn it not merely to influence but also to service. Most, of course, do not. But that is not a condition to be cured by removing privilege and influence themselves, even if that were possible. The only way to remove privilege would be keep us all nonexempt, all lacking in freedom from the harsh necessities. Humanity in general would then not work to live, but live to work.

Some people find exemptions for themselves despite adverse circumstances—I knew a merchant seaman who used his idle hours on ship to read himself into the clergy, an elite group in our society. Others have exemptions they do not use—such nonelites, without influence, can be lazy Rockefellers as well as unaspiring black preachers. Although certain people spend the bulk of their lives "on the job," their job itself creates exemptions. Teachers, for instance, have inbuilt "leisure" to learn: They must keep learning, to teach others well. Teachers have had special kinds of influence on and through their students, the parents, the community organizations that support or work out of the schools. Even when paid less than other professionals, teachers were given the respect reserved for professional status. America's huge education system, unparalleled in the history of the world for its scope and expenditure and ambition, grew in large part because the teaching profession was an elite recruiting an elite, lobbying the community in many indirect ways, upholding the value of its product.

But no matter how one classifies the interacting elites that guide and direct our society, there can be no question that *the* elite in America has always been its "business community." The business of America is business. No other group has had comparable political influence; certainly not the legal profession, which serves as a manpower pool for the filling of public office. The community businessman is the community leader in many areas, including the social (in clubs, charities, civic programs). He is consulted more often and more assiduously by local and national politicians than are other professionals. Even when other elites—doctors, lawyers, teachers, clergy—partake in community leadership, it is often through the patronage or co-operation of businessmen. Anyone who has seen a university president fawning on corporate executives sees at once the true pecking order among elites in this country. In a study of the one hundred presidents of top corporations, compared with the hundred senators then sitting, Andrew Hacker found the former more metropolitan in origin, more WASP, more Ivy League in education, more mobile, more technologically sophisticated (*American Political Science Review*, 1961). The executives had seized the good things in our national life and were using them energetically.

Businessmen claim, of course, that their influence is used for the community. They are needed for the United Fund drive, the ballet society, the Christmas show for kids. More important, they employ those who, however lacking in privilege now, would be worse off without the jobs provided by "the private sector."

But privilege gives power over the *public* sector even for those who do not work in it full time (as politicians or appointees)—indeed, more power over the public sector is wielded by the private sector than by the permanent staff of the public sector. Nothing is more ludicrous than the big-businessman who laments the power of big government. He gave it that power, and he uses it daily. Business and government grew big together, with business leading the way. They expanded by collusion, not by competition. Their growth came especially in two explosive periods—the latter half of the nineteenth century, and the middle of the twentieth.

Looking back from the threshold of the twentieth century, Henry Adams said it was unrealistic for Americans after the Civil War to set themselves the goal of crossing and making habitable the entire continent of America. The nation did not have the capital for such a venture: "Merely to make the continent habitable for civilized people would require an immediate outlay that would have bankrupted the world." Yet the nation created liquid capital in private hands by giving up great quantities of its most basic and stable capital, the public lands. By its system of land grants, the government underwrote business on a scale that, as Adams put it, mortgaged a whole generation to the railroads. In order to protect its stake in this huge gamble, the government had to throw in other forms of subsidy—military protection, the mail, land-grant school systems, protection of gold vs. silver investors (which meant, mainly, big vs. little, railway vs. mining), creation and enforcement of harsh labor laws, which broke railway strikes, seizure of Indian and Mexican land, and use of the Navy to make progress toward the Pacific more inviting. The trains running into California would call, ultimately, for an open-door policy in the Pacific, for seized Philippines, for gunboat diplomacy. The flag followed the dollar, not the dollar the flag. Fortunes were made and lost, and the winners absorbed the losers' stakes. The number of American millionaires climbed from four to four thousand between 1860 and 1900.

It is often said that business took government captive in the late nineteenth century. If so, it was a welcomed capture. Bribes and corruption gave business control over politicians. But the trafficker in bribes is exercising a power of his own, and politicians did not make these deals to lessen their own importance. Of course, the personnel crossed lines more often then than now. That was the period when the Senate became known as the Millionaires' Club, and any suggestion of conflict of interest would have been laughed at. The nation's interest and the businessman's were one and the same. We had all gambled together. But most did not win as well as the few who called the tune.

The businessman may not have been the best and brightest specimen of the Gilded Age, but he was the hustlingest. To quote Henry Adams again: "The men who commanded high pay were as a rule not ornamental. Even Commodore Vanderbilt and Jay Gould lacked social charm. Doubtless the country needed ornament—needed it very badly indeed—but it needed energy still more, and capital most of all, for its supply was ridiculously out of proportion to its wants." The great gamble paid off; and by and large that was what the nation wanted. It wanted the job done, and it was instinctively grateful for being kept in the dark about some of the vicious things accepted as necessary to the job's completion. It was a time of "masculine" impatience with the niceties. That tone so prevailed that what Ann Douglas calls the "feminization of culture" made most other elites look prissy and irrelevant —preachers, teachers, writers, artists, all that "woman's world" of Church and school, books and lectures, tea and travel and good manners. To have bad manners was a sign of serious hurry and efficiency—no time to stop and bow, just grab and move on. A lingering nostalgia for that code was still expressed by Spiro Agnew and George Wallace when they attacked "effete" and "nattering" intellectuals, the donnish high-tea types who cannot park bicycles straight.

Efficiency was the test—getting things done, no matter how— and government had a part in it all. If business grew, so did government—both in the size of the territory (and the ocean) it came to control, and in the powers assumed to exercise control. If we needed a navy, the government needed to own the oil for it, and acquiring that would lead to later cycles of scandal, when those reserves were disposed of to acquire *more* territory. Admiral Perry made Albert Fall possible.

The second great explosion of business and government, of business-*cum*-government, occurred during and following World War II. The New Deal did not create the size of modern government. Federal personnel doubled in the eight years of Roosevelt's first two terms (after a period that artificially inhibited the administrative machinery for a nation our size). But that larger federal machinery was itself doubled in half the time by World War II, and it has never shrunk back. There are still right-wing diabolists who think Roosevelt tried to "do in" the business community rather than rescue it—a good corrective for those still capable of coherent thought is, for example, Hofstadter's essay on Roosevelt in *The American Political Tradition*. But there can be no question that business moved in and ran wartime Washington. Bruce Catton told the story very well, and angrily, after serving in Washington during these years (*The War Lords of Washington* [1948]).

No labor representatives were put on the major "war effort" committees. Business was allowed to say what could or could not be done on the production line, with no criticism allowed and little supervision demanded. If "the customer is always right," then the government—which is the customer when buying bombers and tanks—should have been allowed to call the tune. It didn't, because it didn't want to—any more than it wanted to check the excesses of the Gilded Age. The patriotism of businessmen was presumed; efficiency called for co-operation, not criticism. It was seduction of the willing. Once again, a miraculous economic spurt occurred. A nation still enfeebled by the Depression in 1941 emerged from the war prosperous and powerful as never before, without a rival in the world. All the other major industrial nations had been ravaged, but our shores were untouched. The cold war brought government contracts on a scale to dwarf even the great giveaways of the Gilded Age. Nuclear bombs, rockets, subs, and delivery planes, along with "the space age," continued that merger of research and defense that profited corporations of all sorts, academic as well as manufacturing. Certain professors who would later be war critics had been urgently begging government for funds to conduct defense-related research (by which they meant any kind of research—even, to my knowledge, the study of ancient Greek).

The collusion of government and business has to be sifted through dense riddles of ideology to come out as a clash between the public and the private sectors, with great corporations incongruously voicing what Chesterton called "the rather dirty individualism that talks about private enterprise." Calling the modern corporation private enterprise is, he added, like calling the Spanish Inquisition private judgment. What we have had in America is, rather, a form of state capitalism, with government underwriting and protecting the larger investors. It is not far from the state capitalism (rather than socialism) that Belloc predicted in his distributist book *The Servile State,* but without the worst consequences he foresaw. For the system *with* those consequences, we have only to look to the Soviet Union; for that nation no more qualifies as communist or socialist in the theoretical sense than our society corresponds to "free market" theory.

Apologists for capitalism like to point to the recovery of West Germany as a proof that the free market "works best." But Germany was the most totally industrialized nation in the world before World War II, and our heavy economic aid brought restoration of the razed superstructure on that base. The people did not have to change; they just needed new capital. The Soviet Union, by contrast, was incompletely industrialized before the war; it was heavily damaged by the war; it still had to transform an agrarian society while picking up the pieces of its damage. It did this by state seizure and deployment of the national capital—lands and goods devoted single-mindedly to a rearming as a refashioning process. It also absorbed adjacent territories. Land policy was sacrificed as the nation mortgaged itself to its weapons industry. Hacker points out that some of the same tensions that exist in America between businessmen and politicians show up between the economic managers and political bosses of the Soviet Union.

Russia's recent progress is not as different as we would like to imagine from what happened in our "economic miracle" of the nineteenth century. We, too, seized lands—Indian, Mexican, Philippine. We mortgaged the nation to a rail system, to be protected and made profitable with the help of naval and cavalry power. Our own blacks, Indians, Chicanos, Orientals, and white laborers were treated shamefully. Yet the nation in general supported the effort despite risk and inequities. The *esprit* of the Russian people indicates similar backing for its great economic recovery and industrial breakthrough. If there are dissidents, we had our critics of the Gilded Age—Twain, the Adams brothers, and Henry James.

Yet ours remained a largely free society, at least for whites, in the nineteenth century—despite heavy anti-immigrant prejudices. There were no purges or *putsches*. What explains the difference? The presence of elections in one place and not in the other? Well, the Soviet Union has elections. Ah, but these are rigged, not "real" elections? Ours are better managed, not to say stage-managed. There is less restraint on political initiative in America. But elections reflect an ethos rather than create it—as we have found in trying to impose elections on various countries. Russia's quick transformation from agrarian to industrial society did not change the ethos of the people at the same rate. The Soviet Union tried to cram our three hundred years of change into fifty years—and even our starting point, in the early colonies, was "enlightened" by seventeenth-century standards of British constitutional law. In Russia, traces of czar and boyar, of the great estate owners and the peasants, perdure in commissar and communard, undispellable overnight. Even a dissident like Solzhenitsyn yearns back to the established Church and religious authoritarianism of the old regime rather than to modern democracy.

There are other things that ameliorate the impact of state capitalism in America—things I shall be considering in the next few chapters. I don't mean, here, to say our experience is the same as the Soviet Union's in terms of national freedom. I bring up the comparison to stress just one similarity: Both we and the Soviets adopted state seizure and mobilization of capital because we both wanted to get a huge job done fast—that is, we did it for efficiency. So much for the idea that the free market, even if there were such a thing, is the most efficient economic organization. In war we adopt controls, rationing, central planning, and similar measures, because they allow concentration of resources in the most efficient way. Even Herbert Hoover made that argument while administering World War I controls. No, the argument for democracy cannot successfully be made in terms of efficiency. Freedom is messy. Complex. It lets people work at cross purposes if they want to—lets us all be our potty little selves, a dangerous luxury in wartime. That is why every war for freedom goes forward by restricting freedoms.

And even in nonwarring societies we need some planning, some regimen for efficient feeding of the citizens. Our businessmen are the managers of our economic affairs, our materialist elite. They would like to say that a system takes care of things and needs no management—the old liberal idea of a well-oiled machine automatically co-ordinating people's actions for the best result. That is nonsense. Things are well managed or ill managed according to the skills of the managers. We cannot escape that. We have to use them even if they sometimes abuse us.

And what is there to check such abuse? The political system? The politician? The electorate? Politicians, it is true, cannot as easily say "the public be damned" as some businessmen do. But neither do politicians say, or want to say, "business be damned." Politicians are elected—and, especially, re-elected—in great measure according to "the state of the economy." That means businessmen have great guiding and retaliatory power over politicians. Besides, businessmen are experts at what they do. When politicians need certain kinds of expertise, they have to go to those who possess it. They have to go to an elite—in this case, to *the* elite.

Can the electorate check business abuse? How? Through the clumsy electoral system, meant to prevent hard decision-making and clear choices? At one remove, through politicians? Yet the general electorate cannot bring the daily pressure on politicians that the business community does. The ordinary voter does not have the time, money, organization, knowledge, or friends for the tasks that business lobbyists perform. Elites are not checked by the masses. They can be checked only by other elites—like the ones I am about to consider.

12 · Bureaucrats

In technologically advanced societies, one form of expertise demanded is obviously technological. In the business elite Hacker studied, the second most desirable education after Ivy League schools was training as an engineer. The fear of "faceless technocrats" wielding unseen power has some basis in fact. Some of the most powerful people in our society are never described to the general public. Take, as one of many instances, the people in the Department of Labor who make up unemployment figures. There are several ways of computing those statistics, each with certain flaws, each with scholarly defenders. The impact of those statistics —on investment, on politics, on judgment of other affairs—is immense. A decimal point or two off in either direction can have grave consequences at certain periods in our politics. If the statisticians err, use the wrong method, are sloppy within the method, we all may have to pay for it.

Yet we cannot, with George Wallace, just kick the pointyheads out and muddle along in the dark. We must try to get the best expertise, even when the best is admittedly fallible. The only basis for reasonable action in a complex and interdependent society must be a grasp of the complexities, however imperfect and challengeable. Yet the statistician is not himself a manager. He supplies the managerial elite with the information needed for decisions. Assignment of resources, division of labor, timing of changes—all these things, in and out of government, are also largely out of the public's hands, though it will suffer or enjoy the consequences. So much is this true in our kind of society that some authors have considered the managerial power to be the distinctive one, the real elite for our foreseeable future—for example, James Burnham in *The Managerial Revolution* and John Kenneth Galbraith in *The New Industrial State*. One does not have to agree with them to see how important these decision-makers are, and how relatively free of control (whether electoral or other). Even corporate stockholders find it notoriously hard to affect a large corporation's day-to-day management decisions. Yet, compared with the electorate's limited "retrospective sanctioning" role in our politics, the stockholders are a small and active body with resources for involvement.

Fear of managerial power over our lives tends to merge, as George Wallace proved, with resentment of "big government" and the bureaucracy. Bureaucrats have and use elite training and skills —many are lawyers, economists, professional counselors. The labor statistician is a bureaucrat—so, for that matter, are men like James Schlesinger and Stansfield Turner. But the popular picture of the bureaucrat is of an obscure civil-service careerman whose paper-pushing affects lives invisibly. His power is hard to check or criticize because it is hard to find, even though much of the criticism goes to the comparatively visible "servicing" bureaucracy. This latter is condemned both by the recipients of the services (for being inefficient) and by the rest of the community (for being expensive and "unearned"). The welfare services are damned both for *not* helping the poor *and* for helping them.

Bureaucracy in this narrower sense might be compared to customer-complaint services in business. The citizen is a consumer of government. He or she expects certain services, and complains if they are not forthcoming. People grumble "you can't fight city hall," but they keep trying to do it anyway; and they expect someone to answer the phone when they call to complain. Congressmen find that such "case work" is the principal reason they must expand their staff—even though what this staff does is spend hours talking to people who complain about the size of government. The bureaucracy grows in order to handle complaints against the bureaucracy. Congressmen commiserate with their constituents, and use the bureaucracy to cut through the bureaucracy. Citizens want fast action from people who know how to thread their way through the labyrinth; but having such people on call increases the density of the labyrinth. Government becomes "inefficient," then, by its very effort to be responsive.

Businessmen executives have a narrow producer's view of efficiency—get the job done; for the public's eventual good, of course, but not at the public's direction. "If I listened to you all day I could not build you the generator you need" is the prevailing attitude. That is why production executives are so often at odds with their own sales departments, which are customer-oriented. Politicians, of necessity, resemble salesmen more than production managers. Much of the politicians' energy, their allocation of time and personal resources, goes into "stroking" the public—a performance the public expects and even demands. It is not very logical for people, having issued that demand for personal servicing, to resent the fact that it is time-consuming and expensive not only for the individual politician but also for the government he shapes according to his own sense of priorities. In point of fact, many of the direr predictions about "the managerial society" have not come true because a sales-oriented politics supplements a production-oriented business elite, and does so precisely in the bureaucracies.

Many opponents of "big government" assert or imply that bigness is of itself inefficient. That is an odd complaint to hear from executives of General Motors—who, when they advert to the anomaly, tend to say that bigness is efficient in business and only inefficient in government. They are right, in a way, about our government; but not because government cannot be both big and efficient. We have all experienced the efficiency of the IRS in tracing and extracting revenue from each citizen's income. The only real inefficiency imposed on the IRS comes from politicians drafting legislation in response to a public wish that the IRS should be *less* thorough.

Insofar as the FBI has been inefficient, wasting manpower on silly tasks, it was because of its director's ideological whimsies. The purely "bureaucratic" side of the Bureau can be very efficient indeed—for example, in its computerized fingerprint service. This is the side of government that frightens people when it becomes too efficient. Some of the very same people who claim big government is inefficient turn around and cry that it is becoming an Orwellian Big Brother, knowing too much and doing too much to control our lives. One day we are taught to despise the bureaucracy as a feckless idiot, and the next day to tremble before it as a kind of mad genius.

The Manhattan Project shows us that government can accomplish a task of great scope, complexity, and delicacy. The atom bomb was built and delivered with speed, precision, and secrecy. The thing could not have been done without all the government's power to recruit and commandeer, screen and compel and hush up. And there's the rub. We do not want a government that can take what it wants and do what it wants without letting the public know what is going on. Only the excuse of war seemed to justify such secret control. Government efficiency is at its peak in times of war when the excuse of safety for the citizenry is allowed to override, in importance, the freedom of the citizens. Regrettable as all such war measures are, they obviously destroy the idea that governments cannot act with great—with ruthless—efficiency. Generals are bureaucrats too, and Gilbert Chesterton wrote: "I have never understood, by the way, why Tory debaters are so very anxious to prove against socialism that state servants must be incompetent and inert. Surely it might be left to others to point out the lethargy of Nelson or the dull routine of Gordon."

Government is inefficient not in the degree of its bigness but of its accountability. It cannot "get the job done" because it is always having to stop and explain itself. Pure police work of the technical sort is often improved by size and organization; the better-run police departments are often the biggest ones, where impersonal rules must be enforced and individuals have less chance to color the overall response to criminal problems. In the same way, the FBI's fingerprint operation is superior to "decentralized" local fingerprint banks. But we do not want a government that fronts us mainly as policeman to putative criminal. We think it *should* take time to explain and justify.

The post office, that byword for inefficiency, does not prove that the government could not run a cost-accounted and profit-making delivery system if that were the sole aim in view. It is inefficient because it is expected to service the public, by universal and uniform delivery, by subsidizing the spread of information at below-cost rates (for books, newspapers, magazines, and other printed materials). Readers of *National Review* receive their denunciations of the post office because the government underwrites delivery of magazines at a cheap rate—and even Buckley's magazine wants that scheme of things continued, much as it laments the consequence. Businessmen attack the post office though it subsidizes their advertising and ordering processes, both in direct mail and indirectly (through the delivery of magazines and newspapers that carry their ads). Voters complain about the mail, yet ask their congressman to get them a new post office building and put their second cousin to work in the mailroom. If binding Big Brother down to these menial chores is inefficient, then we owe some of our freedom to that accountability.

It is true that centralization of power can be dangerous. But the servicing side of government is "inefficient" precisely because it *disperses* power, because the government can be tied up with *individual* cases. This is one reason Belloc's fears of state capitalism have not been warranted in America (as opposed, say, to the Soviet Union). Distributism—the English movement represented, from 1910 to 1940, by Belloc, the Chesterton brothers, Arthur Penty, Eric Gill, and Vincent McNabb—was named for its goal of distributing property more equally to prevent the centralization of power in state capitalism. The favored property to be distributed was land, though guild unions would also bestow a kind of property in one's job. Part of the program was simply vigorous anti-trust legislation, more laws to favor small shops and businesses. But another proposal was to give citizens a certain acreage to work or lease, so long as it was not sold to a larger combine. Much in distributism resembles the agrarian values and the decentralized "ward system" of government expounded by Jefferson. So it is not surprising that distributism had great impact within three American movements—the "Fugitives'" defense of southern agrarianism, the midwestern Green Revolution of German Catholics, and the Catholic Worker Movement (one of whose co-founders, Peter Maurin, was a distributist).

The distributist critique of modern capitalism was sound and incisive. But the distributists' proposed alternatives relied too much on mere nostalgia for earlier and simpler days, for medieval guilds and pre-industrial peasants. The radical wing of distributists became Luddite; Father McNabb had agonies of conscience about using a machine as vital to his work as the typewriter. Yet there is an element of vital common sense in Chesterton's dictum "Opposition and rebellion depend on property and liberty." Jefferson also argued that property gives the citizen a place to stand on when making his shove for attention from the government. The difficulty with Jefferson's scheme to give every voting citizen of Virginia fifty acres of land was that the decentralization would only be temporary, even in his pre-industrial days of farming. One had to have a large enough stock of slaves to make early plantations self-supporting. Minor plots would be hard to maintain, and therefore easily absorbed into larger holdings. Some distributists tried to prevent this by saying government grants should stipulate that the land could not be sold to a larger holder. But how is a thing one's property if one cannot dispose of it? Suppose only a larger owner would buy, and the small owner wants or needs something else far more than the land—medicine for his children, travel for his health, an operation, a small store, etc. (This has always been a problem with antitrust laws: How does one limit the power of large firms to absorb small ones without denying the freedom of small-businessmen to sell out if they want to?)

Our society is working out a solution to some of these problems *ambulando*. One way is to give a property right to services. The unions give property rights to a job. One of the things I could not understand about the right wing was its violent opposition to the labor unions. Chesterton's defense of guilds made it clear to me that unions are conservative in the large sense. The original objection to their formation in America came from liberals of the Sumner sort: What right have you to bind a man down to being one thing all his life, a plumber or carpenter, when he can become *anything* on the free market, even *President?* Is this not a retrogression to feudalism, back from contract to status, to a guaranteed life so long as one stays on the fief? Yes, that is just what it is; and that is why it reduces the rootlessness and drift of industrial life. It gives people a stake in society; it makes for social cohesion and stability—conservative values. Chesterton supported the major labor strikes of his time when they were still bitterly opposed.

But the unions affect only a small part of our society. The government has, in its servicing role, been guaranteeing a different kind of property right. Complaints about such services concentrate on comparatively small remedial services like food stamps and unemployment pay. The great expenditures are not widely attacked because everyone so clearly feels their benefit. The greatest of them all is this: Every American citizen, simply by being a citizen, has a right to at least twelve years of education equally bestowed. In an advanced society this is a vital bequest. Early immigrants to America were willing to trade all other property, after providing for the bare necessities, to give their children an education. That shows the property value of the thing. The education can be well used or ill—as Jefferson's fifty acres could be well farmed or ill. But there is this great difference: The right to education cannot be bartered away to others or sold for something else. It belongs to the individual child and to no one else.

This extraordinary social commitment has created a vast bureaucracy, the biggest one in our nation. And it is inefficient because it must service each child individually, addressing the child's particular problems or needs. It is also inefficient because it supplies the community with ancillary services—meeting places, cultural events, policed property in blighted areas; just as the post offices supplied polling places, courtroom space, and public-service distribution points (for tax forms, wanted notices, recruiting offices, etc.).

The government—local, state, and (as supporting partner)

federal—owns the public-school plants. But no one cries "social-ism" over this fact, because the true property involved is the child's ownership of the education system's product. The government must own the means of servicing if the child is to own the service. This differs from classical socialism because it gives own-ership in a service, not "reality" or physical means of production. The problem of common ownership in real property (in the legal sense of real estate) does not arise, since the government owns only what real property it needs—the buildings and facilities—to meet the demands of those owning the service.

The fact that the service is owned as individual property is now asserted by those who call for a voucher system—a money equivalent to the right, to be cashed in as part payment toward a private education. This scheme has been stalled by side consider-ations—the usefulness of vouchers in preventing court-ordered school integration, and a tradition of Church-state separation. Neither consideration affects the principle at stake—that there is a *property* in the right to education. Using that property at a different school is not like selling the fifty acres for something else, since even private schools must meet all the state-accredi-tation standards of public ones, whatever they add to that of their own.

The establishment of this property right to a service should in time dispel the resistance to similar rights to medical service. We have already established a principle of retirement support in the Social Security system. The principle is better than the practice, since Social Security does not cover all the citizenry, and it covers even those included by means of a regressive tax as compelled insurance. But it is hard to construct the equivalent of the right to education in this field because we are dealing with real property as well as a service. We could give retirement pay to everyone falling under a basic income level, if income were the only thing to be considered. But what if the retired person has real property that could produce income, but he or she refuses to sell it—should that disqualify the owner for retirement pay? A more sophisticated approach is needed to make sense of retirement rights.

Another right to service that is being expanded is the right to safety. We all have the right to hold our legal possessions in peace, and police try to guard our homes just as the military guards our shores. I have the right not to be run down by a speeding car, and the patrolman guards that right. But I also have a right not to be poisoned by unknown substances or rotten meat, and the FDA guards that right. This brings us to another part of the bureaucracy that has come under fire of late, the regulatory agencies—the Occupational Safety and Health Administration (OSHA), the surgeon general's office, and others. Once again, the business elite mounts general resistance to these agencies, even though most of them indirectly subsidize the businesses, just as the post office does. A glimpse of the truth was given us in 1977 when President Carter's administration deregulated some aspects of air travel. The airlines themselves at first protested that policy. To see why, we should look at ground travel, where the hazards and rewards are more visible and understandable than in the trackless air.

Stated in the abstract, there is something frightening about the government's control over manufacture, sale, and use of automobiles. What could be more arbitrary, after all, than to say that *no one* can drive on the left-hand side of a road? Speed laws tell truckers and bus companies how to conduct their business. Even the individual citizen must either heed or make all kinds of arbitrary signals before turning, stopping, proceeding. No one can drive without government permission—granted only after a certain age, by license. No one can drive a car the government does not license. The licensing involves inspection of both the car and the driver (who must correct personal defects like bad eyesight under force of law). Mandatory insurance and periodic testing are the law in some states and becoming law in others.

Car manufacturers must heed a whole list of specifications—as to maximum width, placement of wheels and steering wheels, number and arrangement of lights and mirrors and windows. People who complain about government "interference" in the requiring of seat belts can quibble at the gnat, but they should take time to reflect that they have already swallowed the camel. And loud as the manufacturers are against some new proposals (like air bags) they should reflect that government rules have increased business by increasing public confidence in cars and in the conditions for their use. Who would want cars around if children could not be trusted out on the streets, provided there *were* any streets, and not just a jumble of tracks on which anyone could drive any old vehicle any old way he or she wanted? In providing safety services, the government has even more directly subsidized car manufacturers (and truckers and bus companies and gasoline companies). The government owns the means for providing the service: It owns the roads, and it uses that ownership not only to provide for citizen safety but also for communication and mutual access. Once again, we do not think of this ownership as a form of socialism, even though it was built by the exercise of one of government's most awesome powers, that of eminent domain—the evicting of people from homes or forcing of their sale. Everyone profits by the service—but certain kinds of businessmen profit most. Even the courts profit, since they would be tied up far worse than they are if access through a crazy quilt of privately owned roads led to endless litigation.

When the government took over much of the private rail system, there was some loose talk of socialism, but more repetition of the charge that the railroad would be even worse managed now, since the government is so inefficient. The railroads were built with heavy government capitalization—and they only declined because government began to subsidize the airlines, by taking its mail off the trains; and to subsidize trucks, by providing the interstate highways. Trucks, after all, do not have to lay and maintain their own roads, as trains must keep up their tracks. The government is maintaining the trains as a service, not running them as a business.

So it is easy to see why airlines like some measure of federal regulation. Federal standards promote air travel by promoting confidence. If, after a major crash, each private line investigated and reported on the causes, how many people would believe the hired hands of the line itself? How many would trust the airlines to maintain adequate safety standards? Even if I had reason to trust Line A or B, that line would be held hostage to the small maverick firm whose noncompliance endangers every other plane in the air. The lines themselves like to see standards imposed on other craft around theirs. Government monitoring procedures are an extra system of safety in the air, just as the traffic-light system is on the ground.

The Pure Food and Drug Act promotes consumer confidence; so it helps sell meat. As life in the complex world grows more complex, and knowledge tries to keep up with it, safety and health do not involve only crude things visible to every eye, like rotten meat or speeding cars. The conditions of a mine, the effect of smoking, the effect of thalidomide on children, are things about which we must consult the doctors and chemists. They may err—as the labor statistician may. Their findings may be contested by interested businessmen—as the harmfulness of smoking was for so long a time. But the answer is not to expel the expert. After all, his findings will only be proved or disproved in the long run by another expert. Only a better chemist can refute the erring chemist.

Thus the managerial elite, even in its most despised form, the bureaucracy, performs a great service to the nation. For one thing, it helps to check abuses in the practice of the business elite. The mine owner indifferent to the health of his miners, the airline not careful enough of its passengers' safety, the too-hasty pharmaceutical company, the unhygienic butcher—all these can be punished or frightened into compliance. And the principal beneficiary of this is the ethical businessman who can conduct his affairs with a public less distrustful of his product.

This managerial elite has also given us a concept of property in service that does much to disperse governmental power and to spread the individual tools for modern living. The education system is the best model of this, and it shows how an elite can bring about its goals without going through the electoral system. Though funds are voted for schools, the basic decision to have schools of our sort and size was not, primarily, made through electoral debate. An elite persuaded its customers that they needed what only the elite could offer. In doing so, the elite expanded its power as a group by vastly enlarging its own number.

Here we come to the last popular charge brought against the bureaucracy—that it aims to increase the number of bureaucrats as a kind of fief-building; that the principal beneficiaries of social-

welfare enactments are the social workers, not the poor themselves. If one takes the principal sin of *elites* to be exclusion and
narrow hugging of their privileges, then an expanding *bureaucracy*
is a healthy one, one that wants to share its privileges. This shows
that bureaucrats really want to produce more service rather than
retain narrow privilege. That is surely why the school system grew
so fast so far. Teachers by and large believe in teaching, its
benefits and necessity—just as producers believe in production
and salesmen in selling.

George Wallace complains that nobody elected these faceless
bureaucrats, or showed by an election that they were wanted; and
he is right within his normal bounds of exaggeration. The service
elite has always responded best to elite arguments, from the
muckracking of Upton Sinclair against polluted meat to the
charges of Ralph Nader that cars are not as safe as they should
be. The servicer believes in servicing, and when that brings him or
her up against members of the business elite, the people are not
necessarily on the side of the servicers, or on anyone's side. The
question will normally be decided before it can come to the attention of voters. Neopopulists are right to see elitism in the bureaucracy; but they do not oppose it out of consistent opposition to
all elites. They do not want it interfering with *their* side's elite, the
business community, which could make decisions affecting life or
death with relative impunity were it not for the determination of
the regulators to regulate.

13 · Do-gooders

One of the stranger developments of modern politics is the growth of neopopulism on the right. It is not confined to yesterday's "nonornaments," as Henry Adams might put it, like Spiro Agnew and George Wallace. Its current theorists are Tom Wolfe (whose *Radical Chic* made a great hit at *National Review*) and Kevin Phillips (who was at least consistent enough in his populism to resent Buckley's yacht). The anti-elitism enunciated by these men is repeated and distributed by journalists like Pat Buchanan, William Rusher, and Jeffrey Hart; and professed by political activists like Richard Viguery and Philip Crane.

I call the development strange, since Phillips more precisely defines Wolfe's "radical chic" crowd as a nonproductive "knowledge industry." This knowledge elite does not deal in real property or the production of new wealth, but in services—and especially services involving the word. It is made up of writers, advertisers, advisers, bureaucrats, and foundation personnel—

including much of that elite I considered in the previous chapter. In a sense, Phillips is just voicing the age-old opposition of production executives to sales staff. But there are some aspects of his book (*Mediacracy*) that make it refreshingly quirky:

1. The first of these is that Phillips himself is a word merchant. Trained as a lawyer, he became a campaign analyst for Nixon in 1968, served briefly in John Mitchell's Justice Department, and became a journalist. He advises the right wing in his newsletter and lectures. The same role is filled by Richard Viguerie, Pat Buchanan, et al. They are all nonproducers in their own terms. I suppose they justify this by saying that the enemy must be met on his own ground to be vanquished. But the result of fighting fire with fire is usually just a larger conflagration, with the fire and the fire fighters indistinguishable (the story of our aping communist methods to defeat Communists).

2. In the turn of time we often hear from the right what the left was saying just yesterday, and vice versa. In the 1950s it was the liberal establishment that feared "Madison Avenue," the manipulative salesmen with their planned obsolescence and recycled junk. Galbraith and others said we were becoming a nation of packagers with less and less to package. This sounds like some of the more recent pages from Phillips.

3. An even older complaint is echoed here—the turn-of-this-century populist's assault on banks and investors that merely shuffle papers of ownership rather than produce things themselves.

4. But we have to go even farther back to get the full force of this movement's feelings on production. The medieval condemnation of usury was based on the concept that money does not "breed" or reproduce itself; so a charge should not be made for the temporary use of money ("usage"). That was an idea Chesterton and Belloc tried to rescue from its more obvious disadvantages; but their attempt excessively narrowed the idea of the property to be distributed by "distributism." They could not see that the right to *use* property is a *form* of property (proprietorship), just as the right to services can be a property right. The right-wing populist's cry against *intellectual* usury says that *words* cannot breed, any more than coins can—an odd plaint from the

right wing, whose own foundations are placed on the overthrow of medieval bans on usage!

One long-recognized use of capital is to give leisure for planning, inventing, tinkering, teaching new workmen, etc. In that sense, capital has always flowed in to a "knowledge industry." Furthermore, the production of wealth is incomplete without its distribution and protection. It does no good to produce thousands of shoes if you cannot find people who want them, or if the people who want them just come and grab them for free. By considering problems of distribution and protection, the knowledge industry *completes* the production process.

5. But the truly basic question raised by Phillips is one often overlooked by both the right and the left. Do we live to work, or work to live? Assuming everyone could be fed adequately tomorrow, and sheltered, what would be left for mankind to do? Would it have completed its overriding and only task? The work ethic of the right makes work its own end—satisfying, character-forming, virtuous, productive of good to others. To achieve success is to do one's work better than others in the competitive struggle. In a way, the radical left just turns that attitude around and repeats it from a new angle. Politics has no higher goal than to keep the poor from suffering. Equality of possession would complete the human task.

But Bernard Shaw realized there are different kinds of comfort. A clergyman is not any more nonproductive than a baker if his flock feels an acute need for consolation of the spirit as well as for the body's sustenance. Shaw had to recognize the productivity of knowledge because his own sharpest craving was for music. Baffled of that, he would have starved. You could not call musicians nonproductive in his house. Even in the old medieval sense, knowledge "breeds," produces more knowledge in oneself and others, as surely as more grain produces more bread. And the aim of any human production is not simply to turn out more of anything for its own sake. Production is meaningless until it can bring about or increase human satisfaction. Surely religion, the arts, entertainment, and "mere words" are ways of producing that satisfaction. The Phillips analysis, it turns out, is just another phrasing of the Gilded Age's assurance that culture is sissy stuff, that a man's work is to work, and that work blesses the human race with railroads.

This anachronistic snort of Industrial Age masculinity is made to seem timely by the resentment felt for do-gooders in Wolfe's *Radical Chic*. The privileged advocates of welfare for the poor are dismissed as condescending meddlers, people who will not trust the poor to decide what they want. Daniel Patrick Moynihan voiced this complaint in *Maximum Feasible Misunderstanding*, which charged that an elite of the upper middle class had allied itself with the poor to do in the decent working class:

> Social scientists love poor people. They also get along fine with rich people. (Not a few are wealthy themselves, or married to heiresses. In any event, in the 1960s, persons of great wealth have been a major source of support not only for social-science research, but for radical political activity.) But, alas, they do not have much time for the people in between. In particular, they would appear to have but little sympathy with the desire for order, and anxiety about change, that are commonly enough encountered among working-class and lower middle-class persons. The privileged children of the upper middle classes more and more devoted themselves, in the name of helping the oppressed, to outraging the people in between.

This analysis neatly shifts one's concern from the plight of the poor to the plight of the not-so-poor. It also asserts that the protest of the poor, to be authentic, must rise from the unaided voices of the poor. If professors and philanthropists tell them what they should be demanding, we shall never find out what the poor really demand. Moynihan said it:

> The war on poverty was not declared at the behest of the poor; it was declared in their interest by persons confident of their own judgment in such matters.

How, one might ask, were the poor to launch their own war on poverty, at their own "behest"? Presumably by voting. That returns us to all the problems of the electoral system as a means of effecting change. No, it does not return us even that far. Even if the vote were an effective instrument of change, the poor would not wield that instrument proportionately, because of historical inhibitions on their forming the voting habit. (In the case of blacks, of course, the vote was effectively denied them, by law and by social pressure. Even after the do-gooders changed the law, they had to go South and escort frightened Mississippians past lowering sheriffs to get them registered.)

The authors who think the lower middle class needs protection oddly think the poor need none at all—or at least none from the privileged, the elite, the "silk-stocking liberals," or the radical-chic set. All of them treat this alliance of privilege with poverty as anomalous, as something new and monstrous. Did Roosevelt breed a whole line of traitors to their class?

Underlying the argument runs an assumption that shows up elsewhere, too. It is, in fact, one of Plato's deadlier bequests to us. For Plato the real was the immutable, the ideal Forms. Because it *changed,* the shifting world of phenomena verged off toward unreality. In politics, his rulers were to represent and mediate the Forms to those unable to grasp them on their own. This made the rulers represent order and stability to shadowy masses unstable in themselves. Even when Aristotle altered the metaphysical background of Plato's politics, he kept this part of his outlook— change for him, too, came from "below" in social terms. The classical model of politics pits a relatively unchanging ("conservative") privileged set against fluctuant lower classes yearning for change (for "liberation").

It takes little observation to see that this theory, so neat and plausible *a priori,* is cockeyed. Man is a creature of habit, taught and reassured by repetition. Insofar as he must struggle for his daily bread, he accepts the social and religious myths taught him as a child. He never has the time to question them. He fears change because his precarious living depends on anticipatable recurrences. Change comes like an eclipse, "destroying" dependable movements of the sun. The deeply poor have little awareness of alternatives to their world, little ability to explore them. They have not had the leisure and teachers to discover the reasons for eclipses. It is hard to turn astronomer after a long day's work in the fields. And even if the poor have the leisure and tools to consider alternate world views, the means to accomplish any change based on that knowledge would be out of their hands—beginning with the intellectual means, the familiarity with those who hold power, the understanding of how they might be affected.

Change comes, socially, "from the top." That is why all radicals are of necessity elitists, though most of them will not admit this. The secure can (and should) take risks—it is a luxury, like most others, denied the poor. Intellectual risk comes first. The learned feel confident enough to question the social and religious myths. The technologically sophisticated invent things that change our lives. Social theorists ponder in the British Museum what will happen later at the barricades. These truths have often been remarked in their remoter consequences, that it is not the most abject and downtrodden who tend to rebel, but those with rising expectations —that is, room to maneuver. The great eighteenth-century revolutions, of which ours was the more successful, came from a prospering "bourgeois" level of society, impatient with an aristocracy that impeded its already rapid progress. Reform in the nineteenth century was basically middle-class; it came from educated dissenters outside Church and academic establishments. The spirit of rebellion has reached the poor in the twentieth century precisely because they have made strides toward literacy and the envisioning of alternatives. The elite class that spread the doctrine of universal education had more to do with this than did Lenny Bernstein listening to Black Panthers state their case. So did the elite class of inventors and the business class of manufacturers and distributors who put TV sets in the households of the poor, where the business elite can tell them every day what products they must buy to be happy. Capitalists revolutionized our society. Having started that process, the sorcerer's apprentices cannot call it off overnight or blame the whole thing on cocktail parties for Cesar Chavez.

But if most revolutions, even the nonviolent and evolutionary kind, need a mass with rising hopes and envisioned alternatives, they also need in most cases allies among the privileged who will take risks to help them. Tom Wolfe treats the appearance of such allies as a weird creation of the 1960s, some perversion of good American tastes for which the aptest model he could find was Marie Antoinette playing shepherdess in her Deer Park. Privileged reformers are prompted by no nobler motives, Wolfe tells us, than a *nostalgie de la boue*. Yet Mr. Wolfe took his doctorate at Yale in American studies and should know better. Reform in America has traditionally been prompted and guided by elites.

Take, for instance, abolitionism. Most of the charges made against radical-chic lovers of "the black demi-monde" (the contemptuous term is Moynihan's) were brought against William Lloyd Garrison and his like—yes, down to the charge that reformers were especially interested in pretty young black girls. It was said that Garrison supported radicals who would wreck the whole system—John Brown was the "guy" to scare people back then, as Black Panthers were when Moynihan coined his phrase. Slaves, people argued, were actually better off than white workers in the North; slaves were happy with their lot, and the burden of freedom would just make them miserable; Southerners understood the blacks better than "outside agitators" from the North who, in trying to help, would just hurt them. Slave owners were also slave protectors; they had a feeling for "their" Negroes. The litany did not change from one century to the next. So: Are we to call the freeing of the slaves an exercise in elitist arrogance because the slaves did not free themselves, did not declare a war on slavery "at their own behest"?

Why was Garrison certain he could express the real wants of the slaves? Why did Americans not listen to the slaves themselves, rather than this self-appointed spokesman? That is the kind of question asked by people who would not listen to slaves even if they could. One reason abolitionism could be voiced in the North is that runaway slaves and reformers could talk in safety there. Did they expect the slaves' true feelings to be expressed in the slaves' own pamphlets, which they had not been educated to read or write? Printed on their own presses, which they could not possibly buy or work?

Nor is abolitionism an isolated case of reforms brought about by elites. The spread of universal education on the American scale was a silent and most invisible reform in the way most societies have thought of educational privilege—and that was effected, as I have already argued, by a self-expanding elite of teachers and their teachers. We are told now that only the cultured set has the time to worry about the environment, as if they cared only for the spoiling of their own playgrounds. The same thing was said about the muckrakers who attacked rotten meat—they were just fastidious, and were actually driving up the price of the poor man's fare. The labor movement was led and defended by educated and well-traveled men—men like Eugene Debs and Walter Reuther. They, too, were called "outside agitators" not in touch with what workers really wanted. They created dissatisfaction rather than expressed it, hurt people they were trying to help—all the charges brought against Cesar Chavez and his supporters now. It takes a very dull or skewed acquaintance with our history to think that elite interest in reform arose at last (and only then as an aberration) when a composer-conductor got interested in restive blacks awash in the streets of his own town. (He did, after all, compose the song "New York, New York"—why should interest in the "colored" part of the city's population arise from nothing but *nostalgia de la boue*? Is Mr. Wolfe saying that blacks and Puerto Ricans and Chicanos are *boue?*)

Freud asked, "What do women really want?" It is the kind of question people ask when they do not want to know. What do slaves really want? What do segregated blacks in the 1950s really want? What do migrant workers really want? Those who ask the question do not have an answer—but they use that fact to say that neither do reformers have an answer. Now we are told that feminists do not understand what normal housewives want. The elite reformer speaks only for spoiled Radcliffe girls. The same charge was made against the suffragists. They were told women did not want to vote, and would not vote even if they were given the chance. "Then why not give them the vote," some of them answered their male opponents, "since it will make no difference?" As a matter of fact, women did not vote heavily for eight years after suffrage was granted—until an issue came along that broke their habit of nonparticipation. But they have shown us, since, what they really want: They vote more heavily than men do. In the same way, one can argue that blacks do not want to vote, since they have showed up in small numbers even where their concentration would make for heavy voting impact. But voting is a matter of habit, and habits are as hard to form as to break. In time blacks will no doubt follow the pattern of women voters in the twenties. (It is interesting that young voters, just admitted to the polls at earlier ages, have not turned out in great numbers, either. The habit is hard to develop at all social and educational levels).

The suffragist movement is important for anyone considering the uses of elites because it was not only started by an elite, but was intended to express elitist values. Women voters were *supposed* to tell others "what is good for you." Alan P. Grimes (in *The Puritan Ethic and Suffrage* [1967]) made a convincing case that suffrage first grew up in the West, though its ideology had been formed in the East, as part of an effort to make the frontier more genteel. The territories of Utah and Wyoming gave women the vote in the nineteenth century to express cultivated views among transients. The schoolmarms and goodwives were called in to help overrule cowboys. Women voters deliberately spoke for the "feminine" world of Church and lectures that masculine bustle opposed.

It was in the supposedly more cultured East that women's suffrage made slow and hard progress. Not only the big-moneymen who despised culture, but the immigrant machines run by city bosses, resented ladylike reformers upsetting their world of deals. In fact, by getting trapped into an assertion of refinement, the later suffragists discovered they had put on a political hobble-skirt. Aileen Kraditor traces the paradox:

Before the turn of the century [eastern] suffragists claimed the vote principally on the basis of their contention that men and women were identical in their humanness, whereas the antis emphasized the "divinely ordained" differences. On this one point, however, the antis claimed that enfranchised women would melt into the party-ruled electorate, whereas the suffragists insisted that the differences between men and women were so profound that having the vote would not affect women's nonpartisanship. The antis declared that suffrage would make women partisan and unwomanly; the suffragists maintained that it would enable their unchangeable womanliness to undo the evil that men had wrought through their sordid parties.

Many suffragists felt that success depended on their taking only the most lofty and disinterested stand at every turn. The chairwoman of the New York suffrage assembly told the Albany legislature, "I do not want him [the chairman of the committee] or any of his fellow members to vote for reporting the [suffrage] measure until they are convinced that woman suffrage is a good and worthy cause." The absurdity of her position is revealed if we reflect that the chairman of that committee had been buttoning up the measure so politicians would not have to say what they thought of the matter, pro or con. The chairwoman expected men to vote only as conscience dictated with regard to this measure—while on all other matters they were responding to pressure, legislative debts to their fellows, maneuvers for assignments, future campaign possibilities, etc. When Harriot Stanton Blatch used this case to prove that "There did not seem to be a grain of political knowledge in the movement," the ladies answered that they were proud to be unstained by such dark knowledge. There would be no mucking about with *boue* for those ladies.

It is typical that escape from sterile poses to real reform should come from the very top, from a privileged and "liberated" woman like Mrs. Blatch. Strong enough to boss around Bernard Shaw, she had learned her tactics in England, where suffragists were on hunger strikes in jail (a horrid thought to the women who met her when she returned to New York in 1906). In England, where educated reformers remembered that voting was done with stones in antiquity, women used to throw pebbles at antisuffrage politicians on the stump, silently "voting." Mrs. Blatch saw that what the American movement needed was a little imaginative troublemaking. She invited Mrs. Cobden-Sanderson, fresh from jail in England, to come speak at Cooper Union; then she contrived a tour of Ellis Island with the immigration commissioner, and dropped word that the visiting lecturer was a convict—she did not bother to inform him that she was also the daughter of England's leading free-trade politician, Richard Cobden, and the close personal friend of Lord Bryce, then in America as ambassador (and writing his classic work on this country).

The commissioner reacted as U.S. immigration authorities have so often done: He banned the troublemaker from our shores. Ambassador Bryce got the ban lifted, but thought it would be more tactful for his friend to circle into America from Canada, rather than through Ellis Island. Mrs. Blatch made sure this became the more dramatic route, and publicly thanked the commissioner for bringing such a large crowd to the Cooper Union address.

The "responsibles" tried to tame Mrs. Blatch. They gave her money to organize, on the condition that she not open a vulgar headquarters at street level, like any ward boss. When she called for a joint parade of all women's groups, the respectables refused to march—they motored along in coiffed and parasoled dignity. Harriot fixed that, next year, when she organized the march again but banned all cars. As a fillip, she promised free "classes in the art of walking" to any who might have forgotten it. Classes would be conducted by "Josephine Beiderbasse, director of physical training of the Wadley High School." She had corrupted even the schoolmarms. Mrs. Blatch organized, demonstrated, picketed, was arrested. She was mocked as just a society lady off on a spree. She was considered a freak. In other words, she was a reformer. And she won. All the things she fought for are now taken for granted; most people would think a person crazy now if he advocated repealing women's right to vote. Her abnormality has become our norm. That is how change normally comes about. A price has to be paid. And those can pay the most who have the most, unless they make their very possessions an imprisonment, claiming they cannot support the poor because they are not poor themselves.

Neat, isn't it, this argument used against "elitists" who try to do anything except for themselves? Using privilege to bastion privilege is "productive" and authentic. Using privilege to spread privilege is nonproductive and arrogant. For those exempt from harsh necessity to help those still laboring under harsh necessity is somehow to abuse one's own exemptions! How did people back themselves into such a dark little mental cul-de-sac? I suppose—giving them more credit than they do the reformers—we should not put it down to mere selfishness or callousness toward suffering. The horrible thing about bad ideals is their ideality. The American cult of self-sufficiency, of the self-made man, of moral fiber gained only by struggling on one's own, makes spiritual ascetics of some people—even though their chosen rigors are nothing to the unwilled sufferings of the poor. These people truly feel that helping others is a way of showing contempt for them—proclaiming that they need help when we should pay them the respect to think they are above such needs.

When Chesterton ran across the British argument that only "gentlemen" should be elected to political office, because the rich do not need to be bribed the way lower-class candidates do, he answered that the rich were already bribed—most had been bribed before they were born. In the same way, we all need help —but the prosperous class got its help before it was born. Mrs. Blatch was, unfortunately, considered a "maverick" among the rich because she thought one of the advantages of being advantaged is having the means to help the disadvantaged. Admittedly some reformers are condescending, as some experts are mistaken; and they may justly be warned, "Physician, heal thyself." But even their attitude is preferable to that of people who look at the poor and say "Patient, heal thyself." For, in the Kevin Phillips school of self-help, to be a doctor is to express contempt for the ill. To be a teacher is to be arrogant enough to think you can help a pupil. The very profession of lawyer is a smirk at those who cannot establish their own innocence. We all need help. The poor need help, and cannot pay for it—*that* is their crime in the eyes of the self-help school. Let slaves go out and earn the money to hire William Lloyd Garrison; then he would no longer be a "nonproductive" dabbler in radical causes, but a productive man doing his work the way all good people should, for cash on the barrelhead.

Mrs. Blatch noticed that the suffragists were supposed to make their way by pure argument, apart from any baser appeals; while their opponents were free to use all kinds of "lower" arguments, from mutual benefit, log-rolling, and cronyism. In the same way, Messrs. Moynihan and Wolfe tell blacks to make their own way "within the system"—the electoral and court systems, mainly—

while others exercise many kinds of pressure outside the textbook system. Mr. Phillips is not anti-elitist, as he thinks. He just does not want anyone checking the business elite, which happens to be his favorite one. The wealthy can lobby, but the poor cannot demonstrate. The rich can deal with politicians as friends, dinner companions, fund receivers, traders of benefits; but the poor, like the suffragists, must exert influence only by sheer logic and persuasion. The disadvantaged must observe a delicacy beyond that of the privileged. *Faiblesse oblige.* Here all handicapping systems get reversed: The weaker and smaller must have one hand tied behind his back before he enters the ring.

The odds would be stacked against "outsiders" even if the insiders agreed to abide by nothing but the pure electoral system of liberal theory—since the poor have been inhibited by many pressures from partaking fully in the system. They do not have their own parties and candidates, their established polling and vote-getting systems; and the means of forming them are hard to come by. Yet this just begins to touch the problem. Even if the poor worked well and efficiently in the electoral process, that process gives only a muted and fuzzy indication of what all the voters are saying. And here we come to the final rather sick joke on the poor. The very law that reveals to us the limitations on the voting process was not rediscovered for the study of political elections, but in the attempt to find a way of determining what social benefits are wanted most by those lacking them. Kenneth Arrow expounded the "paradox of voting" while laboring to come up with a way to find out "what the poor really want."

Neater and neater this anti-elitist gambit becomes, as we gaze on it. The poor are supposed to make their own way, voicing their grievances through the system—though (1) they do not participate much in the system, and (2) others are free to work outside the system in all kinds of ways, and (3) even if they had full participation in the system their voice could not be clearly heard, because (4) a man taught us to despair of such clarity in the very act of trying to discover what the poor really prefer!

William Lloyd Garrison did not begin by asking what the slaves really want. He began by saying slavery is *wrong*. It was wrong even if slaves did not think it wrong. He set out to convince people it was wrong—including the slaves, if he had to. It seemed to him quaint that others, having crushed the spirit of liberty in the slaves, should say it would be wrong to give them liberty now because they were not asking for it. He answered, in effect, "Give it to them and see if they ever try to give it back to you." If the slave owners did not feel, against their own professions, that the slaves wanted freedom, they would not have been so resistant to giving it. If women will not vote anyway, why care whether they are able to?

Defenders of the system as it is supposed to work are right in feeling threatened by elitists. Garrison does not take a poll among the slaves, before denouncing slavery, to see if slaves dislike it. Mrs. Blatch did not survey housewives before saying women should have the right to vote if men do. Yet why should the best be less useful to us than the brightest? Pasteur did not ask milk drinkers if they thought his system would work. Edison did not wait to start work on the light bulb till a consumer questionnaire showed a majority in favor of developing light bulbs. If people don't want bulbs, they won't use them—as women would not use the vote if they did not want to. It is not the elite's job to go with the majority. Let politicians do that, to the extent they can get things muddled down for a majority to choose them. The elite's job is to be as good and bright as it can, and give as much help as it can in the way of moral teaching and expertise. Opposition to that simple fact of life leads to the weird but popular defeatism of the anti-elitists: Anyone is free to help mankind except those who are most able to.

14 · Good Doers

I can understand the impatience of radicals who say they cannot wait for ladies bountiful to come along and bring reform. This is where radical impatience joins with liberal hope and says, "If the elite does not ride to the rescue, aren't we thrown back on the electoral system as something that, at least, is always *there,* and that might bring about some change?" It would be nice if that were so. But is it so? Of course, elections ratify (retrospectively) change that has already taken place through elite decision (the New Deal) or established consensus (support for the school system). But what *resisted* change for the good ever made its way principally through elections, or got more help from them than hindrance?

Look at the suffragist case brought up in the previous chapter. To the extent that women's suffrage became a hot issue, politicians avoided it at campaign time. Theodore Roosevelt persuaded a delegation of the ladies that he could help them more if they did not bother him during his 1904 campaign. Woodrow Wilson was still evading the issue in 1912, and Mrs. Blatch led a demonstration outside his White House on the day preceding his inauguration. Mrs. Blatch and others asked him to express some kind of support for their movement, and he fended them off by saying it was a matter for the state to decide, not a federal issue— the tactic later used to deny civil rights to blacks in the fifties. Mrs. Blatch then asked Wilson *as a citizen of New Jersey* to express an opinion on this state matter, but he refused. When his party's platform opposed suffrage, he said his hands as a candidate were bound; but the women knew he had influenced the platform committee to avoid a dangerous prosuffrage stand; and when they showed that they knew it, Wilson stalked out of the meeting.

Mrs. Blatch recalled one meeting with Wilson, when he expressed sympathy but refused support:

> Amazed, we asked what the obstacle was and were told it was the Negro question.
>
> "But of course," I urged, "you know the enfranchisement of women in the South would not decrease the proportion of white to black voters."
>
> "Yes, I know it," he replied, "but congressmen don't."
>
> "Can't congressmen be persuaded," I retorted, "to take down a census report, put their elbows on it, and study out the figures for themselves?"
>
> He smiled, and in a low voice answered, "In two states the blacks would still preponderate."

President Wilson was willing to deny the ratio of men to women, to defy mathematics itself, rather than introduce a difficult issue into an election.

Look at another issue: The major social change in the last two decades has been the growth of the civil-rights movement. Through the first part of this century, the rights of blacks and Chicanos and Indians were treated as regional matters, insulated from national debate. The largest body of the aggrieved lay in the South, which the Democratic Party could not afford to alienate— Franklin Roosevelt blocked consideration of antilynch laws and the Klan in Democratic conventions. The matter slept, untouched by elections, until World War II made the issue national, in two ways. It introduced friction into the armed services, where the South's Jim Crow customs were at first imposed on people from all the nation's regions. It was only after the war (and before Korea) that Truman desegregated the services—when a disproportionate number of blacks staying on in the service were officers. Second, the mass migration of blacks to northern jobs during the war made the issue no longer regional. Clark Clifford, in his famous campaign-strategy memorandum to Truman, said that some civil-rights gestures would be needed to head off Henry Wallace's threat—the South could be counted on to swallow this. So Truman proposed a fair employment law early in 1948. The South did not swallow it after all, but threatened retaliation. Truman's people worked at the convention to stop Hubert Humphrey from raising the subject; they failed; Strom Thurmond's Dixiecrats left the convention. But Truman muted the issue from then on and held onto the South. He had demonstrated that civil rights was still an unmanageable topic in election years, and the lesson stuck.

In 1954 the Supreme Court took up the issue politicians had been avoiding and desegregated public schools. President Eisenhower agreed to enforce the Court's decree, but took care to show his displeasure with it, neutralizing that as an issue in the 1956 campaign. The growth of the civil-rights movement, created by activists, not politicians, made it harder for the Democrats to exclude the bitter issue of 1948 from their postfifties conventions. But they did what they could, delaying southern-credentials decisions from one convention to another (1960, 1964, 1968). The reforms and chaos of the 1972 convention marked the point where all these delays caught up with the party and destroyed its chance of picking a strong candidate.

President Kennedy was slow to come up with a civil-rights program, and tried to keep it out of electoral politics by making it something the Republican minority leader in the Senate could cosponsor. The President asked Dr. King to call off the 1963 march on Washington, and sent his brother Robert to beg George Wallace's compliance with the Supreme Court decree on integration. (The transcript of Robert Kennedy's embarrassing conversation is included in Marshall Frady's book on Wallace.) In the mood of national contrition after President Kennedy's death, Lyndon Johnson passed the Dirksen-approved civil-rights bill of 1964, but tried to plead electoral pressure in backing off from the 1965 bill. Elite lobbyists of Church and labor groups held his feet to the fire, using his southern origin as a stick to beat him with— *that* story is told in *The Growing Church Lobby in Washington* by James Adams (1970).

I have dealt earlier with the way elections delayed action on the Vietnam War: slowing things for crucial months while negotiations stalled, along with hostilities; then starting from scratch when the "low profile" time of election had passed.

On issue after issue, then, forces for change were baffled by the inhibition elections impose on debate and consideration of new paths. Yet in all these cases change did, finally, come about. How? Wilson successfully resisted the pressures to support suffrage in the 1916 election. But the movement, though it could not win electoral support, was taking up a good deal of the nation's attention and energy. Mrs. Blatch had been told her disruptive tactics would set back the cause. Yet the movement was now entering an even more radical phase: Alice Paul, also trained in England, had come back to play Stokeley Carmichael to Mrs. Blatch's Dr. King. In 1917 she led a group that chained itself to the White House fence. Some of the picketers were roughed up—including a small pretty girl, unknown at the time, named Dorothy Day. Those arrested were sent to the Occoquan Work House, known for its cruel warden named Whittaker, who boasted he could make anyone work. He failed with these women, who promptly adopted the English tactic of a hunger strike. After fruitless efforts to force-feed them, officials had to free the emaciated women after ten days of the strike. It was during this fast that Dorothy Day, giddy with hunger, picked up a Bible and recognized her own voice in the psalmist's cries to God. Our history turns on such moments, so little known to us.

Wilson is often treated as an idealist too candid and noble to have been a good politician. In this case, at least, the reverse was true. He held off on suffrage in election time; but used the trouble caused by the women, along with his postelection freedom of ma-

neuver, to come out for suffrage. He even had the genius to treat
it as a war measure! Tranquillity on the home front would help
the nation devote all its attention to winning the war. Contrary to
what Mrs. Blatch had been told, the victory went to those working
outside the system. The change did not come about by full discussion in the campaign—that was successfully blocked. It came to
get rid of a nuisance.

In civil rights, the patience of blacks with court challenges to
the Jim Crow laws ran out just as the NAACP won its great case
on the public schools. The response of the white community to
that decision made the end of the challenge look like another beginning toward the same equidistant goal. So all the Jim Crow
laws were suddenly assailed—separate bus seats, separate ham-
burger counters, separate drinking fountains, separate church sections. There were sit-ins, boycotts, marches. Rosa Parks kept her
seat; but the boycott supporting her act was led by a well-read
doctor of divinity—and his fellow clergy from the North came to
stand with him, along with white students who ended all "silent
generation" talk by getting on buses headed South. They did not
get off the bus for a decade—by which time the buses ringed
Nixon's White House.

In writing about Nixon's election I concluded that, whatever
other claims it might make, the electoral system did not bring
about rational debate. It changed things, of course, and was
changed, but only as all human things must change—families,
clubs, schools, whatever. Elections, however, did not stimulate, encourage, or direct reform. They put brakes on that. When Dr.
King was killed, I covered his funeral for *Esquire,* then covered
the war protests. I saw changes effected in society. I began to understand that Dr. King's "direct action" was as clearly justifiable
as other direct influences. Economic and academic elites go direct
to the elected officials as advisers after the electoral pressure is removed. They are not accused of "wrecking the system." Business
and other special interests lobby and advertise, as well as vote, for
what they want.

Dr. King led a lobby in the streets. He did not mute debate, or
remove it from the electoral process. He opened up debate, initiated it after electioneering had stifled it. Roosevelt could damp

down the urge toward new economic measures during his 1932 campaign. But afterward he asked his advisers what the real problems were. There was no one to raise with the President the problems of blacks in 1932—or in 1952; just as there had been no one in President Wilson's entourage to raise the problems of women in 1917. Alice Paul solved that difficulty by raising the issue in chains at the White House fence. She spoke not through a candidate, darkly, not with one silent vote, but as voicing a large "special interest," to be given a hearing along with all the other interests going in the side door and dealing in the back rooms of the White House. The difference between this lobbying and that of "advisers" is that the public at large, resent it or approve, at least has the means to know all about the public lobbying. If the public refused to listen, then Alice Paul would lose. No one who demands an audience is assured of applause. But at least she got her audience, and the public was informed. The public does not know what goes on when lobbyists meet officials for dinner.

I admitted earlier that, even while writing *The Second Civil War,* I did not approve of civil disobedience. The death of Dr. King brushed away my last sophistical arguments against it. I saw in his career something I would find repeated in our history, now that I looked back at it without my blinders: Change is initiated by the principled few, not the compromising many; by the "crazies" in the streets, not by politicians on the hustings; by Mrs. Blatch and Alice Paul, not by Woodrow Wilson.

It is a finding that should not come as a surprise. Change is not an easy thing for most human beings. They do not want to make it if they do not have to. Only when faced with some other discomfort do they consider seriously the difficult steps involved in making change. I had observed this with fascination in the instructive (if cruel) old TV show called "Candid Camera." People were photographed watching contrived little "miracles"—trees walking off, cars talking, etc. The astonishing thing was the refusal to be astounded, or even to notice the oddity. The incredible was countered with an equal and effective incredulity. It would upset a person's world view to admit that the inexplicable had happened; so most people just pretended it had not happened, and dismissed it from their mind.

The direct action of Dr. King was meant to overcome people's refusal to see how blacks were treated. Only, unlike the mule driver who cracked his animal with a two-by-four "to get his attention," Dr. King let himself get hit with a two-by-four in broad daylight, to show us what was going on in different back rooms from the ones frequented by lobbyists.

Only now could I solve one problem in my own view of elections. If they did not initiate difficult changes, what did? Something must, for important and resisted change had taken place. I do not mean popular change, or that introduced because unopposed, or that brought about by technical advisers and inventors. I was interested in the resisted change that politicians find too hot to handle at election time, or even after.

How might a change-resisting creature like the average human being be led to make a change? By listening to all the arguments on all sides, and following logic no matter what it cost—in short, by the liberals' rational-debate model of change? Fat chance. If that were the case, then everything would narrow down to the 50 per cent plus one man or woman unconvinced by the arguments so far, and any distraction from the arguments being offered would be resented as "falsifying the outcome." But that is not what gets people's attention on a wide scale. Dr. King did not just say blacks were being beaten, or introduce affidavits to that effect. He dramatized what he said by what he suffered. This may make for questionable tactics in a courtroom, where theatrical lawyers are criticized (even when they win, or *because* they win). But ordinary life is not a courtroom, with a jury sworn to pay attention and to judge dispassionately.

Resisted changes of a deep sort begin with a few uncompromising fools who just know that slavery is *wrong,* or that voting is a woman's right; that Jim Crow laws are a disgrace, or that the Vietnam War is immoral. They are not running for office, so they do not have to soothe and placate. They are not politicians, so they do not have to say the Emperor is, perhaps, "inadequately" clothed. They are dismissed with a laugh—ridicule may prevent them from becoming a nuisance. They prove their folly by being undeterred. They are scared; but so are others, increasingly, as a few people start listening to the fools. Repression draws attention to their case. The "unthinkable" is thought about. *Sanguis martyrum*. . . . Still, there is no widespread debate. The cranks can still be dismissed for not being realistic. What does it matter that they have attracted more cranks? There is always some audience for the unusual.

If such crazies win, it is not by convincing 51 per cent of the electorate that their cause is right. Perhaps they need only 10 per cent or 20 per cent of the people behind them, but that 10 per cent or 20 per cent is intense. When a majority gives way to them, it is not at first joining them. It is trying to shut them up. It uses a rationalization like Wilson's: It is not worth the trouble carting these women off to jail all the time; we have other more important things to concentrate on; give them what they want, to shut them up; women probably won't even use the vote when they get it. Other rationalizations cluster easily, once it is decided to give way as a means of bringing peace: "Give them an open-housing law; we can always circumvent it with zoning restrictions." Or: "Give them an open housing law; they can't afford the good homes anyway." Or: "The Vietnam War is not immoral; but it is questionably useful on sheer strategic grounds; and it is certainly not worth all this ruckus in the streets." The person whose approval of the challenged situation is marginal will give up that small margin of approval for social peace. As I said earlier, our politics does not go forward as a rational debate but as a series of mutual vetoes. We try to remove from debate anything a significant segment of the population disapproves of strongly—A, whom you cannot abide; or C, whom I abominate. Sometimes, most often, we remove a problem from debate by not discussing it—for example, forgetting the war at election time. But sometimes the only way to remove it is to make a change—for example, to stop the war. It is paradoxical but true that women got the vote "to shut them up." They were allowed to "speak" in electoral terms so we would not have to listen.

Change after change—the minimum-wage law, the voting-rights act—has been admitted into our politics in order to be "tamed," not enshrined. But at this point the conservative tendency of our politics begins to work for the reformers. The new measure becomes part of the established order. Little girls are taught that they should vote. Blacks are taught they have certain rights. In time, they begin to believe those teachings and act accordingly. The sop that was to placate them becomes a platform from which new urges can develop. Giving women the vote does not shut them up but makes them develop new demands, new kinds of feminism. Yesterday's radicalism becomes today's common sense, from which radicalisms take their point of departure.

But the first proponents of that "common sense" must pay a terrible price. They are resented, since they ask for change, and people find change hard. They are put off as long as they can be, dismissed, treated at first as invisible and then as affronts. Such "fanatics" are mocked, threatened, jailed, beat up, shot at—think of William Lloyd Garrison, Frederick Douglass, Bill Haywood, Eugene Debs, Margaret Sanger, Mary Church Terrell, A. J. Muste, Dorothy Day, Cesar Chavez. Political change does not come easily, by way of campaign promises and congressional log-rolling. It begins with individual risk and heroism. By the time passage of the 1964 and 1965 civil-rights bills became feasible, they were eased through with sounding oratory by the politicians. But a lot of people had to die to make that oratory possible—James Chaney, Andrew Goodman, and Michael Schwerner; Herbert Lee, Louis Allen, Medgar Evers; Jimmie Lee Jackson, James Reeb, Viola Liuzzo; Addie Mae Collins, Denise McNair, Carol Robertson, Cynthia Wesley—to name some. Dr. King died in good company.

Prophets are a scandal in democracies. They are not "representative." They cannot be controlled or called off by their "constituents," because no constituency sent them. They create their audience, and compel it. They do not follow or submit to it. They make a claim because it is right, not because it is wanted, even by its putative beneficiaries—normally it is not wanted. The women of Canterbury beg Thomas, their archbishop, to *leave* (and leave them alone); they do not want an awful freedom thrust upon them. Even the prophet is sometimes reluctant to make his or her claim upon friends. But if it is made, it must be made entire and demanding. Dr. King did not make Rosa Parks refuse to move farther back in the bus when the driver told her to. He did not even want to lead the boycott—that was thrust on him by Ed

Nixon, the neighborhood's Pullman porter. But once Dr. King spoke, he was trapped—he was the servant of his message. The God of the Bible's prophetic books directs history's most imperious press gang. The prophet is sent to a people that does not want to hear, and he most often does not want to be sent. Many prophets try to escape, to run off—or throw themselves, like Jonah, "down to the bottoms of the mountains" where "the weeds were wrapped around my head." They would hide anywhere, even in Leviathan's belly—not seeing where it moves. For some, Leviathan gapes in a bottle's mouth, or a woman's. For most troublemakers in America, politics is the great soporific co-opter. *We* are the whale; we softly ingest our prophets with the massaging idea that we need them "within the system."

But the most useful people resist, fight our reasonableness; set up a clatter and threaten to kick out the system's belly slats—until we vomit them up on the shore where their work was set for them all the time. We vainly assure them that we need no prophets. After all, prophets used to be sent to accuse the King, to say he was misusing his power. The prophet spoke out where the people could not. But we no longer have a King. The people can and do speak their will in every election. Where does a prophet fit into this scheme? For whom could he speak? Or against whom? Against the people, whose will is sovereign?

Exactly. Liberal reform in democracies is directed at the machinery of representation, at making it a more adequate reflection of the people's will. If that will is properly carried out, the government will be a good one. The prophet denies all that. If the people's will is evil, if the people have erred and strayed, then efficiency in carrying out that will can never be justified. The prophet will defy even the instruments of the people's will, break the laws. William Lloyd Garrison publicly burned the Constitution behind which slavery was hiding. The prophet is not bound by unjust laws, no matter how popular their backing, how proper their enactment, how strict their interpretation by the courts.

No wonder the prophet is feared. He cannot be bought off, or made to deal. There is often no way to stop him but to kill him. It is fortunate that such people cannot trade their way into power, since they would make the worst of all possible rulers. They are rigid and unyielding; proud and self-righteous; they set impossibly high standards for the rest of us. They make us appreciate the purely political virtues of compromise, easily pleased vanity, and mediocre expectation—the virtues that make for conformity in society. Prophets would impose their message if they could—so it is lucky that they can't. Some realize this; some don't. The prophet's gifts are not those of the King.

But just as a democracy denies the need for prophecy, it reduces all public virtue to that of the politician. It finds that Mrs. Blatch is quick to set aside democratic procedure as an agitator, and concludes she would do the same thing if she were President —therefore she should not be listened to. If she is not qualified to be a politician, she is not qualified to play any role in society. The prophet armed is a terrifying thought, and men fear evil Kings in the most lonely protesters. But most prophets do not want to be armed. John Brown's truth does *not* go marching on—William Lloyd Garrison's does, and Frederick Douglass's. Most prophets are made to suffer, and are willing to; but they feel obliged not to inflict suffering on their enemies. Their fidelity is to their message, whether it is heard or not. Radical reform in America has had a steady nonviolent base, symbolized by the prominence of Quakers in almost every reform movement.

The politicians maintain our country. Keep it running, make fine adjustments, conserve and react—"save" it in that sense. The prophets make it worth saving. They are the people who do not care how many votes they might get for their message; how justice is currently playing in Peoria; what truth Gallup finds acceptable today. George Washington, intent on forms and procedures, is rightly considered the father of our country, the best of our politicians; a Fabius Cunctator settling for what he could get. He bargained our way for us into history. But our founding saint was Anthony Benezet, and one of Washington's officers told Dr. Benjamin Rush, after Benezet's funeral, "I would rather be Anthony Benezet in that coffin than George Washington with all his fame."

Benezet was an ugly little Quaker who conducted school in Philadelphia. He furtively taught slaves to read at night, and cared for the sick by day. His pamphlets, more sincere than learned, ignited the antislavery movement in England. His attacks on war reached Kings and generals in Europe. He fought the rum trade. Benjamin Franklin dressed as a Quaker in Paris partly to share in the reputation of Benezet, who perfectly embodied the eighteenth century's ideal of *l'homme bienfaisant*. When Quaker friends sent Patrick Henry to meet Benezet, the plantation owner was lectured on the evils of slavery. When General Howe took Philadelphia, Benezet explained to him the evils of the military life. When Philadelphia's own Quaker rulers were treating Acadian refugees with less than perfect charity, Benezet committed civil disobedience to help them out. Benjamin Rush described how Benezet would bustle about the streets of Philadelphia: "In one hand he carried a subscription paper and a petition; in the other he carried a small pamphlet on the unlawfulness of the African slave trade, and a letter directed to the King of Prussia upon the unlawfulness of war."

We are more likely to see another George Washington than another Anthony Benezet. The political system *is* a system; self-perpetuating. There are thousands of bright lawyers wanting to run for office. And thousands of professors wanting to write their speeches. The machinery is fueled with huge amounts of money, talent, and ambition. But there is no school for prophets, no office they get elected to, no way to produce a succession of them. Each is unique, a mystery of human freedom. Still, there is a line of obscure saints that descends from Benezet. Part of his mission is taken up again, decade after decade, by people like Jane Addams, Maria McLeod Bethune, Randolph Bourne, A. J. Muste, Dorothy Day. The national life owes more to these people than to the long line of Presidents. The officer at Benezet's funeral was right—the saint matters more than the general—or the President—even in practical terms. Businessmen make up our material elite. The saints constitute our spiritual elite. They have the greatest exemption of all from life's harsh necessities. They have so few needs. They do not need our approval, or fear our laughter. They are fully exempt. They are free.

Benjamin Rush, himself a radical, had a strange eighteenth-century dream, showing how deep the fear of blacks is in white America's psyche. He arrived alone on a strange shore peopled only by blacks, who came at him with great hostility. But suddenly their faces softened—he did not see why—and they embraced him. Then he looked around, and understood. Benezet had come up behind him, and was standing with him. That saved him. Politicians depend on us. We depend on the saints.

15 · Politicians

When Judge G. Harold Carswell was nominated for the Supreme Court, Senator Roman Hruska made a lot of people laugh by innocently asking if mediocre people are not "entitled to a little representation." The ridicule was less enlightened than it seemed, and the senator need not have worried. We have taken very good care to be represented, in the main, by mediocrities. I do not use mediocre to mean inferior but, precisely, "middling." Only this "middle" is not the national "average." We used to be told that anybody in America can grow up to be President. Maybe so. But in almost two centuries no one has done it who was not white, a male, a Christian, solvent, married only once (if at all), and educated beyond mere literacy. It has also helped to be rich, from certain regions, socially mobile, yet with usable roots—we are already down to a minority of a minority. We are obviously sifting people not in terms of excellence, or even of representativeness in the sense of averageness—the average American is not a male white Christian married to his first wife and with photogenic children. What we are looking for is the safe person, one who comes from our ruling tradition, from the political background most familiar to voters who have grown up watching other politicians in action. This, it is ingrained in us by repetition, is how a candidate should look. Fannie Lou Hamer did not look quite presidential.

Politicians form an elite, of course. How could "the elect" not include the elected? But their influence is all for accommodation, for adjustment. Their real gifts are for *being* influenced. Because politicians try to accommodate everybody, they even pretend to put principle above compromise—to please those who expect that kind of thing. Yet compromise is not only *a* virtue in politicians, it is *the* political virtue.

Of course, there are occasions when a politician *must* compromise, and therefore does. So do we all. There are even more occasions for compromise in politics than in most pursuits (except marriage). Every man does what he must. The real test of a politician comes when he does not have to compromise, yet finds a way to. Each time a politician indulges his or anyone else's single opinion or principle he is losing an opportunity to ingratiate himself with those who hold different views or standards—a criminal waste. Compromise involves, at the minimum, two views to be accommodated—and often more. A skilled politician never acts without deferring to several opinions at once. Admittedly, in the hypothesis I raise, he does not *have* to defer to any opinion but his own. Still, he *can* do so, and sheer economy demands that he seek out unnecessary compromises.

Consider. By the accumulation of compromises, concentric circles of people are, with varying intensity, obliged to the politician. Maximum inclusiveness is built into the dynamics of election. In this way the politician first got disparate elements within his constituency to support him in the first place. By the same arts, he got the attention and allayed the fears of his fellow elected officials. By careful attention to each opportunity for compromise as it arises, he makes sure that any enemy he must make on Point A is already partly a friend on Points B, C, D, etc. When he cannot offer or feign agreement on any of these points, he must at least maintain a benevolent neutrality as long as possible. He becomes an accountant of little courtesies rendered and due, slight debts, accumulating favors. By such constant increments of advantage or leverage, power is attained and entrenched, and the politician is able to act, to fulfill his mandate. This is the moral foundation of political compromise. It makes the compromising of principle a politician's only principle.

Looked at in this way, compromise is just another name for the discipline all vote-getters must profess. It is representation. Without compromise, a politician would not represent anything or anyone but himself. This matter is most often misstated by our moralists. We all grant that a man can suspend his private judgment when he is speaking for others—in the politician's case, for his constituency. But which part or parts of his constituency? It is a complex little world he appeals to—a delicate coalition he must forge from competing interests, even among his own supporters (to say nothing of his opposition, which must also be placated). Some voters want A and some want non-A and some want A with this qualification while others want a different set of qualifications, and some do not care about A at all. The politician must get elected by suggesting that he would support all these people in one way or another. Then, once he gets elected and takes his seat with other representatives, a range of issues comes into view that were never considered in his dialogue with constituents. Some "back home" will be interested in the new issues, while others will not. Which of these constituents' views should he solicit and which ignore? On what points should he take care to inform them, while rejoicing in their ignorance of others?

Or suppose a topic comes up about which his constituents as a whole have no direct interest or discernible opinion. It is, for them, a neutral issue. Is he allowed, here at least, to indulge his private views? By no means. Insofar as he combines with men whose constituents *do* care about this topic, he will acquire the likelihood of their future co-operation on matters of vital concern to his own constituents. He thus represents their interest even on matters where they do not know they *have* an interest.

It will readily be seen that consistency is a fault in politicians. Imagine a resolution that a congressman opposes or must oppose, before his constituents, to be re-elected. But the resolution has no

chance of passage at this time. By encouraging his fellow representatives' view that he really supports the resolution, he can induce one or more of them to vote for Point X, vital to him and his
constituents at that moment, and whose passage is a close thing.
No politician would hesitate a moment in so clear a matter. And
later, when the first resolution gains ground and becomes a matter
of concern to many, and is in danger of passage, it would be
wrong for the politician to stay consistent with his earlier qualified
approval of the resolution. Nor would colleagues blame him for
this kind of reversal. There are many gradations of intensity in the
commitments, agreements, and disputes among such men. Weigh-
ing each one, its binding force, its probable effect, is at the very
center of the politician's art. After all, by reversing himself on the
one resolution, our imagined hero gives hostages for future ingra-
tiation to the men who supported him on Point X.

All this is clear, in theory and practice. It presents no moral
cause for the slightest hesitation on a politician's part. But greater
and less obvious demands follow from our clear example. No man
knows today what might be politically important tomorrow. A
subject not yet in debate may soon be up for negotiation, one way
or the other. It is best to have one's options open when these
topics emerge by making no prior record on such matters at all. A
reckless indulgence in private judgment, an indiscriminate "view-
iness," deprives a politician of bargaining opportunities. Besides,
when a man has indulged private standards on one point, or two,
where is he to draw the line? Many would-be politicians have
been tempted down this path of gradualism toward the politician's
hell of principle. And his fellows know this. They will not trust a
man who squanders his views all at once, and has nothing more to
spend in representative "deliberation."

One common way of defending the politician's morality is to
say that he must compromise on a thousand little things to gain
breathing room for his own conscience on some Big Thing he
cares deeply about. But no. Unless his Big Thing has a chance of
instant passage, premature commitment to it can take away his
chance for doing all the small good things within his reach. Indeed, if the one Big Thing has a chance to win, it will be as a
compromise built on compromises, and the politician's role is best

played by refusing to give up all his bargaining power on the pre-
liminary compromises necessary to the final one. It may even help
him to have voted against the Big Thing beforehand. The politician is not a prophet crying out against power, but a technician
learning to wield it. (Admittedly, we need prophets more than
politicians; but, as their roles are different, so are their separate
skills.) Senator Everett McKinley Dirksen of Illinois spent most of
his career working against civil-rights bills of the kind he helped
to pass, after suitable dilutions, in 1964. He was not ultimately responsible for the bill—prophets like Martin Luther King were.
But Dirksen was its principal servicer when passage became politically desirable. He was in the right place, exercising the right
skills. Others thundered a claim into the heavens so that he, later,
could tinker it into law. A minor achievement, but necessary.

The apparent enemies of a bill have more power over its passage than do admitted friends of the measure. The people who
could do least for the House effort to impeach Richard Nixon in
1974 were those who had clamored for it in 1973—a Bella Abzug
or a John Conyers. Holding out, deliberating, bargaining—those
were the ways to gain power over the President's fate, as Peter
Rodino demonstrated. Walter Bagehot has written the best sustained description of the political virtues in his essay "The Character of Sir Robert Peel"; and his description of Sir Robert's general strategy could be applied directly to things like Dirksen's
passage of the civil-rights bill:

> From a certain peculiarity of intellect and fortune, he was
> never in advance of his time. Of almost all the great measures
> with which his name is associated, he attained great eminence
> as an opponent before he attained even greater eminence as
> their advocate. On the Corn Laws, on the currency, on the
> amelioration of the criminal code, on Catholic emancipation,
> he was not one of the earliest labourers, or quickest converts.
> He did not bear the burden and heat of the day; other men
> laboured, and he entered into their labours. As long as these
> questions remained the property of first-class intellects, as
> long as they were confined to philanthropists or speculators,
> as long as they were only advocated by austere intangible
> Whigs, Sir Robert Peel was against them. So soon as these

same measures, by the progress of time, the striving of the understanding, the conversion of deceptive minds, became the property of second-class intellects, Sir Robert Peel became possessed of them also. He was converted at the conversion of the average man. His creed was, as it had ever been, ordinary; but his extraordinary abilities never showed themselves so much. He forthwith wrote his name on each of those questions; so that it will be remembeded as long as they are remembered.

It is not accidental that most of our politicians were educated as lawyers. Of the fifteen Presidents in this century, only five have not been lawyers—Harding, Hoover, Truman, Eisenhower, and Carter. Congress is dominated by lawyers, as are most state houses. We have just the kind of regime the Russian Emperor derided in the nineteenth century, a *gouvernement des avocats*. Many have criticized the pettiness of legal training, and its effect on the politicians who share this kind of training. Jimmy Breslin grumbled at it yesterday, and Macaulay a hundred years ago. It is easy to understand their objections. The lawyer's skills are negotiatory, technical, mediating, neutral. He acts as an expert adviser or as an agent for a client, not as a creative thinker or framer of his own views. It is his job to make the maximum claim on his client's behalf—whether to a jury, an insurance company, the IRS, a sued or suing opponent, a partner in divorce proceedings. He speaks for one client today, another tomorrow; one side now, a different one later. The neutral agent is not a friend of one side, and therefore no enemy to the other side. Legal adversaries can exchange their lawyers, and the only difference (if any) will be in their technical skills. Having made the maximum claim for his own client, and expected a similar maximum claim from the other side, the lawyer must forge the terms of settlement and advise his client on them. If our own lawyer made less than the maximum legal claim for us—out of ignorance, or reticence, or rectitude—we would feel cheated. His services were not fully at our disposal; part was kept to indulge himself.

So the critics of the lawyer background shared by so many of our politicians are dead wrong. No better training could be found for them. They, too, must struggle with each other, yet be friends the next day; make maximum claims as bargaining points, but aim at a compromise settlement; satisfy most people somewhat rather than a few people fully; represent diversity by muting differences; be always more neutral than hostile; deal in increments and margins only, but deal constantly; always adjusting, hedging, giving in a little, gaining a little; creeping toward one's goals, not heroically striding there; always leaving oneself an out, a loophole, a proviso —what Willmoore Kendall used to call "a verbal parachute," so that no alliance is irrevocable, no opposition adamant.

If compromise is a virtue in politicians, so is egotism. Not pride —pride digs in its heels, endangering the first virtue of compromise. Egotism, on the other hand, is flexible; relaxes to the tickle of acclaim; seeks polymorphous cosseting; is easy of access. Its wants are constant, but its demands are small. It is widely believed that men become politicians to enrich themselves or to wield power. They are not above such considerations, because none of us are. But neither are they signally vulnerable to them. Most politicians have the gifts—ambition, education, hard work, obsequiousness—to make money in any pursuit, and most could in fact make more money outside politics. Lyndon Johnson became rich in politics, but he moved in those Texas circles where the very air is sticky with money—when you come indoors, you must scrape it off with a strigil. (If you are very fastidious, you throw it away; if less so, you try to wash it off; if you are Lyndon, and in a hurry, you just jam it in your jeans.) Eisenhower died rich, but mainly because he was a famous general—the foundations of his wealth were laid before he went into politics. He would have been as rich, or richer, if he never ran for office. Nixon is more typical —through most of his career, he lost money by being a politician; and when he finally decided to steal, he was not very good at it.

Admittedly, politicians service the forces of wealth, both to get help in their own campaigns and to govern this plutocratic society. But their personal return is often in the form of "contacts," favors, flattering solicitude, campaign support, rather than personal wealth. Indeed, it often shocks people, when a financial scandal breaks, that our politicians can be bought for so little— airplane rides for Tom Dodd, paper bags of money for Spiro

Agnew. Perhaps these are merely down payments—politicians often retire to money, cashing in on favors done while they were in office. But few retire before the voters force them to. By that time, the money is a consolation for loss of office. It was rarely the first motive for seeking office.

Much of what looks like corruption grows up naturally from a politician's circumstances. There are lots of people trying to do him favors, often quite innocently. It is hard to separate these from less innocent benefactors without alienating the well-disposed. I was with Senator Lowell Weicker and two of his aides, once, in the Hartford airport. When Weicker checked in for the Washington flight, the airline agent invited him to have a free drink in the lounge. Mr. Weicker, who endeavors to be preppy-clean, declined; but the rest of us wanted drinks, and tried to pay for them. The waiter had been ordered not to take money from us. He was caught either way—between his orders and the senator's arguments, briefly raised. Nothing short of a major scene could have prevented the favor. Airlines should not do such things, but they always do—and politicians begin, however reluctantly, at first to accept, then to expect, these many little favors. Senators rage and bellow when commercial planes are not held for them, or other passengers are not bumped from first class. This is not a pleasant side of the politician's character; but neither is it dogged pursuit of wealth.

Besides, think of all the men already wealthy who go into politics. What are they after? The normal answer is power. But that answer must be severely qualified to make any sense. Real unchecked power is wielded by more executives, corporate lawyers, or establishment advisers than by politicians of any but the highest level. And men do not reach those high levels without undergoing long service lower down. Even the most unfettered politicians must defer to voters, bosses, and backers in a way that would disgust the executive in his private jet with his squad of flunkies.

A Nelson Rockefeller hardly got more raw power when he became governor of New York—and he had to kowtow to many party regulars and plain voters in order to get there. It is not power, as such, that men of his sort seek, but recognition. They like to be known, photographed, flattered. They like to do things like making speeches, a futile exercise so far as power-wielding goes. They have the same itch that performers have to be at center stage, in the limelight, soaking up applause.

Pride, stiff and prickly, rarely comforts its possessor. The proud man will not stoop to woo strangers, peddle his own praise up wide streets and down back alleys, risk heckling and insult at factory gates and subway outlets. The proud man is Coriolanus, too dignified to buy favor with his wounds, however honorable—in fact, *because* the wounds are honorable in themselves, he would not cheapen them. But egotism lives on handshakes, praise, and autographs given. It is fed with small things—but it must be fed constantly. It screens hostile recognition through a private converter that makes the recognition matter more than the hostility.

The politician's ego is a very specialized development. It is insatiable, yet yielding—to get what it wants it will face tasks not only difficult but demeaning. Politicians must meet with people they do not want to see, praise and flatter those they despise, show interest in silly constituents and courtesy toward impolite ones. They must show up at dull affairs not only for their own campaigns but for those of other people in the party. They must submit to showy contributors who like to prove their access to the candidate or office-holder, suggesting that the contributor is not only a patron but an owner of his client. Even a performing ego like that of Frank Sinatra would not submit to the things most politicians undergo. They must smile when insulted by a stranger. When, once, George McGovern refused to smile—when he told a heckler at an airport fence, "Kiss my ass," this struck some as refreshingly different. But he only allowed himself this freedom when his campaign was almost over, at a moment of fatigue and frustration. And few other politicians will take that risk—you never know who the heckler is related to.

Politics demands a great capacity for self-deception, which rescues the politician from hypocrisy. He can normally manage to believe what he is saying for the time it takes him to say it. This gives him a certain sincerity even when he is saying opposite things to opposite people. Since he loves to be pleased, he tries to please people back. He genuinely dislikes disagreement with anyone. It interrupts the reciprocal laving of egos; it puts grit in the butter bath. Bagehot knew the type:

> Providence generally bestows on the working adaptive man a quiet adaptive nature. He receives insensibly the suggestions of others; he hears them with willing ears; he accepts them with placid belief. An acquiescent credulity is inherent in such men; they cannot help being sure that what everyone says must be true; the *vox populi* is a part of their natural religion.

This capacity to induce the appropriate belief at will shows up in almost every campaign. Onlookers have noticed that no politician thinks he is going to lose an election. No matter how bad his chances, he clings to the desperate hope that some miracle will save him in the end, and is usually the last man around him to know that he has lost. This self-induced blindness is an act of charity to the candidate's followers. Every day he must watch them struggling for him, giving up time and money and effort—often, indeed, losing health and mental balance and family in his cause. He cannot realistically tell them that they are wasting their time, that it is all for naught. On the other hand, it would be hard to lie to them day after day and know that he is lying, at such cost to his devoted followers. It saves psychic wear and tear on all involved if the candidate can just manage to believe he will win, no matter what the facts are. By the end of the campaign, much of the hoopla around the campaign tour is meant to keep up this confidence in the candidate, so he can dispense it to the tiring army of workers. Sometimes withdrawal from the campaign plane toward reality becomes too cruel. The candidate needs his daily "fix" of crowds, even though it is draining all his energy. So it is unfair to call politicians liars. Most of them cannot tell, any longer, what the truth is—and therefore they cannot lie. They have sacrificed their capacity to distinguish facts from what their ego wants the facts to be. They deserve credit, and not scorn, for this act of self-immolation to the nation's good.

Politicians fascinate because they constitute such a paradox: They are an elite that *accomplishes* mediocrity for the public good. Hilaire Belloc, after spending a term in the House of Commons, wrote: "The standard of intellect in politics is so low that men of moderate mental capacity have to stoop in order to reach it." He meant this as a criticism; but it is good that some men are willing to stoop. How else would our politics get done? Eugene McCarthy spent a good deal of his time trying to prove he was too good for politics. What use was that? Most of us are too good for politics; but we do not make a career of demonstrating it.

Any fair person must recognize the positive uses of mediocrity. There is no mystery in the matter. We have admitted that a politician must be representative—and that means he must be predictable. He must be chosen because his general circle of thought is known. He is not likely to depart too markedly from that agreed-on area of thinking. If he were startlingly novel in his approach, liable to strike off on his own, capable of bold invention, unafraid of its consequences, only an idiot would ask him to represent the mass of common man. Bagehot put it best:

> Those who desire a public career must look to the views of the living public; an immediate exterior influence is essential to the exertion of their faculties. The confidence of others is your fulcrum. You cannot, many people wish you could, go into Parliament to represent yourself. You must conform to the opinions of the electors; and they, depend on it, will not be original. . . . People dread to be thought unsafe in proportion as they get their living by being thought to be safe. . . . This world is given to those whom this world can trust.

We have also said that a politician must compromise. This militates against rigidity of opinion. On the other hand, a politician is expected to speak often and on all kinds of subjects—to show his wares, as it were, so people can decide whether he represents them, or can bargain with them, or will yield enough to them. He must have a wide if shallow stock of knowledge and oratory. He must convince people just enough without committing himself too much. A shallow mind is necessary for this, even if it has to be developed by men with the gifts to be profound. Listening to parliamentary debate, where men say one thing now and another thing

later, where they are plausible for a moment without being bound
for the morrow, Macaulay concluded:

> The talent for debate is developed in such men to a degree
> which, to the multitude, seems as marvellous as the perform-
> ances of an Italian *improvvisatore*. But they are fortunate
> indeed if they retain unimpaired the faculties which are re-
> quired for close reasoning, or for enlarged speculation. In-
> deed, we should sooner expect a great original work on po-
> litical science—such a work, for example, as *The Wealth of
> Nations*—from an apothecary in a country town, or from a
> minister in the Hebrides, than from a statesman, who, ever
> since he was one-and-twenty, had been a distinguished de-
> bater in the House of Commons.

Even in the comparative leisure and privilege of the eighteenth
century, it was noticed that Burke was ineffective as a practical
politician to the extent that he was bold and deep in his theory of
politics. Even when he was right, Charles James Fox said of
Burke, he was right "too soon." He could not do anything about
being right; so, *politically,* what good was his brilliance? (It
served, of course, outside politics, for those able to read and be
enlightened by him.)

A man very original must shape his own life, make a schedule
that allows him time to reflect, and study, and create. But politicians live with a crowded schedule largely out of their control;
they must turn their minds quickly from one thing to another,
with the same kind of instant response that interrupts longer
courses of reflection. It is fortunate that, where having fixed or individual opinions would be a disadvantage, the very nature of politics makes it hard to have such opinion. Bagehot's formulation
of the case is definitive:

> It requires a great deal of time to have opinions. Belief is a
> slow process. . . . Our [political] system, indeed, seems
> expressly provided to make it unlikely. The most benumbing
> thing to the intellect is routine; the most bewildering is dis-
> traction: Our system is a distracting routine. . . . It is rather
> wonderful that our public men have any minds left, than that

a certain unfixity of opinion seems growing upon them. We may go further on this subject. A great administrator is not a man likely to desire to have fixed opinions. His natural bent and tendency is to immediate action. The existing pressing circumstances of the case fill up his mind. The letters to be answered, the documents to be filed, the memoranda to be made, engross his attention. He is angry if you distract him. A bold person who suggests a matter of principle, or a difficulty of thought, or an abstract result that seems improbable in the case "before the board," will be set down as a speculator, a theorist, a troubler of practical life. To expect to hear from such men profound views of future policy, digested plans of distant action, is to mistake their genius entirely. It is like asking the broker of the Stock Exchange what will be the price of the funds this day six months? His whole soul is absorbed in thinking what that price will be in ten minutes. A momentary change of an eighth is more important to him than a distant change of a hundred eighths. So the brain of a great administrator is naturally occupied with the details of the day, the passing dust, the granules of that day's life; and his unforeseeing temperament turns away uninterested from reaching speculations, from vague thought, and from extensive and far-off plans.

We must remember that Bagehot is considering the work of a *great* administrator, the peculiar genius of a master politician like Sir Robert Peel. The intellectual limits he describes would be even more apparent in a less talented, educated, dedicated man. It is the very best political mind he is describing, not that of political hacks:

If we bear in mind the whole of these circumstances; if we picture in our minds a nature at once active and facile, easily acquiring its opinions from without, not easily devising them from within, a large placid adaptive intellect, devoid of irritable intense originality, prone to forget the ideas of yesterday, inclined to accept the ideas of today—if we imagine a man so formed, cast early into absorbing exhausting industry of detail, with work enough to fill up a life, with action of itself enough to render speculation almost impossible—placed too in a position unsuited to abstract thought, of which the conventions and rules require that a man should feign the other men's thought, should impugn his own opinions—we shall begin to imagine a conscientious man destitute of convictions on the occupations of his life—to comprehend the character of Sir Robert Peel.

Bagehot was writing at a time when politicians composed their own speeches, when the pace of life was less jagged, when the demands of quick travel and communication had not been added to the life of a politician. Stress on appearances, on quick yet careful adaptability, has multiplied many times since then. The modern politician is watched constantly, one way or another. He is onstage to a wider and less discriminating audience than Robert Peel had to suffer. No wonder he has no time to write his own speeches, or the books he lends his name to. Even when he retires from office, the effect of such scattered intellectual attentiveness remains. He cannot collect his wide experiences into writing that makes reflective use of them. We no longer even expect it—nor should we.

We have said that the politician must indulge a constructive egotism. This drives him to seek flattering company, which means light company, even when he is not performing political duties. The only distraction from showing off is to show off in company even more certain to be obsequious than a rally of one's own party would be. The principal distraction from politics is talking about politics with one's cronies. The garrulous politician off-duty is often a more amusing performer than the polished man on the stump—witness the private Lyndon Johnson. But politicians are bound to collect a penumbra of toadying listeners, an uncritical audience that soon becomes necessary to them. There is nothing more conducive to mediocrity than such a crew; that is why there is very little to choose between a Red Fay and a Bebe Rebozo. Here is the former, engaged in his regular duties for the prince (as remembered in Ben Bradlee's *Conversations with Kennedy*):

There was a bunch of toasts, including Red Fay's vaudeville act in which he sings, if that's the word, "Hooray for Hollywood." This act panics the Kennedys, and they've heard it a hundred times. No one else quite understands why.

Thus we must judge politicians' minds by the natural level they seek, the company they keep, and the company that puts up with them. Men who acquire great power are allowed, by those seeking things from them, to blossom into previously unsuspected charm. Cambridge academicians, who could not wait to get out of Henry Kissinger's company when he taught there, tried to wheedle their way into his presence when he went to Washington. But once that spurious glamour is removed, and one has heard the politician's stock of stories once or twice (they recur diurnally), few would seek out his company. Not many want to spend much time with politicians, even when they are in power. That takes a positive thirst for mediocrity like Theodore White's.

When I first advanced the thesis of this chapter, several years ago in *Harper's,* some people thought it a sardonic exercise, an indirect assault or satire on politicians. But my praise of them was genuine. They give cohesion to society, ease frictions, promote mutual deference. If we all got up every morning to argue over ultimate justice, there would be a continuing state of civil war where there is now a society. Just as it is wrong to look to elections for choice and rational change, so it is wrong to look to politicians for a reckless principle and rectitude. Politics does not provide us with justice, but at least it gives us some peace, some convenience. And one should not underestimate the virtue in that. Peace, St. Augustine argued, is the precondition of every other social activity. It is the very soul of society. And, for us, peace is the gift of the politicians.

PART FOUR

MULTA TENENS ANTIQUA

16 · Wheat and Weeds

The old lament is familiar, and true: *Quantula sapientia mundus regitur.* (How ignorantly are we ruled.) But that misses the point. There is no other way we could be ruled representatively. Virtue and brilliance are uncommon, volatile, distrusted. We need men we can trust, to bargain for us with each other. Elites will lead us. But we balance elites against each other by electing the supreme accommodationist, the politician type, to speak for us, to "represent." So true is this that we probably cannot be led by people much better or worse than the nation deserves. Too much virtue would be a vice in government. Imagine, for instance, McGovern winning by some electoral fluke in 1972 (assuming, for the sake of argument, that his position was more virtuous than Nixon's). McGovern would not only have represented a minority, but a minority deeply resented by a great many other minorities. A plurality candidate can have a mild majority against him and survive. But a President so little trusted, so little felt to represent or understand his countrymen, would have no leverage on Congress, no strong voice in foreign affairs, no ability to hold the country together, no favors to do other politicians, no way of earning favors in return.

Nixon in 1968 and 1972 represented a country disrupted by change and feeling repressive. When Spiro Agnew asked why we could not hear the good things about America for a change, he was signaling that he would shut up those freaks saying bad things. That was a popular stand to take at the time. Add Wallace's vote to Nixon's and you have a landslide victory for that mood even in 1968. In 1972, Nixon appealed to the same majority. The middling-in process makes the candidate resonate to what the great central mass of citizens tells him to tell them. When Nixon tried to dump Agnew in favor of John Connally, Nixon's own party would not let him. The audience was still there to clamor for Agnew's "red meat."

Liberals complained that the system had failed by giving us Nixon, and they wanted to tinker with it, reform it, make it give us "the best man" again. But the most an electoral scheme like ours can give us is a middling man, one trying to accommodate himself to the central moods of the voters. If those moods are repressive, the man chosen will probably be repressive, or at least willing to go along with repression. Going along is what politics is all about.

Why should even the best machinery of choice guarantee a good product? What if the people are vicious? To the extent that the system reflects popular will, the product will be vicious. How could the machinery automatically turn vice to virtue? That *would* be "falsifying the outcome." The axiom about programming computers applies here: garbage in, garbage out. If peace is the soul of society, it is probably better to keep body and soul together, even if they are the body and soul of a bad society. A bad man can reform if he is kept alive. Keeping society alive, at peace with itself to the degree that it remains one society, is the first thing necessary: Let the wheat and the weeds grow together. Don't uproot the whole society to get at the weeds.

Only when Nixon had forfeited public confidence through his procedural faults (tampering with the electoral process, and then lying about that), when he was in effect politically crippled, could he (or should he) have been removed. When I made that argument to fellow critics of the Vietnam War in 1972, some thought me just as immoral as the war. A friend told me, "When you're not defending the crazies in the street, you defend the crook in the White House." It felt odd to be called a defender of Nixon—all I was saying was that the system worked when it gave us a man who fit the national mood. Anyway, defending crooks was what I had been charged with when I quoted Newman in my "convenient state" essay. It was a charge made against St. Augustine when he said that the state is not supposed to be the seat of justice. Perhaps the best way to defend "crooks"—or, at least, politicians—was to read again, more carefully, the *City of God*.

God's City and the Earthly City are not, as some medieval misreadings of the book had it, church and state. They are not only (though they are mainly) heaven and hell. But *neither* of them is Rome in any historical sense; because neither is an earthly polity, despite the name of the Earthly City. In working out the logic of the two cities, Augustine found himself compelled to define the characteristics of a third, which is the secular polity in our sense. There is no doubt that he began with only two cities, and some Augustinian scholars believe he ended with only two. But I think he did not, because he could not.

Consider his problem. He set himself the task of explaining how one order is falling to ruin and another is rising. The scheme is simple, but its fit with experienced reality was complex; and it got more complex in the thirteen years he spent on this, his lengthiest work. The city falling to everlasting ruin is first symbolized by Rome in its besieged state—but not pagan Rome; Rome in its post-Constantinian stage, when Christianity was the established religion. Pagans blamed the Christians for doing in Rome by deserting Rome's real gods. Christians themselves were still swayable by such comments. Much of the Christianity experienced by the people at large was a mix or amalgam of old auguries and the comparatively new Eastern faith. Murray Kempton said America's liberals never bowed so readily to the cross as when it was taken from Bill Buckley. Henry Adams said much the same thing about the fourth-century fight between God and the gods after Constantine started "using the cross as a train of artillery, which to his mind it was."

In one sense Augustine's task was simple. The *individual* Christian suffered as much here on earth as the individual pagan. So why should anyone expect a Christian *society* to suffer less? But Augustine made the argument complex in ways it did not have to be, because he meant to attack the whole mentality that could raise the charge occasioning his book. Ever since his conversion from Manicheism—one of several conversions leading up to his famous garden scene of accepting the Gospel—Augustine had been fighting the tangle of superstitions that had overgrown the fourth-century mind. When Augustine discovered that the great Manichean guru Faustus was a mountebank, he developed a healthy skepticism about all those who claimed a secret knowledge. (This would come in handy when he argued with Porphyry over the oracles.)

An example of his questioning approach is the treatment of astrology in the *Confessions* (7.6). His friend Firminus was born at a time so close to a slave child's birth on his father's estate that no distinction could be made in the children's stars. Using the slave as a "control," St. Augustine convinces Firminus that if the very same birth constellations (so far as man can measure them) produce two such different fates, then reading the stars is a waste of time: "To hit the truth, I should have to tell two different stories from the same stars, or else speak false by telling but one story. So, judging only by the stars, any truth discovered comes from luck, not art; and any error comes not from lack of art but of luck." This theme is developed at greater length in the *City of God* (5.1–7).

Yet to us, the *City of God* itself seems a colorful hodgepodge of oddball beliefs and superstition. One of its values to the historian is as a record of popular views at the time. But Augustine expresses an acute protoscientific spirit—as one can see by comparing his work with Pliny's uncritical collection of old wives' tales in his *Natural History* (21.7). Augustine wittily satirizes pagan superstition (see especially 4.8, 6.9), but he also criticizes Christian superstition (8.27). The book traces a growing realization that there can be no manifest providence, in the lives of individuals or society, only a hidden providence (4.33, 5.17, 20.2). All attempts to know God's purpose in sending prosperity or affliction are presumptuous. Augustine opposes millenarians and chiliasts and all attempts to extract historical timetables from the *Apocalypse* (18.52–53, 20.7–8). His attitude is the one Chesterton would give expression to in his *Ballad of the White Horse:*

> The men of the East may spell the stars
>   And times and triumphs mark,
> But the men signed with the cross of Christ
>   Go gaily in the dark.

Thus Augustine severs "secular" history from any narrowly theological reading. In that sense the common statement that Augustine gives us "a theology of history" is wrong. Outside the specifically revealed history of the Jews, Augustine often insists on the *dis*continuity between our knowledge of God's will for the soul to be saved and any knowledge of his purpose in the vicissitudes of life. His originality in all this is lost to the casual modern reader; we lack the background of accumulated ingenuities devoted, in his time, to reading God's will in every accident, turning event into omen.

God, of course, foreknows the course of things. For Augustine, providence and prescience would mean the same thing: foreseeing. God knows, for instance, that the outwardly pious Christian of today will fall from grace tomorrow, or the pagan become a Christian (18.47–48). There is, then, no correlating a man's final membership in the City of God (heaven) with his membership in the Church at any moment. Seen in this light, Augustine's doctrine of predestination results in a kind of agnosticism about the mystery of each other person's destiny. He has not so much made God the tyrant of the universe as rescued man from the tyranny of omens and spells and mumbo jumbo, sealing up all their partial and feigned "revelations" in the unknowable knowledge of God alone. Augustine himself had been first a Manichean, then an Academic, then a Neoplatonist, before becoming a Christian. He prays for perseverance in the faith, but cannot know his own future as a Christian, any more than he knew where he was bound when he professed those earlier faiths. And if his own destiny is a mystery to him, how much more must other people's be?

This theological humility about the fate of the individual soul has important political consequences. Those whose final citizenship will be established in heaven or hell must have different orientations—love of God in the one case, a self-defeating self-love in the other. So, if they are to live together at all (and they must, for no one knows who is a citizen of either of the final cities), the basis of their consorting must not be long-run but short-run. It must not be the perfect justice of the City of God, because membership in that is a mystery, and how can one bind nonmembers to a justice they will finally oppose? Even the true members of the City of God (who do not know, yet, that they are true members) must "settle for less" than the final order of things, or they would exclude erring members of the final city still on their way to Christ (for example, Augustine in his Manichean days). The test of secular citizenship therefore cannot be theocratic or even "just" in any ultimate sense. That would arrogate to man the right to distinguish members of the two cities, a right God has reserved to himself for the last day of judgment (20.1–3).

At this stage of his thought, two parables from Matthew's gospel became almost obsessive for Augustine—that of the mixed catch of fish (18:49) and that of the weeds mingled in with growing wheat (18:48, 20:5, 9). What man cannot separate, God will, but only at the end of time. If you try to uproot the weeds in normal politics, you will just pull up the wheat—that is, exclude from membership in society Christians still on the way. The parable actually understates the difficulty, for it only deals with the problem of *uprooting* the weeds. For Augustine the difficulty does not lie simply in getting rid of weeds once they are identified. For him there was no way of telling what was a wheat stalk and what a weed (that is, who was finally saved, who damned). Despite this limit to the parable, Augustine now saw depths of political wisdom in it that he had not discerned earlier.

Even wheat and weeds can only grow together if they share basic ground and nutriment (air, water, sunlight). But the Earthly City does not, in its final identity as the hellish city, share in the vision of order based on God's love and justice. That is what troubled Augustine in Cicero's definition of a people: "A people is a gathering of those united by agreement on the right and by shared interests" (2.21). The words that troubled Augustine were "agreement on the right." All societies are flawed, none more so than government, including as it does all those born into national territory. Are the evil to be excluded from citizenship, since they do not agree with good men on the nature of right? But who can be sure he has the true and only right? In Augustine's theological categories, who can say with confidence that he is a citizen of the lasting City of God? And if one cannot even be sure of citizenship for oneself, how can one presume to mete out the justice of that final city? Men are not to think of themselves as performing little days of judgment ahead of God's ultimate judging act. (Augustine had a very low opinion of human courts in general, of their pretensions to the knowledge and the meting out of justice—19.6, 20.2.)

But the nature of flawed man returns Augustine to one of the basic insights he earned in his escape from Manichean dualism. Evil is not positive or self-existent. It is flawed good. All things, simply by *being,* are to that extent good. If the flaw ever outweighed the good, the thing would simply go out of being; disappear (19.13). Evil, in that sense, is its own cure. Augustine was constantly seeking out ugly or ignoble things to show the inescapable evidences of rhythm, unity, and coherence that hold them in being at all. He traced the beauty of a monkey, of a cockfight, of the devil himself (19.12, 22.24). He wrote:

I could descant in all candor on the glories of the worm, when I look at its glancing color, its perfect corporal rotundity, its intermeshing of end with middle, middle with end, each contributing something to a thrust toward oneness in this lowest of things, so there is no part that does not answer to another part harmoniously. And what of the principle of life effervescing its melodious order through this body?—its rhythmic activation of the whole, its quest for that which serves its life, its triumph over or revulsion from whatever menaces it, its reference of all things to a normative center of self-preservation, bearing a witness more striking than the body's to the creative unity that upholds all things in nature? [*True Religion,* 77].

Augustine is considered a pessimist in his politics and theology. The maxim often cited to enforce this view is: "Justice absent, what are political realms but gangs of robbers, what are gangs but smaller realms?" (4.4). But few people follow Augustine when he takes up the positive side of that reversible coin and dwells on it to bring out the good in any association manifesting human concord and internal peace: "Even robbers desire peace among their confederates, the more swiftly and brutally to shatter others' peace" (19.12). Augustine has just been defining peace as the thing that makes a society a society. Just as "peace" between body and soul constitutes the human being, so peace between man and man creates society. Even the robber gang shows that a good can exist in evil—*had* to exist, to bring it into being—*even when justice is absent.*

The point is crucial with Augustine, and he pursued it with dogged thoroughness. Even the hypothetical presocietal individual (almost an anticipation of Hobbes' individual in the state of nature) wants peace with his environment, present and future—wants not to be at odds with other things, though he may not see how that can be accomplished. The antisocial monsters of myth have the same desire for concord, if only as the resolution of some more immediate discord (19.12). Even devils must have some concord among their selfishnesses to constitute the final society of hell (the robber gang made eternal). Peace in itself is a good, no matter how unjustly those at peace may act in other ways. And there are many good things that unite in earthly peace the citizens of the two opposed and final cities. A household seeking only temporal things can unite on that basis with a Christian household seeking temporal peace along with the eternal love of God (19.17). Peaceful union is the nutriment, as it were, for both wheat and weeds. By ordaining that both should need the same things, God ordained a certain unity of goal and co-operation between them. His fields nurture both the wheat *and* the weeds, till harvest. Thus Augustine makes a momentous change in Cicero's definition of a people.

This—

> A people is a gathering of those united by agreement on the right and by shared interests.

becomes this:

> A people is a gathering of many rational individuals united by accord on loved things held in common. [19.24].

When Augustine says the Roman state was not a people in Cicero's sense (19.21), he is not saying—what he has been made to say—that the Roman people were not a people, but that the definition is faulty; and three chapters later he gives his own definition, by which the Romans clearly were a people (19.24).

But why, if political realms make up a third order of society, does Augustine refer always to *two* cities as the basic components of human society? (This is the problem that has made scholars like Gilson, O'Meara, and Knowles deny the existence of a third city in Augustine.) Well, first of all, it is misleading to say that there are only two cities in the book. Both the key terms are taken from Scripture—the City of God from the Psalms (87:3) and the Earthly City from St. Paul (1 Co. 15:47–49). Each of these terms has a range of different meanings within itself. St. Augustine's last intellectual conversion occurred when he adopted the Ambrosian method of reading Scripture symbolically.

Thus the heavenly city is Jerusalem (20.17). It is Mount Sion. It is also Christ, whose members are "edified" into the heavenly Jerusalem (22.18). It is the Church in heaven with triumphant citizens. Yet we can also use the term for the pilgrim Church on earth with a secret citizenship (18.47).

The Earthly City, by contrast, is Babylon (16.4, 18.41). It is also hell (11.1). It is Rome of the Apocalypse (that is, ranking with Babylon and Jerusalem as an historical city lifted to an eternal realm of symbol for the Bible's teaching purpose). It is any terrestrial city considered insofar as it sacrifices to false gods. And —here is where people have stumbled into the easy identification of the Earthly City with historical polities—it is the temporal considered *merely* as temporal (that is, as deliberately *excluding* the eternal). Thus when Augustine talks of pagan and Christian households adopting a common "earthly peace" (19.17) he cannot be using earthly to mean *confined* to the temporal, because it is used as well by God's citizens, who go *beyond* the temporal in their concerns. The shared earthly peace is "common to the good and the bad alike" (19.26), so it cannot be the eternal order of hell that Christians are serving. We might put the problem to ourselves as one of punctuation in the modern translations of Augustine. Most translators capitalize City of God; but not all of them make the logically correlative capitalization of the Earthly City.

Yet when we talk of the earthly goods that even Christians can and should use, including the earthly peace of politics, it is clear that we should not capitalize the adjective as belonging, in that case, to the devil's realm. If that were true, men would be holding membership in *both* the *eternal* cities, which is absurd in Augustine's scheme of things.

It might be objected that Augustine does call the shared earthly peace a "peace of Babylon" (19.26). But (1) Babylon has a range of symbolic meanings not entirely coincident with the Earthly City in Augustine's scheme, and (2) the use of worldly goods by Christians was often described in patristic literature as "spoils of Egypt," taken out by Israel into the desert, and (3) Augustine is employing a scriptural language that was always double-edged (something his Manichean background made him especially sensitive to)—the condemnation of "earth" and "flesh" and "the world" when considered as principles deliberately militant against the spirit. That Pauline meaning did not preclude, even in Paul, a favorable use of the same terms as God's creatures, indeed as parts of his redeemed cosmos.

Since the City of God is the mystical body of Christ, the Second Adam, Augustine built his contrast with the Earthly City around the treatment of the two Adams in 1 Corinthians 15:47–49. The "earthiness" of that passage is nature as unredeemed, the principle of death. But this does not imply that earth or the world are evil in themselves (see 19.7) or will not be "saved" in the order of the New Jerusalem (20.17). Thus the terrestrial order can mean, according to context, the Earthly City (diabolically at odds with God), or earth as the middle area of shared goods, or the cosmos of God's final disposing.

Earthly peace, though a good thing shared by both cities, can be said to be a more natural "home" for the Earthly City, since this latter does not aspire to the higher things of eternity (though it does lead to eternal torment). Augustine did not read Paul as being opposed to flesh in itself, which as God's creature is good, but to the disorienting isolation of fleshly considerations from things of the spirit. In the same way, Augustine is not saying that earthly peace belongs to the devil's reign (the sure final meaning of the Earthly City). If it did, Christians could not share such a peace, any more than they can sacrifice to false gods. No one who reads Augustine's hymn to peace as beautiful in and for itself (19.11–12) can think he makes a politics of temporal peace the devil's proper realm.

And note that St. Augustine introduces the concept of love into his definition of a people. Since the phrase that bothered him in Cicero was "agreement on the right," he could simply have removed that and maintained a purely utilitarian basis for politics: "A people is a gathering of those united *by shared interests.*" That is very different from the definition he gives us as his own: "A people is a gathering of many rational individuals united by *accord on loved things held in common.*" Here we have proof that Augustine is considering the "third city" as something categorically similar to the final two cities; for they, too, are defined in terms of love— love for the all-embracing good that is God, or exclusionary love of self that leads to self-defeat. The earthly with a small "e" is that place where the two final cities mingle on pilgrimage, indistinguishable as yet, settling on the good things they love in common as a basis for their transitory unity. This does not make the third city unreal, just because it is not eternal (see the general definition of a city at 15.8). It is a society based on love, even though that love is not coterminous with either of the two final loves. It is a third thing, compatible with both for now, till the harvest.

It is not odd that Augustine would talk of only two cities as the basic division within human society *sub specie aeternitatis.* In fact, sometimes he talks of only *one* true city, in which concord and love are completed and satisfied. Even though hell is eternal, it is in a state of eternal dissolution never quite accomplished. In the same way he talks of the two hopes proper to citizens of the two cities, but adds that there is only one real hope and only one real peace (19.17). It all depends on the level of meaning whether there is one city, or two, or three. Scripture gives each symbol a range of meanings. Jerusalem and Babylon are historical cities for Augustine, yet symbols as well, *and* the things being symbolized, since "signs 'impersonate' as it were the things they signify" (18.48).

I believe that one reason St. Augustine did not promote the third city to equality with the other two was the lack of a proper city symbol in Scripture. Yet that, too, was fitting in his view of things. History is not a visible revelation, to rank with Scripture. It is not even a puzzle that can be unlocked with Scripture as the key. The secularization of the historical process that resulted from Augustine's agnosticism over omens and the fate of souls made it wrong for politics to exist on the same plane with the central symbols of the human drama of salvation (to which alone Scripture looks, 21.15).

Thus, instead of referring to the political realm as a scriptural *city,* Augustine treated it regularly in terms of a scriptural parable. The third city does not rank with the symbolically rich but simple cities of Jerusalem and Babylon, because the only way to describe the third city is in the complex image of a field in which wheat and weeds grow, inextricably tangled, toward the harvest time. The other two cities have both process *and* finality. Their members are pilgrims before they reach final citizenship. The third city has no *final* citizens. It has only process, not finality. At the harvest time its components will be separated, to make up the membership of both other cities. The third city will cease to be, like time itself.

St. Augustine reduces the pretensions of politics in order to give primacy to the great destiny of the soul, to a drama of salvation not reducible to things the state can judge. This has offended those who make politics the supreme activity of men in their search for justice. A. J. Carlyle regretted Augustine's "persistence in leaving out the moral or ethical conception of the state." And Carlyle said: "It is a notable fact that this passage of St. Augustine [denying that a common view of justice is the basis of the state] is hardly ever quoted at all in later Christian writers." He is correct there—the insight was too novel to be grasped at once. Classical modes of thought perdured even in the medieval politics (and helped pervert Augustine's work with all kinds of odd misreadings). But it is not true that Augustine's insight stands alone.

When Donald Greene, in *The Politics of Samuel Johnson* (1960), denied that Johnson believed in a natural-law basis for the state, he was accused of soiling the great man's thought with an irreligious pragmatism. But Greene was able to find the same approach in Blaise Pascal—hardly an irreligious man. In fact, the few times I have seen the Augustinian insight repeated, it was by people whose theological grasp of the purity and transcendence of

God made them deny any replication of that purity in the justice of the state. For them politics can only be accommodationist, not revelatory. They know that God's kingdom is not of this earth.

A clear example of this is Cardinal Newman's political thought. He gained his experience of politics opposing the Erastian establishment of his own (Anglican) Church—not for giving the Church too much, but for limiting its freedom to be a moral guide, connecting it with political bargains and deals. He wanted the Church disestablished so it could exercise a prophet's freedom. He knew this was quite a different thing from serving the conservative interests of politics in its quest for earthly peace.

Newman was directly influenced by Augustine, and repeated some of his better-known maxims about the lack of justice in earthly realms: "All states of the world, all governments, except so far as they are Christian, except so far as they act on Christian principles, are scarcely more than robbers and men of blood" (*Subjects of Day,* pp. 263–64). But this did not lead him to desire a Christian establishment; quite the opposite. He wanted a moderate state, the kind expounded in *Who's to Blame?*—a state in which Christians contribute their share of effort toward an earthly peace. The Christian Church, he said,

> upholds obedience to the magistrate; she recognizes his office as from God; she is the preacher of peace, the sanction of law, the first element of order and the safeguard of morality, and that without possible vacillation or failure; she may be fully trusted; she is a sure friend . . . [*Differences* I, p. 175].

Christian politics is, for these men, placatory and minimizing. (Newman was known as a minimalist even in matters of *Church* authority and politics.) This was doubly necessary for Augustine and Newman—not only to keep the individual free in his quest for God, but to keep the Church free for its prophetic office, which involves spurs and sanctions quite different from those of the law.

I apologize if anyone thinks this chapter too lost in discussion of past theology. The more anfractuous that discussion, the more astonishing its close fit and usefulness in explaining modern politics.

17·War and Peace

St. Augustine reached his final view of politics almost perforce, since it involved a total wrench from his background of classical thought about the state. His theological beliefs (in heaven and hell, in the predestination of souls to those different goals, in the unknowableness of one's own goal, in God's love as the ultimate category of being)—put together and reacting on each other—led him to his break with the idea of a state founded on justice. But no matter what led him, he accomplished the breakthrough; and even those who lack his theological presuppositions can follow an analogous process to similar conclusions.

Apart from the doctrines of heaven and hell, we can see that people in the same society differ in their deepest values and orientation. Modern man, in fact, sees a bewildering variety of ultimate beliefs exemplified in any society, not just the two goals that divided everyone in Augustine's view. How are we to bind such disparate human judgments on the nature of reality into the kind of agreement that gives society its unity and effectiveness? Only, it seems, by finding some common ground *other* than deepest commitments or most inclusive beliefs. The more precisely we define the nature of justice and truth and reality, the more we must exclude from our fellowship those who disagree. This causes problems for any government "dedicated to a proposition" with specific controversial content. A proposition-test for citizenship is, not very far down the line of spelled-out concepts, as objectionable as a religious test. Because it *is* a religious test for those who, like Augustine, consider it unrealistic to talk of justice apart from God.*

The difficulty is immediate and practical, not remote and hypothetical. People constantly put the challenge to their fellow citizens, "How can you be part of an order that legally condones slavery, segregation, unjust war, a suicidal weapons race, murder of unborn children?"—or whatever any citizen finds unjust. If it were true that our very citizenship "says," as it were, that the state is just, that its principal claim on us is adherence to justice, then we would all, sooner or later, have to renounce citizenship in order to stop saying such things—since the state commits unjust acts in someone's eyes every day. Only what is unjust in the eyes of some citizens is a basic right for others. Abortion is killing babies in the considered judgment of many Americans. To others, the banning of abortion is a violation of a woman's privacy, freedom, and right to care for her own body. Politics cannot, usually, solve such a disagreement by forcing the matter to sharp debate and a single conclusion; politicians intuitively avoid the issue as long as they can, then bargain over it, trying to give something to everybody—for example making abortion legal, but not supporting it with federal funds.

Some people do renounce citizenship, really or symbolically, entirely or in part—Garrison burning the Constitution, conscientious objectors refusing military service, antinuclear protesters refusing to pay taxes that finance our weapons system. These can be valua-

* Augustine's full theory of tolerance, reached toward the end of his last great work, does not square with his earlier practice, even when we recognize, with Peter Brown, all extenuations for that practice (*Religion and Society,* pp. 260ff.).

ble teaching acts and testimonies of conscience. But they are not things every person is obliged to do as a logical consequence of citizenship in an unjust regime. We are not forced to that position every time the state acts unjustly because our citizenship does not really "say" the state is just or founded on justice. All it says—all it can say in our system—is that we citizens have a love of certain good things shared that makes us one community trying to remain at peace with itself.

One can "go along" with an unjust regime in many ways without condoning the injustice. I even argued, in the *Nixon Agonistes* chapter that Buckley turned down, that one can participate in an unjust war (so long as it is defensive). Robert E. Lee hated slavery; said he would release all his slaves to avoid war, and did not want to fight when war came. But he had only three options: to fight against his own Virginians (since the North offered him command of the Army of the Potomac), to abstain entirely from combat, or to defend the lives of his erring fellows. It was a tragic choice, and perhaps he did not make the best decision; but it was a morally defensible one, even though a war fought to retain slaves can hardly be a just one. In the breakdown of earthly peace that created two societies where one had been, he stayed with the society in whose good things loved he had a greater actual share.

This view of political reality would not preclude the overthrow of an unjust regime, but it would make it far less eligible in theory as well as practice. Classical teaching on tyrannicide can suggest that unjust regimes should be overthrown at once if the side effects of a coup are not foreseeably worse than the present injustice. That would have justified, in some people's eyes, the overthrow of Richard Nixon. If the state is unjust, what further claim can it have on people who think the state exists precisely to embody justice? It has undermined itself, removed its own *raison d'être*.

An Augustinian view would "settle for less" in the state's claims on us, and be more permissive of its performance, since such a view promotes a lower opinion of the state's ability to enunciate just teaching. It would also discourage people from seeking a political remedy for all earthly ills. It is not true that radicals are necessarily opposed to peaceful working of the normal political system. Many see it simply as irrelevant to deeper issues of conscience. That is why intransigent prophets do not so much run for office, or support candidates, or even vote, as preach and teach in the name of something higher than compromise. This does not mean they will not compromise at one level in their actions. The wheat can grow with weeds, even while individual stalks preach the value of wheatness.

The radicals I most admire have instinctively sided with Augustine on the norm of "earthly peace" even while troubling people with hard truths. Dr. King, the Berrigans, Dorothy Day—all have been nonviolent. Some other radicals think they have been nonviolent to a fault. Dan Berrigan, while honoring Dietrich Bonhoeffer's good intentions and heroism, thinks his change from nonviolent opposition to the planned assassination of Hitler was a falling off from grace, a use of evil means to fight evil. I would not, myself, preclude tyrannicide in the case of a regime engaging in mass murder—but I see the horrible temptation that such a stand opens up. Was the napalming of children in Indochina mass murder? Is the killing of fetuses mass murder? Start pulling weeds by force, and the wheat itself is endangered. The presumption against violence should always be *almost* overwhelming. Without earthly peace we cannot communicate with each other or hold good things in a common love.

But if a lessening of the state's claim to embody justice logically entails nonviolence by making earthly peace our political norm, the same lessening lifts some of the moral barriers to civil disobedience. If the state is not the sole or best guardian of justice, and the electoral system does more to maintain than to innovate, and the moral impulse has manifested itself outside the system in voices of unyielding principle, then the objection to civil disobedience is not so much moral (one must never break the law) as tactical (will it hurt more than help?) and personal (have I the courage to risk obloquy or worse from those resisting painful change?). The civil disobedience of America's proved moral leaders, back to that of Anthony Benezet defying the ban on help to Acadians, should be seen as one of our great historical treasures, the renewing of moral impulse that has made the country's earthly peace worth preserving.

When I began to cover antiwar protests, I found that radicals had grasped the difference between procedural liberalism and moral testimony. The former asks, "Is the war legal?"—declared by a legitimate regime, through constitutional procedures, carried out by a military subordinate to civil authority, etc. The latter rightly notes that Hitler's war was probably legitimate; it was also unjust. Garrison said not only that slavery was *wrong,* but that the laws protecting it were wrong.

The prophets in our society, no matter what they have to suffer, do have a certain hold on politicians, who try to placate everybody. This means that politicians try to accommodate the unaccommodating. (After all, they even try to please those who think they should stand for principle, not compromise—that is, their compromising vein makes them feign, for that audience, an opposition to compromise.) Even when change originates outside the system, the system tries to absorb what it can as a way of defusing the protest, softening the position, giving the protesters less than what they wanted, bargaining only part of their claims into wider social acceptance. Senator Dirksen, finally giving way on the Civil Rights Act of 1964 said, "There is nothing more powerful than an idea whose time has come." He had done his best, in the past, to keep this idea's time from coming; but Dr. King and his fellows had made it come. So Dirksen yielded with grace and upheld now what he held down then.

A modest politics is only a blessing if it makes room for the immodest claims of conscience outside the essentially compromising political arena. This involves a kind of mutual trust among citizens that is lacking in places like the Soviet Union, one that can break down even here—as it almost did in the sixties. We are a stable country thanks to the inertial forces of our normal politics. We are a prosperous country (and reform normally needs some room to maneuver, some easing of the harsh necessities of life) because of our business and technological elite. We are a moral people insofar as we raise up voices of protest at injustices among us. The voice of such protest does not normally come from the White House, or Capitol Hill, or a campaign platform. That voice comes from jails, at times. Or schools. Or slums. Or pamphlets. Or picket lines. Or pulpits. It is not the voice of Washington or Jefferson, but of Benezet.

During the Chicago convention of 1968, I was standing with Murray Kempton when Dick Gregory, to protest the penning up of Chicago's blacks, invited us to cross a police line and go to his home. Murray went—and went to jail. I did not. I had not yet run out of excuses. But it was getting harder to stay "uninvolved," a mere journalistic spectator, as our society's earthly peace was troubled. I was beginning to chafe at the long lead time of the magazines for which I was writing. Too much was happening too fast to be treated in articles that would appear months after they were written. I had turned down two offers from syndicates to write a newspaper column (it costs a big syndicate practically nothing to try out new columnists, so the offers were no honor). After Kent State, I asked a new syndicate (Universal Press) if I could do a column just for a few months. I wanted some chance to say something about the meaning of that event as I saw it. Civil peace was being destroyed not by protest, but by repression—as rioting police had caused the Chicago turmoil, responding to Mayor Daley's self-defeating "toughness." The readiness to shoot was now out in the open and being applauded—as I saw men applaud the beating of kids in a Chicago bar when I stepped out of the tear gas on the street. A sizable part of the nation had even reached the point of honoring Lieutenant Calley for shooting women and children in a ditch. The readiness to shoot, and shoot to kill, had given us "Four Dead in Ohio."

The Vietnam War crept into the ordinary American's consciousness as a kind of unwanted but inevitable growth. There was no clear enemy, no conscious war aim. The war began on a rickety basis of weak and partial aims to "stop communism," to help the Vietnamese, to maintain our stance as guardians of the free world, etc. But most Americans felt it was a tar baby we had got accidentally stuck to. Now we had to prolong our involvement to remain "credible" as a world power. But in 1968 something horrible happened: Those deprived of the satisfaction of waging war with a strong feeling of righteousness now *developed* that feeling, directed less at a distant and unknown enemy than at America's own students and moral leaders. The war became a civil war, with certain Americans telling others they had no right to criticize their country. The atmosphere of a Wallace rally in that year was something I had never experienced before. There was an implicit willingness to kill Asians in order to silence domestic critics, to fight our civil war by proxy with the bodies of other people—like the lord of a plantation who has a slave boy whipped to show his son what *might* happen to him if he is unruly.

America has never been very good at self-criticism. "Then conquer we must, for our cause it is just," we sing in our national anthem. Yet the sixties brought a wave of criticism to public attention. Not just riots or demonstrations, but presidential reports on assassination, violence, drugs, pornography, and racism said that there were deep things wrong with our country. Presidents had to reject those findings, because the voters were not used to self-criticism on this scale and wanted it shut up. That was the meaning of Agnew and Wallace.

Of course, in this breakdown of civil peace, each side blamed the other for the violence. There were crazies on the left; but only one person was killed, by accident, when a man working at midnight died from the Wisconsin bombing of a military research building. (Some other bombers blew themselves up in New York. The crazies are not very competent in "practical" matters.) Most demonstrators were adherents of Dr. King's teaching on nonviolence. They were less quick than policemen to hit out, or than National Guardsmen to shoot. The initial violence to the American people was their involvement in a war they never really chose, never supported but for vague and slippery reasons that cried out for additional motivation—until the aim of "showing the kids" they could not "get away with" opposition in the streets became the twisted intent of this weird war's later stages.

I tried to say these things (the column was extended when the syndicate sold it to enough papers). I felt a share in my country's responsibility. The crusading anticommunism of my upbringing and my Richmond editorials was the kind of thing, magnified many times, that brought us to this scuffle in one of the world's back alleys, where we hit out blindly and could not distinguish (or disentangle ourselves from) friend and foe. Not that anybody had listened to my opinions except those already converted. Yet I had expressed one mood that led us here, and had special reason to regret that as I read my Augustine more carefully. We had imperiled our internal peace while ravaging that of others. We did it for their own good, confident we knew what that was. We did it because we were right, our cause just. We were a little City of God arranging our own day of judgment, separating noncommunist wheat from communist weeds. We tried to impose on others a "just regime" we cannot even lay claim to for ourselves.

If the state should not try to embody ideal justice even in domestic affairs but "settle for less," for the modest goal of protecting our shared good things, then it is absurd for us to tell other societies what they are allowed to settle for. A society's peace depends on its agreement about the real things held in common, the things that citizens unite in loving. What right has an outsider to tell people what they may love? The national ethos is shaped, in each country, by the things its citizenry wants, whether they *should* want them or not. We wanted Nixon in the sixties. We wanted to tame the West in the Gilded Age, at whatever cost. Other countries have wanted Kings or dictators. Our country would have been unrulable under an unwanted leader like McGovern; how can we expect other countries to take rulers (or rules) of our choice and call them *their* choice?

If a country directly threatens us, we have a right to defend our lives and just possessions. But the modern game of playing world stage-manager or choreographer of nations, trying to create governments sympathetic to us, overthrow those not sufficiently sympathetic, impose "good" elections, spread loyalty tests out from our own citizenry to foreign countries (asking that they be loyal to their own country only if that country is loyal to us)—all this was an exercise in unreality that rightly led to the civil-war-by-proxy of Vietnam: We jeopardized our internal peace by thinking we could arrange internal peace for others. I felt obliged to say this as many ways as I could, though it contradicted (*because* it contradicted) what I had written as recently as the summer of 1961. Yet I could not think of this as a departure from conservatism, but as a rather late arrival at it. The belief that one's own nation had to defend justice in every other nation, no matter what that nation thought of the matter, is not conservative or liberal so much as lunatic. It is extravagant, and radical, and antihistorical.

What interested me now was the way America, apart from its anticommunist grandiosity, adhered in fact to the way politics should be conducted in the Augustinian scheme of things. We are often told that America has a conservative loyalty to a liberal tradition. But the matter is more complicated than that. We have a conservative loyalty to a liberal theory that purports to explain a *conservative* system. The electoral process that is supposed to bring about change actually inhibits it. My analysis of that system had been taken as an attack on it, because people do not adequately value the conservative impulse that must bind a people together for protection of the things they share. I do value that impulse, and find it exemplified in a politics that—domestically, at least—is willing to settle for less, to exclude the divisive as much as possible from the stringencies of legal obligation, to muddle in toward a middle and choose candidates who are "safe." None of this precludes change and originality of spirit; it just gives us a legal framework in which people can argue and preach and teach without bringing in the law's final arbitrament on every subject affecting justice. The turmoil of the sixties occurred, I was convinced, because the anticommunist crusade had revived in our system, whose whole genius is bargaining and compromise, an absolutism not in accord with our normal politics. We could not administer final justice around the world through a political apparatus not meant to administer final justice even to ourselves. America had, in and after World War II, come to think of itself as the giver and arbiter of justice. We would put the whole world on a kind of continuing Nuremberg trial, ourselves both jury and executioner. The Augustinian morality could only look at this spectacle and ask: When did God turn the day of judgment over to you? We wanted to pull up all the weeds in the world; and we only disturbed our own roots.

18 · Re-membering the Past

I would now "resume my story" if there were one worth telling in this context. My experience over the past dozen or so years has been much like that of other journalists following the civil-rights and antiwar movements, presidential campaigns and Watergate. Those stories have been often told, and better than I can tell them. My contribution, if I have one, is in my starting point: Few of those covering the turmoil of the sixties and seventies had begun writing for *National Review*. A different starting point can, despite errors in that start, give one a different way of looking at things, useful perhaps even to those who did not share my errors. Besides, the "givens" of one's life can be narrated. What one makes of the givens tends to take the form of reflection and argument. Perhaps that is why the childhood sections of so many autobiographies are the best.

My political childhood was retarded; but it gave me a set of experiences to reflect on, and a desire to puzzle out the attraction I

felt and feel for the very term "conservatism." It was easy from
the outset to see that libertarians lived in a dream world of hypothetical atoms interacting with each other dynamically, not chemically. No society can ever be formed on the basis of individualism,
togetherness deriving from apartness. It would take me longer to
see through the authoritarian side of conservatism, trying to
uphold religion and morals by law, turning communism into the
new anti-Christ against which justice must be done, *ruat caelum*.
In St. Augustine's last view of things, to do apocalyptic battle with
anti-Christ is to arrogate Christ's role to politics. Augustine's
agnosticism about the souls of other men was what I ultimately
needed, not the certitudes of right-wing righteousness.

Yet the instinct toward conservatism remains. Some of this is
no doubt a matter of temperament, the mere accident of birth. I
am by taste and training a classicist. My Church puts great emphasis on tradition. I respond to the praise Ennius gave his hero
as *multa tenens antiqua* (tenacious of the ancient things). Yet so
far as I can tell in my own case, the positions I have reached by
reflection seem conservative in a way that goes beyond quirks of
my own taste.

I am certainly not a liberal. I don't believe our politics works
the way liberal theory claims. And I admire the system's workings
because they guarantee coherence and continuity: They soften
difference and mute change, so it may enter the social body as nutriment, not as a knifeblade. These surely are conservative values.

On the other hand, I admire the voices calling for moral renewal and difficult change. I find in them the mystery of free will
and heroism, and know we depend on these. No system can automatically turn human selfishness into "checks and balances" with
benign results. The liberal wants a "system" that works automatically, a government of laws and not of men. But until we can
mass-produce prophets and martyrs, we must listen constantly for
whatever light is given us from human ingenuity and courage. We
cannot produce wisdom or sanctity or genius—though all of these
can be crushed, can be starved or broken or killed. This should
dispose us to allow as much freedom of preaching and teaching as
we can, within our large politics of compromise.

Conservatism is a title deserved by a view that tries to value and retain the politician as well as the prophet, the bureaucrat as well as the technocrat, the business elite as well as the unions, the poor and oppressed along with the elites. That kind of politics would be elitist, but not partially so, like our other political philosophies; not covertly so; not attacking "elites" when all that is intended is destruction of elites opposed to one's own favored group. The right wing in America is stuck with the paradox of holding a philosophy of "conserving" and an actual order it does not want to conserve. It keeps trying to create something new it might think worthy, someday, of conserving. My own conservatism is simpler and more accepting. I like our political order because I don't believe for a minute it is trying (and failing) to do things liberals keep praising it for trying to do and accusing it for failing to do.

I know the term "conservative" is often misleading, that people will take it to mean "right wing" in either its libertarian or authoritarian senses. I tried for a while to do without it. But people *do* keep asking what one is; and while I do not want to fight for a term, neither do I want to acquiesce in the mindlessness that calls a hodgepodge of anarchic and repressive resistance to our "liberal establishment" by so improper a title as "conservative." I could make up a third name, a new one; but that hardly solves the problem. If I were to call myself a "convenicntist," that would involve more explanation than conservatism itself. If I called myself "Augustinian," I must recognize that Augustine's thought labors under centuries of misapplication and misunderstanding, and I would have to isolate those elements I find applicable today.

Chesterton described the problem when he said his opposition to capitalism was constantly being mistaken for an opposition to capital or the basic facts of investment:

> The truth is that what we call Capitalism ought to be called Proletarianism. The point of it is not that some people have capital, but that most people only have wages because they do not have capital. I have made an heroic effort in my time to walk about the world always saying Proletarianism instead of Capitalism. But my path has been a thorny one of troubles and misunderstandings. I find that when I criticize the Duke of Northumberland for his Proletarianism, my meaning does

not get home. When I say I should often agree with the *Morning Post* if it were not so deplorably Proletarian, there seems to be some strange momentary impediment to the complete communion of mind with mind.

Yet Chesterton did get stuck with the term distributism, not of his own making; and the idiosyncratic title attracted cranks or little cultists, much as Chesterton tried to maintain common sense in his movement. There is a sense in which I could still call myself a distributist, as I did in 1957, but I would have to distinguish between my form of distributism and all others—there is no using a simple term simply in the complex world of our politics.

America faces the special problem that it applied ideological judgments from the Old World in a new situation. In Europe's *ancien régime,* the "haves" at least had many fiefs and established properties or rights—the churches, universities, estates, guild monopolies, townships, etc. The comparative have-nots wanted to loosen up tenure, cause movement through these entrenched powers. Conservative and liberal were terms one could fairly clearly apply to those views (though they were not common at the time). In America, however, there was a continent to be seized and tamed. No elaborate structure of legal holdings had to be cleared away, "just" nomadic bands of Indians. The law was not pre-existent on the side of such holding, to be changed or broken if the establishment was to be challenged. Our seat of power was an expanding capitalism aided by the state. Our only duchies were held by "robber barons." Capitalism is of its nature expansive, risk-taking, wanting new markets and materials and products. It has wrought more change in the modern world—often senseless change—than any revolutionary force. It overturns and runs on. It has of itself no sense of tradition. It tears down old to keep building the new in a perpetual gamble on tomorrow. It is of all things the least worthy of the name conservative. Then how did it get it?

King and Church were seen as the seat of established power in the Old World, intent on conserving that power. The source of power in America was the business class of expansionists and investors pushing across the continent and then out over oceans.

We rather simple-mindedly kept the nexus *power=conservative,* even when the power involved was a revolutionary and unstable one. And with equal originality we called "liberal" any challenge to the business world's power—even unions, promoting stability and cutting down the ruthless bargaining of a "free market." A politics of compromise, insofar as it clogs the single operation of the profit motive, is called "liberal" though it makes for cohesion rather than dispersal. We are in a topsy-turvy world of terms. Yet the puzzles of our history will not go away if we just stop using the terms. The tangling of the terms reflects our own ignorance of our own history, the acceptance of slogans for thought and of official explanations that do not explain. There is no way to approach this problem without redefining, renewing any language we start with. So we might as well use the language that reflects the problem as we try to inspect it.

But once again, I am not a stickler for the term. I observe some terminological niceties myself, just to help my own thinking. I do not expect others to follow my practice; but I have to use it, when asked to explain myself, since it is the most adequate I have been able to come up with. I use *right wing,* then, where many others use conservative. Right wing applies to part of a political *spectrum,* on which people of very disparate political philosophies have huddled for their own purposes, whether libertarian or authoritarian, anticommunist or racist or whatever. The collection of actual voters and politicians does not deserve the name of a philosophical school, but of a political force. *Liberal* I use for the belief in the market system of social organization. Historical liberalism believed in the economic free market as well as the political and academic markets. It is a respectable school of thought, though now met mainly in fragments. I don't believe in its individualist basis or its assumption that market interplay can make an economy, or the play of ideas, or the political parties, "self-correcting," productive of the best result. So I am not a liberal.

Conservatism looks to the cohesion and continuity of society— what makes people band together and remain together with some satisfaction. The answer that Augustine and Newman give to this question is empirical: People band together in stable ways to conserve the shared good things they love. Conservatism looks to possession—but to the *common* possession (Augustine's *concordi communione*) of a language, a history, a concrete set of loyalties; to possession in the large sense as what links countryman to countryman; not to property in the narrow sense of individual possession, that which one holds apart from one's fellows. Conservatism is the sphere of social affections, exercised not by the imposition of "raw justice" on others but by participation in what Newman calls "a certain assemblage of beliefs, convictions, rules, usages, traditions, proverbs, and principles." We do not agree on everything with everybody, but *we agree to agree to as much as we can* without doing positive violation to our soul's higher destiny. In Augustinian terms, we share what we can of earthly peace so long as that does not jeopardize our hope of a higher and ultimate citizenship.

Because it values continuity, any sane conservatism cannot be opposed to change. Cohesion and stability are not insured but doomed by mere brittle resistance to inevitable change. The constant adjustings and compromisings, pushings and shovings, takings and givings, settlements and half measures that are ridiculed in our politics are the signs of life reacting as a whole; making society responsive to a number of needs, so we can move and change together.

The kind of conservatism I am describing can be doctrinaire—it was, for instance, in St. Augustine, who was forced to his politics precisely by religious doctrines of the most forbidding sort (hell and predestination). But the only appeal it can have to modern man is, I think, empirical—and that is why I have spent so much time as a journalist trying to observe the way our society actually works, our political system of compromise, our elite system of leadership. I had, by the accident of my entry point into political life, less stake in providing any *theory* of how things work than I might otherwise have felt. The liberal theory was neither hateful to me nor a cherished possession. There was little conservative theory of how things work, just a distaste for much of our "liberal" past—a distaste I soon felt leave me as I looked at the largely successful way we do political business with each other. It is a flawed world, a tragic world; but we cope with it as well on the social level as we do in our homes or private lives. Who can expect more?

Having observed the way our politics work—the electoral compromises making for stability, the challenging elites making for renewal within that continuity—I approved of things in the main, and wanted to conserve the precious social affections expressed in our national life. If that cannot be called conservatism, what can?

Life is a continual process of shuffling off error, as breathing in absorbs nutriment and breathing out sheds noxious residue. But I can hardly speak for continuity without expressing gratitude for the hints and guidance given even when I was supporting views I now reject. Willmoore Kendall did more, I suppose, than anyone else to make me see that liberal theory does not account for the supposedly liberal conduct of our affairs. Frank Meyer pushed on my reading of the political classics and argued me toward better understanding of them. Bill Buckley has a genuine and infectious reverence for the past which, though it sits ill with capitalism's harum-scarum pressure for change, is something I still admire and aspire to.

Later teachers of a different sort, like friends in and around the Institute for Policy Studies, or various editors who made me explain myself again and again, have probably been more helpful to me, though they remain less vivid, than my first mentors. In fact, it is the *very* first ones who have counted most. I told earlier how, till 1961, my political reading had been mainly in literary sources —Chesterton and Ruskin, Newman and Johnson. It was only after some years of reading in political theory that I realized my best lessons were still to be learned in my first loves. The instinct that drew me to them was in need of correcting; but it was still the strongest motive in my thinking on man's polity. Bits of distributism or Ruskin's economics, of Johnsonian realism and the moderate politics of Newman, are things I am still exploring.

Is this, again, a matter of mere temperament or accident? In part, of course, it is. We are the products of our circumstances, though not only that. It will be seen, for instance, that much of my thought came from Catholicism, for the simple reason that I was educated in Catholic schools. But other students took very different attitudes toward what we shared. I never had a single course that dealt with St. Augustine. But I had, it seems, endless ones explicating St. Thomas Aquinas. My admiration of Thomas remains distant, and has not really affected my thought, while

Augustine has. In the schools of my time and place, Chesterton was rather looked down on by the better teachers as a shallow fellow; if anything, an embarrassment to Catholics. Newman, by contrast, was an ornament. Some made it seem that the only way to protect Newman was to jettison Chesterton. Yet Chesterton's thought was always more congenial to me; and I am convinced that he was fully as profound as Newman, and with far broader interests. (But Newman had that great gift for self-dramatization Victorians specialized in—men like Ruskin and Carlyle, the criers of doom, themselves doomed.)

I have tried to look at the conservative instinct apart from my own biases of temperament. This is not the same as a conservative philosophy of government, and can exist apart from it. We are all conservative *and* liberal by instinct—nostalgic and curious, to put it simply; savoring the past and anticipating the future. We could not shed either aspect of our lives even if we wanted to. Nonetheless, I find certain things that encourage the "innovating" side of life a bit misleading, if not morally dangerous. I mean the attitude that says the dead past is over and we must turn to the future, look to *it,* treat it as the real, as the realm of meaningful endeavor. One would almost think that such singers of a brave new world had adopted the creed of Clifford Odet's Golden Boy: "When a bullet sings through the air it has no past—only a future—like me."

Even to search for a metaphor is to reveal the emptiness of that view. A bullet, if it has any rational purpose, has a very stable past indeed—the moment when a person took aim at a pre-existing target. The lifeless thing flung at a life is teleologically fixed, not free; its target is the *telos.* Now some people do talk about the future as if it were a target "out there" ahead of us, toward which we might "shoot" ourselves, with a velocity determined by our escape from a launching point in the past. But there is no target already out there in the not-yet. The future, after all, does not exist; it *is* what *isn't,* yet.

Insofar as we steer rationally toward the future, we do so by our rear-view mirror. There is no windshield, because there is nothing to "see" up ahead. We go forward by seeing backward. By tracing the trajectory of past events we extrapolate to future positions. But if we trace only one trend, the chances of steering well are slim; too many other things will jostle and interact with the simple arc we are imagining. That is why so many simple reforms or five-year plans or platform pledges are bound to go awry, even with the best of wills. The best guides to the future are those whose knowledge of the past is broadest and deepest, who are most cautious and aware of complexity, least confident that they can "see" something up ahead.

Even the prophet, who says moral change must come, should not dismiss the past. Bill Buckley calls himself a radical conservative. But Dorothy Day has a better claim to that title, going all the way back to the Gospel through that higher hero worship called hagiography. It is also called the communion of saints. Chesterton puts the matter in terms of a certain generosity:

Man is like Perseus, he cannot look at the Gorgon of the future except in the mirror of the past. . . . It is utterly useless to talk about enlarging one's mind with visions of the future. The future does not enlarge one's mind in the least. The future is a blank wall on which I can paint my own portrait as large as I like. If I am narrow, I can make the future narrow. If I am mean, I can make the future mean. I cannot make the past mean. I cannot make St. Catherine of Sienna mean. I cannot make Plato narrow. In the past I have real antagonists, men certainly better, braver, or more brilliant than I. Among the dead I have living rivals. In the future all my rivals are dead because they are unborn. I know I could not write *Paradise Lost,* but I could easily write a Utopia very favorable to the sort of poetry I can write. . . . We are fleeing from the faces of our fathers because they are faces. We are attracted to the future because it is what is called a soft job. In front of us lies an unknown or unreal world which we can mould according to every cowardice or triviality in our own temperaments. But if we look back at our fathers as they gather in the gate of history, we see it like the gate of Eden, described by one of them in verse which we cannot imitate: With dreadful faces thronged and fiery arms.

In choosing our teachers we do not have to depend on lucky accident—on finding the one person among our contemporaries who has the time and will and means to enlighten us. The great Academy of the Past is open to all who would use it; no admissions board can exclude us. Chesterton calls tradition a "democracy of the dead." We should not exclude a man's opinion because of the accident of death, any more than we should for the accident of birth.

There is a meanness of spirit in the effort to "escape" one's past. I have already argued that the concept of "historical guilt" is the other side of conservative tributes to the wisdom of the past. Chesterton was right to see a kind of heroism in dealing with the past. There is so *much* of it (as opposed to the thin and hypothetical nature of the future). The best image of this truth comes, in fact, from one of the oldest poems of heroism in our tradition, the *Odyssey*.

Odysseus' return home is presented as a psychological problem —how to re-enter one's past—imaged under the cruder external job of outwitting the suitors. With great tact the poet makes re-entry hardest where it matters most: The more reason people have to know Odysseus, the more recognition signs they require. A shallow relationship is easily resumed—the dog sees his master and dies for joy. His son was only an infant when he left; but he has been aspiring to his father's height and heroism, has almost *become* him in his official role, so he knows him without trouble. But his old nurse and his father need special signs and testing, and his wife needs most of all. The long scenes of mutual quizzing do not show distance between Odysseus and Penelope but an intimacy not to be resumed too lightly—so many nerve ends meeting all at once, the complicated meshings of emotion. For each, recognition of the other requires entry into one's deepest self. This is a heroic quest more challenging than the mere itch for novelty expressed in Tennyson's *Ulysses*. Homer is dealing with a higher thing than wanderlust when he has his hero circle with infinite caution the secret of the marriage bed.

As true and tactful, as quiet in brilliance, as all this is, the poet has an even more stunning effect to arrange as his poem ends. Odysseus voyages into his past, steering by recognition signs (the scar and the trees and the bed that convince nurse and father and wife). Telemachus has an identifying sign that reveals him to himself as well as others—the trick of stringing his father's bow, a secret given him long before, but one he did not have the strength to use till now. Telemachus about to string the bow just as his father returns is a narrative device with a deeper meaning: Odysseus returns when Telemachus takes up his bow—just as Achilles went back to battle in the armor worn by his dead friend.

The final identity of Telemachus and Odysseus, who have journeyed toward each other throughout the poem, is confirmed in one of the most astonishing scenes of all poetry. On a literal level, the returned father and the grandfather almost "resurrected" from the fields go out to fight together with Telemachus—three lone men with their retainers against an army of the suitors, that new and restless crowd trying to take away the settled fields and bed, the long-worked realm of the heroic family. As they face the enemy, the first spear thrown is by the oldest arm—yet Athena speeds it with such impact to its goal that it breaks the spirit of the suitors and ends the battle. Telemachus goes out with his ancestral ghosts to battle. He not only draws his father's bow but throws his grandfather's spear. They fight with and in him, for him.

Telemachus is the only "individual" who can stand against a mob; for he is a crowd in himself. He is all the good things loved that have been passed down to him in the mystery of human tradition, the community that lives on even in the single self. His spear flies shining into the future because his whole race threw it—the human race, the past, the Fathers.

19 · Remembering the Future

It is not enough, I think, to say that respect for the past is natural and necessary in man. Anybody will grant as much—along with the equal truth that a readiness to face unknown things around the corner of the future is a needed part of the soul's equipment. But even those who grant these complementary truths tend a little too easily to sort out different virtues for each attitude. Willingness to "cast off" leads to innovation and creativity, we are told. The conservative mood digs in its heels with a certain stubborn virtue of resistance. There is rough truth to those kinds of statement; but they *isolate* the overlapping and reinforcing aspects of reverence toward the past and creativity in facing new tasks. Once more my warrant is St. Augustine.

I have noted the daring break Augustine made with classical thought in order to arrive at the concept of a state not founded on justice. He made a series of such breaks, finding God in the flesh against all Neoplatonic prejudices. He made an even riskier leap when he made *change* and process a vehicle of teaching and truth, not of ignorance and unreality. The changes that teach are those recovered by memory. Creativity grows in the travel back toward origins—to creation.

Our culture's artist, spelling things from chaos with a "solitary alphabet," is the iconographic heir of God in the Book of Genesis. Jehovah is a God who makes things—fish, animals, birds, and finally man—and then rests from his labor. It is this banausic note of labor that separates the Jewish God from Greek divinities. To preserve the impassibility of their higher gods, Greek philosophers thought of emanation or reflection rather than creation, the world as derived by a leisurely divine overspill. But in Genesis, as in its Mesopotamian analogues, God *labors* forms out of the pliant water and awesome wind.

Early Christian thinkers upped the creative ante when they turned the water of Genesis into an abyss of nothingness, and the wind into God's own Spirit, so that creation takes place radically *ex nihilo*. This startling development colored all later talk of creativity. The romantic artist, off alone in his storm-battered castle, fuming whole worlds from his brain, reflects his culture's most persistent myth, of God creating from a primal loneliness. The poet is battered by storm as a sign of inner turmoil; if he creates out of himself alone, his must be an exceeding *busy* self—like the God he images. In the Trinity of Christian thought, all the demiurges and emanations of Neoplatonism were absorbed within the Godhead, concentrating a high "charge" there that could explode outward. God creates by acting on himself:

> At the origin the Concept was in being
> and the Concept faced toward God,
>   and was God as his Concept—
> this is what faced God at the origin.

God *faced* God — the active Greek preposition, ἦν πρὸς τὸν θεόν. God's only leverage, as it were, is on himself, since he has no other material to use in the creation. And from this self-confrontation all things other than the self must be derived:

> Through It all things came into being,
> and except through It nothing came to be at all.

The way this concept of God affected man's understanding of himself can be traced most readily in St. Augustine. He refers continually to the two great points of origin, the opening of Genesis and the opening of John, and builds his whole psychology on them. There were many obstacles to this project, including the Neoplatonist equipment he brought to the task. He must think of the Creator as immutable. But then how can man, mutability's prisoner, be called the image of God? The *Confessions,* his first masterpiece, arrives at one answer to this problem. The book is an exercise in self-recovery; the author "saves" his youthful self by calling it up in memory, an action that is musically enacted in the Tenth Book. The very act of remembering becomes salvific.

It is odd, on the face of it, that a Christian Neoplatonist should dwell so on the particular circumstances of his timebound life. A common early argument for the soul's immortality—one that Augustine had used—was based on the mind's ability to enunciate (to "contain" in the spatial metaphor) eternal truths. But the *Confessions* challenges that argument. Even if we enunciate a profession mentally, as opposed to verbally, we do it within time's processes; there is a *motion* involving temporal lapse (however split-second) from one aspect of the known to another—from, let us say, the subject of a proposition to its predicate. Our knowledge is in progress always, which means it changes in the very act of asserting what is changeless. Not only are we different today from yesterday's self, we are different people by the time we end a sentence from the ones who began it. Augustine had an almost haunted awareness of this constant dropping of reality over into the abyss of time past, second by second disappearing, dying from him. We used this awareness against the astrologers of his day, saying that a fatal interval occurred between the birth of one and the next, no matter how fast the mother's birth throes succeeded each other. No astrological measurement was precise enough in any man's case. The astrologer's problem with births that are close yet fatally sundered was, for Augustine, the philosopher's problem with terms of a proposition, no matter how quickly enunciated by the mind. To *move* to a conclusion is to change in the very act of concluding. How to say, then, that the subject is the same subject by the time one reaches a predicate, when the "I" who enunciates the subject is already a different "I" from the one who asserts the predicate?

St. Augustine's problem was to turn time the enemy into time the friend. He does this by entry into the basic experience of memory, in which the I-now somehow recovers an I-then, by an act that is neither of the two I's taken simply. I can in effect resurrect a former self, not exactly as it was, but transcended: I-happy can recall a me-sad, without undergoing that sadness. I can without sinning remember a sinful me (the whole of the *Confessions* does that). I can recall an erring me without re-enacting the error. This helps explain what some have isolated as the principal problem of the *Confessions,* finished fifteen years after Augustine's conversion—the inconcinnity in tone between his writings at the actual time of conversion (which often seem more Neoplatonic than Christian) and the description of that period he gives us in his middle forties. But the terms in which scholars pose the problem would not have made sense to Augustine. For him, the self recovered is always a self transcended. What matters to him is not objective fact detachable from him, but the miracle that allows him to stay in contact with himself, to perdure across the disjunct points of an instant "present" always disappearing. For just as the I that is recollected is also transcended, so is the I recollecting. I become more than the I-now of each moment by achieving continuity with my former self. I can witness the growth of certain fruits in my present from seeds contained in the past, understand myself dramatically straining forward to what fruit will grow from the present's seed time. Thus memory becomes St. Augustine's primary experience of transcendence.

By a paradoxical development, the urge to escape time drove Augustine back into time, to discover his own continuity there. Metaphysical presuppositions led him to treat time as a medium of dispersal. But he experienced it as a mode of retrieval. The dilution out into temporality (*distentio animi*) is also a triumph of perdurance (*extentio animi*) and the medium of self-regulation (*intentio animi*). From memory we first quarry a self recognizable to us, and therefore *constituting* the self. Memory is creative—we come to *be* what we can recognize as the self; and man is not an agent in history until he has acquired this intimate history, the working identity through which other things can be identified. The first human act of creation is such *self*-creation.

In his next masterpiece, his book on the Trinity, St. Augustine went even further in treating self-knowledge as self-creating. Here his theological warrant is, expressly, the fact that God and his Concept (*Verbum*) are coeternal and mutually constitutive, that they "face each other at the origin." In the same way, he argues, man's knowledge becomes a self-generating *verbum:*

> Although every knowledge takes an image resembling the thing known (the object of its knowledge), self-knowledge is similitude carried to the perfection of equality, since the knowing mind is itself the known object. So one and the same thing is expression and expresser—the former is only received in an act of recognized correspondence with the latter. What is begotten is thus the begetter's equal (*De Trin.* 9.11).

Man begets himself in his act of knowledge, delivers himself back to himself in his own *verbum.* Gerard Manley Hopkins invented a verb that is properly neither active nor passive (more like a Greek middle)—"to self"—for expressing this outward act that delivers oneself back. Each mortal thing, he wrote,

> Selves—goes itself; myself it speaks and spells,
> Crying, What I do is me.

Having gone thus far in treating man's own *verbum* as creative, Augustine was bound to go further. In his third and last masterpiece, his *City of God,* he went so far indeed that Martin Luther felt he had to scold his master, rebuke him for arrogating too much to man, playing down God's creativity in the Genesis account. God, Augustine observes at the outset, not only knows himself in his own Concept, but through It conceives a world:

> Through It all things came into being,
>   and except through It nothing came to be at all.

So it is with man's *verbum:* We know other things only through and in our self-knowing. Every proposition we enunciate is also an assertion of the enunciating self. We know creatively—otherwise that fatal gap in our continuity of consciousness would separate subject from predicate (by separating the *enunciator* of the subject, that endangered time-frayed self we always have to rescue in the energies of remembered identity, from the enunciator of the predicate). We are creating ourselves in every act of knowledge—that is the real force of St. Augustine's famous statement, *Si fallor, sum.* There is hidden truth in every false statement, a secure recognition below each deception, recognition of oneself. Now, as a man entering his sixties, Augustine would give a radical reinterpretation of the Genesis text. In the Eleventh Book of the *City of God,* he uses the Greek argument that God cannot labor through six days in time; but Augustine uses it to emphasize man's creative action on the world. If God knows no first or second day or evening to limit his action, man conceives things in a light struggling through the darkness of sin, a knowledge asserted through lifting and lowering mists, the twilight and dawn of his temporal extension and effortful remembering. Here is the passage that offended Luther:

> Whenever human knowledge is turned back to the Creator in love and praise, night yields to day. When man achieves self-knowledge, that is the first day. When he achieves knowledge of the world's fundamental stuff, intermediate between the upper and lower liquids, that is the second day. When he comes to know of earth and sea and all living things that grow from the rooted texture of the earth, all kinds of stars, the fourth day; of all the live things swimming the sea or flying in the air, the fifth; of all animals, and of mankind itself, the sixth day (*De Civ.* 11.7).

Genesis signifies, for man, the acts of creative recognition that take place within our enabling first self-recognition, the *verbum* of "day one." It is therefore man who says "Let there be light," as knowledge of himself reveals a world.

Once formed as an agent within history (by becoming a subject *with* a history), how does man use his power? How create things in the future with the energies of a remembered self? It is a question that Augustine worried constantly: How does one travel toward an unknown goal? Terms and imagery were given him in the myth of Aeneas. He had been saturated in Vergil's epic from childhood. He tells us how, as a boy, he wept over Book Four, was thrilled by Book Two, declaimed from Book One, and could not have been prevented from reading it if his teachers had ordered him not to. It was the text he taught as a professional rhetorician; and even as a Christian convert he read half a book of the epic with his fellow catechumens every day. His own *City of God* is a kind of anti-*Aeneid*—which means, of course, that it had to be cast in terms of the *Aeneid*. Vergil's hero leaves Troy and moves on, resisting the allure of Carthage, weathering Juno's hostility, fated to reach an unknown place. The Christian, in his turn, goes out from the earthly Rome, called elsewhere, he knows not where, opposed by devils and helped by a supernatural machinery of angels. The similarity of the two quests is spelled out in Books Two and Five of the *City of God*—though a passage from an early work betrays how soon and naturally Augustine framed his journey on the contours of the *Aeneid*. In the dialogue *De Ordine,* Augustine and his friends are intoxicated with the rich promise of Christian philosophy. Augustine prays for fidelity to this call, borrowing in his prose the verse prayer of Aeneas to Apollo:

> What leader send you, whither shall we roam:
> Where, father, should we settle our new home?—
> Inspire us, and by omens make it known.
> (Aen. 3.88–89)

Augustine writes: "For he shall guide us if we take him as leader, make us roam where we can settle a new home; for he inspires and does by omens make it known" (*De Ord.* 1.4.10).

What does human creativity mean, if like Augustine we study it in the light of the *Aeneid?* What keeps Aeneas moving toward his unknown goal? *Piestas,* the poet answers—fidelity to one's parentage, roots, homeland, and the gods of home. And Aeneas' home has been destroyed. Troy no longer exists. Except within Aeneas. The hero takes his hearth gods out with him. He must find a worthy resting place for them. Troy remains as a set of demands upon him, and through a remembering faithfulness to those demands he goes into the future, not content with Carthage. His inner Troy yearns out toward Rome, as memory transcends its object.

Augustine, in his hard antipagan polemic, mocked Rome's preservation of gods already conquered in Troy, as if they could preserve domination for Rome. But in the soul's *Aeneid* he was always fashioning, he felt just that piety toward his own past, even when it was a time of personal sin and defeat. One must preserve a self in order to wield and perfect a self. In the *Confessions,* he carries even his false gods—the sinful memories—forward into the present, praying "to circumvent in the act of memory the past cycles of my sinfulness" (*Conf.* 4.1). He regularly presented the pagan view of life as a cyclic imprisonment, from which repentance moves free, breaking the chains of recurrence. But this happens only in history, in the personal drama. One must resurrect the past self of sin—it is the only self we have—for purification in the present. In his commentary on John, Augustine tells his auditors that they must lift up their hearts, knowing what they lift and whither they lift it—a heart of sin to the sinless God. As he later put it: "Peter was in a healthier state when crying from displeasure with himself, than when pleased with his own boastings." We must be fully man to become more than men.

In his work on the Trinity, Augustine says creative men must love themselves, just as God loved himself in the act of creation. He applies here the fourth verse of John's first chapter:

> And that which already dwelt within the Concept
> was life, and this life was a light for men.

Self-love is the warming, energizing principle of man's activity. But how, Augustine demanded, can man love himself knowing his own sinfulness? The answer is that our love is for our acquired *knowledge* of error, not for the error itself. That answer is not a bit of pre-Scholastic hairsplitting; it grows directly from Augustine's experience of the remembered self as a transcended self. What we love is the recoverable self of possibility. We know and love a self in the very act of disengagement from the past that has allowed us to perdure into the present—and beyond. This energetic remembering, described so often by Augustine, is the memory of a process, of a duration *through* change *to* change; the self is a becoming. Love, focusing on this self, urges us out to become more. Augustine loves the past because it led him to the present, gave him a self with a history, gave him an entry into salvation history.

How does one journey to an unknown goal? By loving a yet-unknown self. This kind of love is creative, adumbrating an unknown self through dialogue with the recognition (*verbum*) of our known self. Such self-love prompts further self-knowledge, generating it as it was generated, forcing man to move out from himself toward himself. This interaction of love and knowledge fascinated Augustine, in his endless effort to love knowing and know love:

> The impulse present in all seeking goes out beyond the seeker, and hovers as it were, unable to rest in a goal, until what is sought has been found and the seeker achieves it. This impulse, or seeking, does not seem to be love, for love is of a known thing, and this is an effort toward knowing. Yet it has a quality cognate to love's. It can be called an act of will, for the seeker wills to find, and if something knowable is being sought, then the seeker has a will to know. And if the willing is urgent and focused, he is called a student, our term for those who pursue and master an area of knowing. So an impulse of some kind precedes the mind's generative act, and through this will to seek and find knowledge, the knowledge itself comes to birth (*De Trin.* 9.18).

The student of mathematics wants to know what he does not know; but he must act from a kind of preknowing love that makes him seek to know. In the same way, the lover of self has a mysterious precognitive urge to call up the self in memory, achieving the *verbum* of man's "first day." The human trinity is therefore constituted for St. Augustine in these terms: We exist, and we know we exist, and we love that existence and our knowledge of it, all in a creative mutuality. This trinity is as active as the divine one of which Augustine thought it the image; for man not only grasps himself *in* a creative act, but *as* a creative act, as something becoming more, echoing God's own ceaseless single act of creation.

For Augustine, man cannot look simply to the past or to the future; each must be used to escape the other, in the dialectic of creative memory. History makes man as man makes history—they are mutually constitutive, like the reciprocally generative acts of man's *verbum* and his self. The truism is also a mystery: To have a future we must have a past. Truisms are often things too obvious to be penetrated; it takes something like Augustine's lived description of memory to turn the truism into a truth. He argues that man must simultaneously penetrate and contain his past, recover and escape it, transcend it by re-entering it. The more intense the act of self-recovery, the more energetic the act of self-transcendence. As was his practice, he summarized this psychic truth in a pun, playing with the idea of "recollection," interweaving the Latin words *cogo* (gather) and *cogito* (reflect). Memory "recoils," winds in on itself the spring that drives man forward. *Reculer pour mieux sauter*. To pounce, one must crouch.

It is often said that the genius, the creative person, seems somehow fresh and childlike, appears to tap the springs of his actual childhood, to feel life still in his deepest roots. Augustine's own curiosity about his childhood, undiminished over half a century, is a type of this truth. His action is the very opposite of nostalgia or make-believe, the Disney cult of childhood. It does not seek to re-enter a world of illusion, but to bring forward some of the risk-taking first awareness in the human mind, that *verbum* which recalls the first day when the world was young. Such energetic recollection escapes imprisonment in the past—but it does not try to "escape the past" as that phrase is normally understood. The whole reality must be encompassed, sin and all. The genius does not remember childhood as islanded off somewhere away from him, as Never-Never Land. His memory goes back to roots through the entire trunk. A total sense of perdurance gives forward inertia to his work. It goes forward because it has always been grasped as ongoing.

For if creativity must have a past, its use is to give man a future. Troy must impel toward Rome. St. Augustine adapted a phrase from Plotinus to express this: "We must *escape* to our homeland" (*De Civ.* 9.17). So restlessness, dissatisfaction, a certain *traveling* mentality, mark the creative person—the troubled heart of Augustine's most famous saying, refusing to be quieted until God gives it rest. This is not a dissatisfaction with others— the fake genius could always have done great work but for some external check on him (the silent fifties intervened, or Nixon's Middle America depressed his spirit). No, the creative man's self-dissatisfaction comes out of creative self-love, an impatience to become worthy of oneself. A very Augustinian paradox: "to become worthy of oneself"—that is saying the self is still unworthy; and that is the creative contradiction man experiences.

In *The Trinity*, Augustine says man's knowledge should rest in itself as one foot "rests" while walking. Augustine himself was not only growing all the time, but always examining this process of his own growth—which reminds us of Heraclitus' saying, that man's quest is a matter of self-inquest: ἐδιζησάμην ἐμαυτόν. Genius is a kind of controlled obsession, the ability to keep asking the same questions and a dissatisfaction with all former answers. Augustine manifests this in his six major commentaries on the creation passage from Genesis, the last of which is the freshest and most daring. A Beethoven re-creates the quartet form, as Verdi did that of opera, because he never feels he has exhausted its possibilities. The artist creates the form while the form is creating the artist, in that mutuality of love and knowledge by which man becomes aware of his own endless possibilities.

It is the creating-created self that is cast forth in individual works of human art. The greatest works made are those that involve a remaking of their maker. This is a more useful distinction than the old division between "fine arts" and mere cobbling (the "banausic" tasks). The carpenter who makes a cabinet at full stretch of his skill (thus pushing that skill out), who exercises care on a work, exploring all the potencies of this particular piece of wood, is taking human responsibility for the result, opening new powers in himself as he goes. This makes him more creative than, say, a rote musician or some hack arranger for Guy Lombardo. Creativity advances through works that bring about the artist's continued self-creation.

In his artifacts man incarnates himself, an act Augustine

expressly compared to the fourteenth verse of John's opening hymn:

> And the Concept came to be flesh
> and housed itself among us.

The artist conveys himself into his work—we recognize him there, know him in the stuff he wrought, though we never met him elsewhere. We can tell at a glance the work of Michelangelo from that of Botticelli, the prose of Ruskin from that of Newman. Their work breathes with them, it is their spirit's home. A self recalled, collected, "recoiled," has gone out beyond itself, animating a new world. Man is like God, and never more like him than when making things. This calls up some dim memory of our first myth, the time of all beginnings. "In the beginning, God made the heaven and the earth." And tomorrow morning, when we wake up, we must make it all over again.